Emerging Trends and Insights on Economic Inequality in the Wake of Global Crises

Shilpa Deo
MIT World Peace University, India

A.V. Senthil Kumar
Hindusthan College of Arts and Science, India

IGI Global
PUBLISHER of TIMELY KNOWLEDGE

A volume in the Advances in Finance, Accounting, and Economics (AFAE) Book Series

Published in the United States of America by
IGI Global
Information Science Reference (an imprint of IGI Global)
701 E. Chocolate Avenue
Hershey PA, USA 17033
Tel: 717-533-8845
Fax: 717-533-8661
E-mail: cust@igi-global.com
Web site: http://www.igi-global.com

Library of Congress Cataloging-in-Publication Data

Names: Deo, Shilpa, 1989- editor. | Senthil Kumar, A. V., 1966- editor.
Title: Emerging trends and insights on economic inequality in the wake of global crises / Shilpa Deo, and A.V. Senthil Kumar, editors.
Description: Hershey, PA : Information Science Reference, [2023] | Includes bibliographical references and index. | Summary: "This book discusses how Covid-19 has worsened the inequality across the economy and presents research chapters meant to educate governmental and international agencies for the need for intervention in order to reduce these inequalities"-- Provided by publisher.
Identifiers: LCCN 2022027234 (print) | LCCN 2022027235 (ebook) | ISBN 9781668452899 (hardcover) | ISBN 9781668452905 (paperback) | ISBN 9781668452912 (ebook)
Subjects: LCSH: Equality. | Equality--Government policy. | COVID-19 Pandemic, 2020---Influence.
Classification: LCC HM821 .E64 2023 (print) | LCC HM821 (ebook) | DDC 305.5--dc23/eng/20220815
LC record available at https://lccn.loc.gov/2022027234
LC ebook record available at https://lccn.loc.gov/2022027235

This book is published in the IGI Global book series Advances in Finance, Accounting, and Economics (AFAE) (ISSN: 2327-5677; eISSN: 2327-5685)

British Cataloguing in Publication Data
A Cataloguing in Publication record for this book is available from the British Library.

Advances in Finance, Accounting, and Economics (AFAE) Book Series

ISSN:2327-5677
EISSN:2327-5685

Editor-in-Chief: Ahmed Driouchi Al Akhawayn University, Morocco

MISSION

In our changing economic and business environment, it is important to consider the financial changes occurring internationally as well as within individual organizations and business environments. Understanding these changes as well as the factors that influence them is crucial in preparing for our financial future and ensuring economic sustainability and growth.

The **Advances in Finance, Accounting, and Economics (AFAE)** book series aims to publish comprehensive and informative titles in all areas of economics and economic theory, finance, and accounting to assist in advancing the available knowledge and providing for further research development in these dynamic fields.

COVERAGE

- Public Finance
- Investments and Derivatives
- E-Accounting
- Accounting information systems
- Field Research
- Finance and Accounting in SMEs
- Applied Finance
- Statistical Analysis
- Economics of Intellectual Property Rights
- Applied Accounting

IGI Global is currently accepting manuscripts for publication within this series. To submit a proposal for a volume in this series, please contact our Acquisition Editors at Acquisitions@igi-global.com or visit: http://www.igi-global.com/publish/.

The Advances in Finance, Accounting, and Economics (AFAE) Book Series (ISSN 2327-5677) is published by IGI Global, 701 E. Chocolate Avenue, Hershey, PA 17033-1240, USA, www.igi-global.com. This series is composed of titles available for purchase individually; each title is edited to be contextually exclusive from any other title within the series. For pricing and ordering information please visit http://www.igi-global.com/book-series/advances-finance-accounting-economics/73685. Postmaster: Send all address changes to above address.

Titles in this Series

For a list of additional titles in this series, please visit:
www.igi-global.com/book-series/advances-finance-accounting-economics/73685

Handbook of Research on Changing World Economic Order in the Post-Pandemic Period
Sushanta Kumar Mahapatra (IBS Hyderabad, The ICFAI Foundation for Higher Education, India) and Vishal Sarin (Lovely Professional University, India)
Business Science Reference • © 2022 • 470pp • H/C (ISBN: 9781799868965) • US $325.00

Perspectives of Management Accounting for Sustainable Business Practices
Ionica Oncioiu (Titu Maiorescu University, Romania)
Business Science Reference • © 2022 • 310pp • H/C (ISBN: 9781668445952) • US $250.00

Wealth Expanding Theory Under the Principle of Efficiency-Equity Equilibrium
Fred Y. Ye (Nanjing University, China)
Business Science Reference • © 2022 • 335pp • H/C (ISBN: 9781668449356) • US $215.00

Handbook of Research on Stock Market Investment Practices and Portfolio Management
Renuka Sharma (Chitkara University, India) and Kiran Mehta (Chitkara University, India)
Business Science Reference • © 2022 • 335pp • H/C (ISBN: 9781668455289) • US $250.00

Opportunities and Challenges for Multinational Enterprises and Foreign Direct Investment in the Belt and Road Initiative
Miraj Ahmed Bhuiyan (Guangdong University of Finance and Economics, China) and Isidora Beraha (Institute of Economic Sciences, Serbia)
Business Science Reference • © 2022 • 323pp • H/C (ISBN: 9781799880219) • US $250.00

Advanced Machine Learning Algorithms for Complex Financial Applications
Mohammad Irfan (CMR Institute of Technology, India) Mohamed Elhoseny (American University in the Emirates, UAE) Salina Kassim (International Islamic University of Malaysia, Malaysia) and Noura Metawa (University of Sharjah, UAE)
Engineering Science Reference • © 2022 • 335pp • H/C (ISBN: 9781668444832) • US $270.00

For an entire list of titles in this series, please visit:
www.igi-global.com/book-series/advances-finance-accounting-economics/73685

IGI Global
PUBLISHER of TIMELY KNOWLEDGE

701 East Chocolate Avenue, Hershey, PA 17033, USA
Tel: 717-533-8845 x100 • Fax: 717-533-8661
E-Mail: cust@igi-global.com • www.igi-global.com

Table of Contents

Section 2
Sectorial Inequalities

Section 3
Inequality in Changing Times

Detailed Table of Contents

The developed, developing, and least developed countries have been experiencing differing levels of inequality over the years. The economic and financial crises have also been aggravating the extent of inequality. The Sustainable Development Goal (SDG) 10 emphasizes reducing inequality that is prevalent within and amongst the countries. The COVID-19 pandemic is expected to reverse the progress made so far in reducing inequality. Hence, the average Gini coefficient is expected to increase by 6% for emerging and developing countries. Therefore, the present study aims to undertake an analysis of the impact of past crises and the current COVID-19 crisis on global inequalities. The world inequality database has been utilized for analyzing the impact. This study will certainly enable the policymakers to implement policies with the help of which the SDG 10 can ultimately be achieved by 2030.

Trade plays an important aspect in broadening the aperture to international merchandise and services; for instance, it allows nations to handle distress by changing suppliers when domestic or international links are disrupted. The COVID-19 pandemic's health and economic catastrophe has been a tremendous pressure for every national system, causing unparalleled distress to universal supply networks and trade associations. In nominal dollar terms, the global GDP fell by 3.3% worldwide, and trade in goods and services declined by 9.6% in 2020, ensuing in the most terrible recession since World War II. Countries that share boundaries with many other countries are predominantly susceptible to interruption in the delivery of crucial provisions due to transportation problem. The purpose of this chapter is to focus on the prevalent inequalities across all countries amidst diverse segments.

The global spread of COVID-19 in the post-pandemic situation had a very drastic impact on various aspects of livelihood. The deaths have risen to more than 3.1 million wherein majorly the aged people remained in danger. The other aspects include the inequalities in sectors like unequal income, prices, opportunity, vaccine access, global recovery, extreme poverty, rising debt levels, etc. The major causes of these are regional trends, migration of skilled workers, the impact of policy, climate mitigation, and adoption policies, etc. Due to sudden switching of teaching in online mode, the education levels have drastically fallen causing learning poverty too. The extreme increase in basic commodities and fuel prices is seen in post-pandemic situations. The climate conditions are also drastically affected causing the people to migrate from one place to another place globally or locally. This chapter details the various causes of post-pandemic situations and the measures to overcome them for eradicating global inequalities.

The chapter analyses gross domestic saving, household consumption, and inequality in African countries. The study covers the period from 1989 to 2019, a length of 31 years, for 24 Africa nations from all the regions of the continent. The main econometric methods of analysis employed for the work is panel cointegration analysis. The variables used for the study to explain both gross domestic savings and household consumption trajectories in Africa include income, inequality, financial development, and government final consumption expenditure. The results show that inequality has negative effects on gross domestic saving but positive effects on household consumption in countries across Africa.

Happiness supports growth, this chapter aims to further explain how developed countries achieve peace and prosperity by keeping their population happy. The aim of this chapter is to analyze the interdependence between the various factors that affect the happiness of a population measured on happiness scale. This analysis is done by using the World Happiness Report 2020. This report includes the data from 154 countries from different regions of the world taking into account the country's GDP per capita, freedom to make life choices, social support, health life expectancy, among other factors. The research results are based on descriptive and inferential statistics methods. The target of this chapter is to explain the possible reasons behind the success or the failure of the country to provide for its population. This chapter investigates the positive relation between factors like GDP per capita, freedom, health life expectancy, and social support to the happiness of the population.

Preface

Global inequality has been a burning issue for years now. Just as the economies progress, it is expected that the benefits of growth will percolate to the lower sections of society. However, this percolation takes place in a discriminating manner. Inequality can be observed in terms of health, income, education, wealth, gender, other socio-economic parameters, and availability of opportunities as well. Rather, the wealth of the world's richest 1% is more than twice that of the world's 6.9 billion people.

The governing authorities and international agencies have been taking various corrective measures to reduce the widening levels of inequalities. However, certain external factors like pandemics can just wash away the efforts taken and deteriorate the inequality levels in the economies. Barring the Black Death, which was a horrible plague that killed around half of Europe's and the Mediterranean's population, almost all the past pandemics have resulted in an increase in inequality.

COVID-19 has not been an exception in comparison to the past pandemics and has worsened the inequality across the economies. The inequality has widened in terms of health, income, education, and gender to name a few. Moreover, inequality is expected to worsen in the days to come. In 2021, the richest two deciles are predicted to recoup about half of their losses from the previous year, while the poorest two deciles are expected to lose another 5% of their income. Rather, COVID-19 has directly counterbalanced the decrease in the gap between countries seen between 2013 and 2017. The end of the COVID-19 pandemic is not in sight and the future of economies is bleak amidst the increasing inequalities. Hence, there is a dire need for the government and international agencies' intervention to reduce these inequalities.

Reducing inequality within and across the economies (Goal 10) along with ensuring inclusive growth and development has been one of the essential Sustainable Development Goals (SDGs). An overview of the evolution of global inequality over the years, increasing different forms of inequalities amidst the pandemics, corrective measures are taken by the national and international agencies, and the way ahead for the economies with the worsening inequalities can certainly enable all of us to collectively reduce inequalities. Once the researchers, governing agencies, and citizens become aware of the past, present, and likely future scenario with respect to global inequalities, inclusive development, and reduced inequality will soon be a reality.

The target audience of this book will be composed of students and faculties studying development economics and professionals and researchers working in the field of global inequalities. The book provides an overview of the evolution of global inequality over the years, increasing different forms of inequalities amidst the pandemics, corrective measures taken by the national and international agencies, and the way ahead for the economies with the worsening inequalities.

ORGANIZATION OF THE BOOK

The book is divided into three sections with three chapters in each section. The brief description of each section and chapter is as follows:

Section 1 of the book portrays the way in which inequalities and crises have been influencing each other. Certain inequalities like income and racial ones can cause social unrest and crisis at the societal level. On the contrary, economic crises can aggravate income gaps, education, and health inequalities to name a few.

The developed, developing and least developed countries have been experiencing differing levels of inequality over the years. The economic and financial crises have also been aggravating the extent of inequality. The Sustainable Development Goal (SDG) 10 emphasizes reducing inequality that is prevalent within and amongst the countries. The COVID-19 pandemic is expected to reverse the progress made so far in reducing inequality. Hence, the average Gini coefficient is expected to increase by 6% for emerging and developing countries.

Therefore, the first chapter addresses the core theme of the book and highlights the influence of global crises on inequalities across countries. The World Inequality Database has been utilized to graphically present the impact of four major crises viz., the Great Depression, East Asian Economic Crisis, Great Recession, and the spread of COVID-19 pandemic on the mainly affected countries. It also discusses the policy measures that have been implemented by national and international agencies to tackle the growing inequalities.

Trade plays an important aspect in broadening the aperture to international merchandise and services; for instance, it allows nations to handle distress by changing suppliers when domestic or international links are disrupted. The COVID-19 pandemic's health and economic catastrophe have been tremendous pressure on every national system, causing unparalleled distress to universal supply networks and trade associations. In nominal dollar terms, the global GDP fell by 3.3 percent, worldwide and trade in goods and services declined by 9.6% in 2020, ensuing in the most terrible recession since World War II. Countries that share boundaries with many other countries are predominantly susceptible to interruption in the delivery of crucial provisions due to transportation problems. Deforestation, intensive farming, and climate change are all examples of environmental problems that can be aggravated by the business. Trade may not be the main source of pollution, but it does contribute to emissions through transportation and increasing output. These emanations contribute to environmental tumult and to the danger of climate-related natural catastrophe in the dearth of effective climate change policies are ardent.

Hence, the second chapter focuses on the prevalent inequalities across all countries amidst diverse segments. The information from various countries has been scrutinized. It examines the relationship of diverse aspects of inequality that hinders the advancement of the economy amidst the pandemic and provides insights on the course of action to be taken up by policymakers across the world.

The global spread of COVID-19 in the post-pandemic situation had a very drastic impact on various aspects of livelihood. The number of deaths and infected people has created havoc. The other aspects include the inequalities in sectors like unequal income, prices, opportunity, vaccine access, global recovery, extreme poverty, rising debt levels, etc. The major causes of these have been regional trends, migration of skilled workers, the impact of policy, climate mitigation and adoption policies, etc. Due to the sudden switching of teaching to online mode, the education levels have drastically fallen causing learning poverty, too. The extreme increase in basic commodities and fuel prices is seen in post-pandemic situations. The climate conditions are also drastically affected causing people to migrate from one place to another place globally or locally. Thus, Chapter 3 details the various causes of post-pandemic situations and the measures to overcome them for eradicating global inequalities.

Section 2 of the book sheds light on the sectoral inequalities prevalent in certain countries. It makes one realize how inequalities can be more taxing for some sections/sectors calling out the need for more context-specific policies.

The tourism industry has been one of the fastest growing sectors of the world economy since the second half of the 20th century. However, due to the spread of the COVID-19 pandemic, the sector has suffered huge losses Hence, the fourth chapter discusses the measurement and management of the economic effects of the pandemic on the tourism sector. A survey was conducted with 322 participants working as managers in different units in various travel agencies operating in Turkey. The construct validity of the scales was carried out by exploratory factor analysis. It was seen that crisis management practices were gathered under four dimensions. The total variance explanation rate for the marketing factor was 57.291%, for the human resources was 10.132%, for the government support was 7.937%, and the maintenance was 5.286%.

South Africa has been experiencing the highest level of inequality. The recent COVID-19 pandemic can further aggravate this inequality. However, with the right kind of strategies, it can certainly be reduced. The fifth chapter emphasizes the role that can be played by corporate entrepreneurship amidst the fourth industrial revolution era to turn this challenge into an opportunity thereby reducing the widely prevalent inequalities in the long run.

We can survive and have food on time due to our farmers. However, they also have to bear the brunt of various kinds of inequalities. Hence, the sixth chapter highlights the need of increasing the usage of digitalization by the farmers to reduce the inequalities. Hence, it is stated that with the development of digitalization, agriculture in Indonesia, which still uses little technology, must be encouraged to be more technologically literate. In the future, the government must pursue agricultural digitalization to increase the level of farmer welfare. It can enable agriculture to become a driving sector for industrialization and economic growth.

Section 3 of the book depicts the relationship between inequalities and other macroeconomic indicators and their influencing role in the economies. Economic inequalities can accentuate other forms of inequalities thereby influencing other macroeconomic indicators negatively.

Chapter 7 highlights the relationship between gross domestic saving, household consumption, and inequality in African countries. It covers the period from 1989 to 2019 for 24 African nations. The main econometric method of analysis employed for the work is panel cointegration analysis. The results show that inequality has negative effects on gross domestic saving but positive effects on household consumption in countries across Africa.

The relationship between happiness and inequalities has been discussed in Chapter 8. It has made an attempt to further explain how developed countries achieve peace and prosperity by keeping their population happy. The authors have presented an analysis of the interdependence between the various factors that affect the happiness of a population measured on the happiness scale. This analysis is done using the World Happiness Report 2020. The research results are based on descriptive and inferential statistics methods. The positive relation between factors like GDP per capita, freedom, life expectancy, and social support to the happiness of the population has been investigated in the chapter.

The COVID-19 pandemic itself has caused an increase in different forms of inequalities. Unless this problem is identified and addressed, it can result in the reversal of progress made in the past few years and intensify the socio-economic problems in the economies. Therefore, Chapter 9 analyzes the impact of the COVID-19 pandemic on economic and social inequalities in five dimensions: health, income, education, gender, and digital. Cases from developed countries are provided as evidence of the stimulating effects of the pandemic on inequalities.

Chapter 10 summarizes the key results, and policy suggestions, and discusses the way ahead for the economies amidst the prevalent biological wars, global supply chain disruptions, declining demand, resulting government and monetary actions, geopolitical tensions, and stagflationary tendencies causing global turmoil.

This book will be of immense use to the students, faculties, independent researchers, and policymakers across the countries as it throws light on the interrelationship between past and present crises and economic inequalities. It also highlights other forms of inequalities and their staggering impact on certain sectors/sections in the economies. It is highly interdisciplinary in nature as it emphasizes the correlation between inequality and macroeconomic indicators like happiness, GDP per capita, savings, and consumption to name a few, and the cumulative influence of such indicators on the inequality levels in the economies. It is believed that every problem has a solution. The first step to solving it is to identify it and then formulate the policies to uproot it. Hence, every book chapter throws light on the socio-economic problems that are prevalent across the countries and then suggests certain policy recommendations that can enable us to reduce the extent of inequalities and achieve SDG 10 by 2030.

Shilpa Deo
MIT World Peace University, India

A. V. Senthil Kumar
Hindusthan College of Arts and Science, India

Acknowledgment

This book would not have seen the light of the day without the backing, supervision, and cooperation of many people. Firstly, I would like to thank the IGI Global team for providing us with the opportunity to work on the book project. I am highly obliged to them for their consistent support and guidance. I am grateful to Prof. Senthil Kumar A V, co-editor of the book, for working relentlessly with me to maintain the quality of the book. I feel indebted to the authors of the book chapters, especially Dr. Fatma Feyza Gunduz, Ms. Neelima K., and Dr. Gayathri R., for not just submitting good quality research work but also assisting us in reviewing other chapters. Last but not the least, I am thankful to my family members and friends for their continuous support and encouragement.

This book is dedicated to my daughter, Ms. Saanvi Soman, for being very understanding and encouraging me to do research always.

Editorial Advisory Board

Section 1
Inequality and Crises

Chapter 1
Global Inequality and Global Crises:
Past and Present

Shilpa Deo
Dr. Vishwanath Karad MIT World Peace University, India

Senthil Kumar
Hindusthan College of Arts and Science, India

Sushil Sharma
Texas A&M University, USA

ABSTRACT

The developed, developing, and least developed countries have been experiencing differing levels of inequality over the years. The economic and financial crises have also been aggravating the extent of inequality. The Sustainable Development Goal (SDG) 10 emphasizes reducing inequality that is prevalent within and amongst the countries. The COVID-19 pandemic is expected to reverse the progress made so far in reducing inequality. Hence, the average Gini coefficient is expected to increase by 6% for emerging and developing countries. Therefore, the present study aims to undertake an analysis of the impact of past crises and the current COVID-19 crisis on global inequalities. The world inequality database has been utilized for analyzing the impact. This study will certainly enable the policymakers to implement policies with the help of which the SDG 10 can ultimately be achieved by 2030.

DOI: 10.4018/978-1-6684-5289-9.ch001

INTRODUCTION

For centuries, the economies in the world have been grappling with several pressing socio-economic, political, environmental, and cultural problems other than inequality. It is not the case that inequality is the most severe of all issues. However, these problems can be accentuated further due to the increasing economic inequalities (Champernowne & Cowell, 1998). For instance, poverty concentration as a form of economic inequality can cause an increase in the crime rate and unrest in societies (Kang, 2016). "Inequality refers to the unequal and/or unjust distribution of resources and opportunities among members of a given society" (Koh, 2019). Different forms of inequalities have been experienced by people like social, economic, regional, and political, to name a few.

Further, though economic inequality and income inequality terms are interchangeably used, the former is a broader term (Sen, 1997). The impact of economic inequality on economic growth and other social factors like crime, political conflicts, health, and education has also been explored in the past (Thorbecke & Charumilind, 2002). Kuznets (1955) found that after the second world war, the income distribution in underdeveloped countries was more unequal than the developed countries. He also emphasized that income inequality initially increases but later decreases during long-term growth. The term inequality of opportunity is frequently discussed and widely researched these days. However, it is not a very new concept. In 1937, Franklin Roosevelt emphasized the necessity to have equality of opportunity. The inequality of opportunity differs widely across the countries, and the circumstances like gender, family background, race, religion, disability, etc., are causing much higher income and consumption inequalities. In addition, though the inequality of effort results in an increase in the growth of the countries, the inequality of opportunity is causing a decline in their development. It can further lead to intergenerational inequalities. Hence, macroeconomic stability and sustainable growth can be at risk due to growing inequalities (Ferreira, 2019; International Monetary Fund [IMF], 2022).

Literature Review

According to Thomas Piketty, world inequality has increased since the 1980s, and much higher taxes must be imposed to bring down the wealth inequalities that cause resentment in societies. Further, in his book titled "Capital and Ideology," he argues that unequal societies create ideologies to defend disparities as it is believed that the increase in wealth will trickle down to the poor as the richer ones may contribute through philanthropy. Instead, racial discrimination is experienced in its extreme form in countries like Brazil, the USA, and South Africa (Kuper, 2020). According to the World Inequality Report 2022, wealth inequality seems more severe than income inequality, with the top 1% owning 38% of the wealth compared to 19% of income.

Figure 1. Global income and wealth inequality (Chancel et al., 2021)

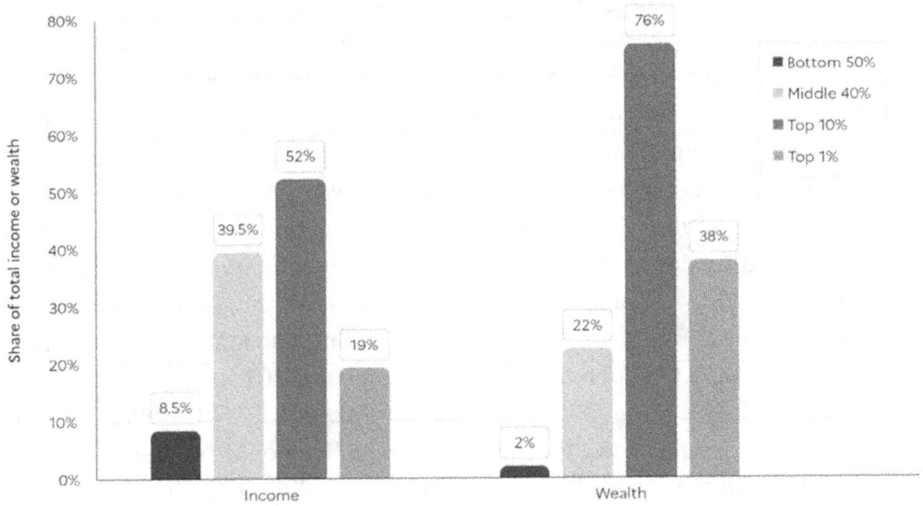

Figure 2. Top 10%, middle 40%, and bottom 50% world income shares (Chancel et al., 2021)

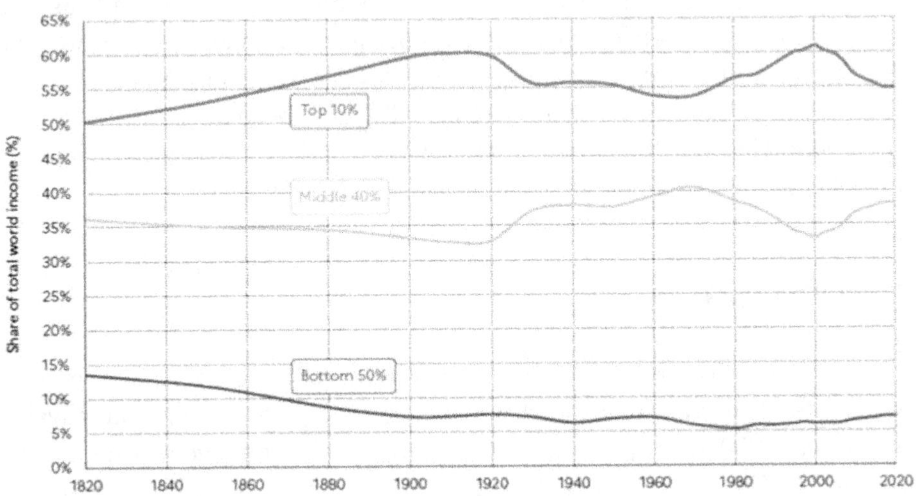

Rather, the income inequality has also worsened over the years as the top 10% continue to own more than 50% of the income from 1820 to 2020 (see figure 2).

Several crises that have been experienced in the past have resulted in significant changes in the economies. The present study aims to analyze the influence of substantial problems like the Great Depression, the East Asian Economic Crisis, the Great Recession, and the COVID 19 pandemic on the inequality in the affected economies. The crises may lead to equal distribution of resources in the countries, just as the Great Depression and World War II led to more equality in the USA. However, it remains to be seen whether the increase in equality may be long-lasting, as inequality has gone up in the USA since the 1970s due to the kind of policies that favored the employers rather than the employees (Piketty & Saez, 2003; Schmitt, 2009). The East Asian Economic Miracle that preceded the economic crisis had reduced poverty and inequality due to rapid growth. However, inequality has increased since then in some of the East Asian region's economies like China (Ahuja et al., 1997; Rao, 1999). The Great Recession also increased income inequality and slowed the pace of recovery of the US economy (Perri & Steinberg, 2012; Meyer & Sullivan, 2013; Thompson & Smeeding, 2013; Cynamon & Fazzari, 2016). Instead, Maloney & Schumer (2010) emphasized that income inequality could be one of the root causes that triggered the Great Recession. The spread of the COVID 19 pandemic exacerbated gender, education, health, and economic inequalities across the countries. Moreover, the pandemic is expected to increase economic inequality further due to the changes it will bring to the workplace (Stiglitz, 2020). It has counteracted the reduction in inequality between the countries from 2013 to 2017. In addition, inequality has increased within the country due to the pandemic (Goldin & Muggah, 2020; Yonzan et al., 2021). However, Deaton (2021) anticipated that the pandemic has caused a decrease in inequality. He stated that other studies had emphasized an increase in inequality between the countries because the countries are weighted by their population. Therefore, it mainly reflects India's worsening inequality.

Therefore, a lot of studies on global inequality have been undertaken in the past. Still, the world inequality database has rarely been utilized to estimate the influence of global crises on economic inequalities across countries.

METHODOLOGY

The world inequality database has been utilized to analyze global crises' impact on inequality levels in some developed and developing countries. The data is available from the year 1930 to 2021. The global crises that mainly emerged during the stated period are the Great Depression 1932; the Suez Crisis 1956; the International Debt Crisis 1982; the East Asian Economic Crisis 1997-2001; the Russian Economic Crisis

Figure 3. Income inequality in USA, 1913-2021 (https://wid.world/)

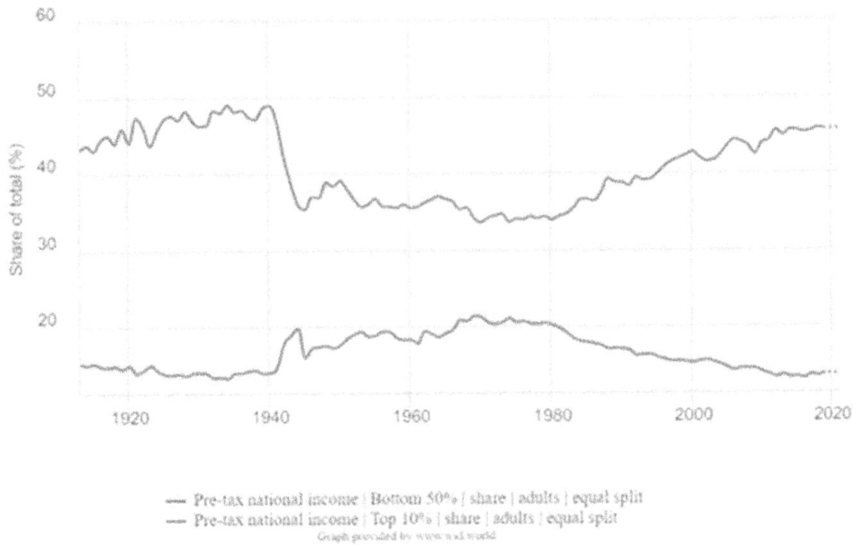

1992-97, the Latin American Debt Crisis in Mexico, Brazil, and Argentina 1994-2002, the Great Recession 2007-09, and the spread of the COVID 19 pandemic 2020. Out of these crises, since the Great Depression, the East Asian Economic Crisis, the Great Recession, and the COVID 19 pandemic had a widespread impact on several economies, the present study aims to highlight its influence on the inequality in the affected countries. Therefore, the changes in global economic inequalities across the nations, particularly during these four crises, have been discussed in this study.

Inequality and Crises

Though Schmitt (2009) found that the Great Depression led to more equality in the USA, the World Inequality Database indicates otherwise. The top 10% of the population owned 46.5% of the income in 1930. In comparison, the bottom 50% owned a meager 13.6% of it. In 1940, though the percentage of income held by the bottom 50% hardly changed, that of the top 10% increased to 49.2%. After that, the inequality declined to its lowest till 1970, which economists call the "Great Compression" as the workers had more bargaining power than the employers. However, as stated earlier, after 1970, inequality has been increasing again due to the policies that favored the employers over the employees (O'Brien, 2015).

The inequality in the USA also increased during the Great Recession (Perri & Steinberg, 2012; Meyer & Sullivan, 2013; Thompson & Smeeding, 2013; Cynamon

Figure 4. Income inequality in Malaysia, 1980-2021 (https://wid.world/)

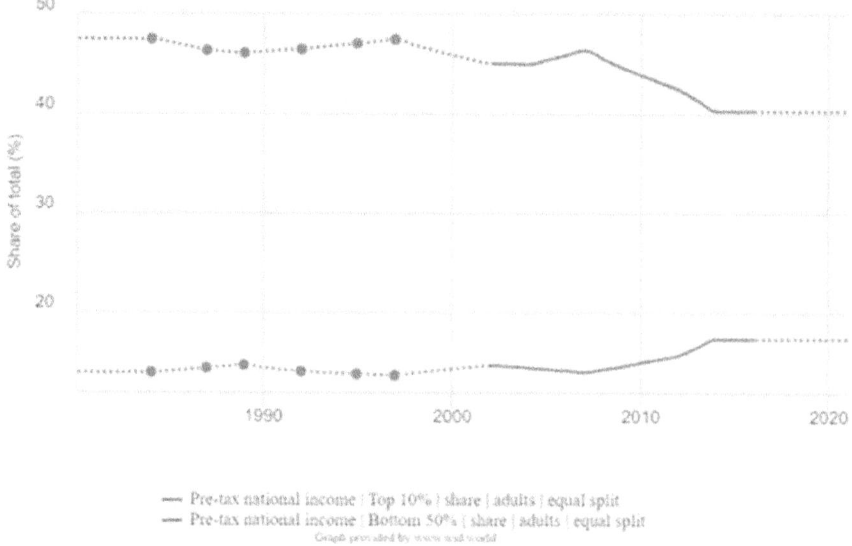

& Fazzari, 2016). Instead, economic inequality has been increasing across the countries after the 2008 financial crisis (Ishikawa & Vorranikulkij, 2019). Figure 3 clearly illustrates that inequality was very high in the USA from 1913 to the 1950s, stagnated from the 1950s to the 1980s, and continued to widen thereafter.

The East Asian Economic Crisis that followed the East Asian Miracle, had mainly influenced Korea, the Philippines, Malaysia, Thailand, and Indonesia (The World Bank, 1998). Rather, these countries had experienced rapid growth, an increase in living standards, and a drastic reduction in poverty. However, the factors that led to this rapid growth fueled the financial crisis in 1997. The stock market and property values were inflated, and overheating pressures had developed. In addition, the political uncertainties and governance issues worsened the crisis. The resulting capital flight further deteriorated the financial stability of the countries. Hence, though there was an increase in financial inflows due to the rapid growth, it was not followed by changes in the regulatory regime, and the weakness in the financial sector led to the crisis. Since Indonesia, Korea, Thailand, Malaysia, and the Philippines were the worst hit, the present study aims to study the impact of the financial crisis on inequality in these three countries (Ahuja et al., 1997; IMF, 1998).

Inequality has been alarming in Malaysia, the Philippines, and Indonesia (Ahuja et al., 1997). However, it seems to stagnate in Malaysia since 2014 and the Philippines since 2018 (see figure 4 and figure 8). The Malaysians seemed worried about the increasing income inequality, as the 2014 Pew Global survey suggested that they

Figure 5. Income inequality in Indonesia, 1992-2019 (https://wid.world/)

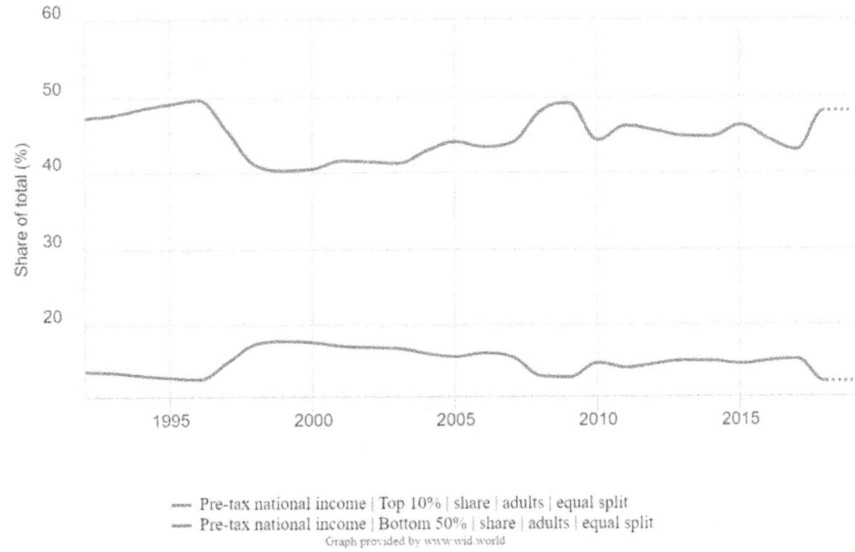

considered this gap a considerable problem (Sander, 2015). The government has been providing cash transfers to poor and vulnerable households to reduce poverty and inequality in the country (World Bank, nd). The inequality was at its peak in

Figure 6. Income inequality in Korea, 1976-2021 (https://wid.world/)

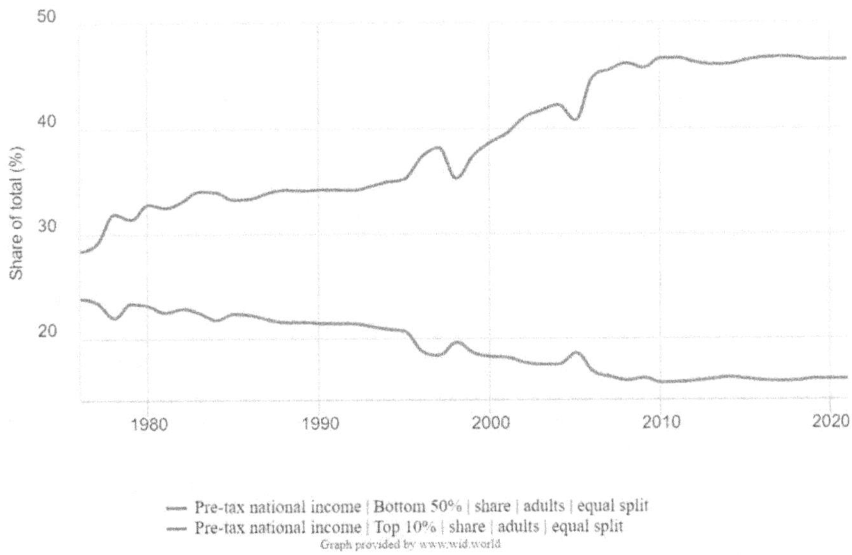

Figure 7. Income inequality in Thailand, 2001-2019 (https://wid.world/)

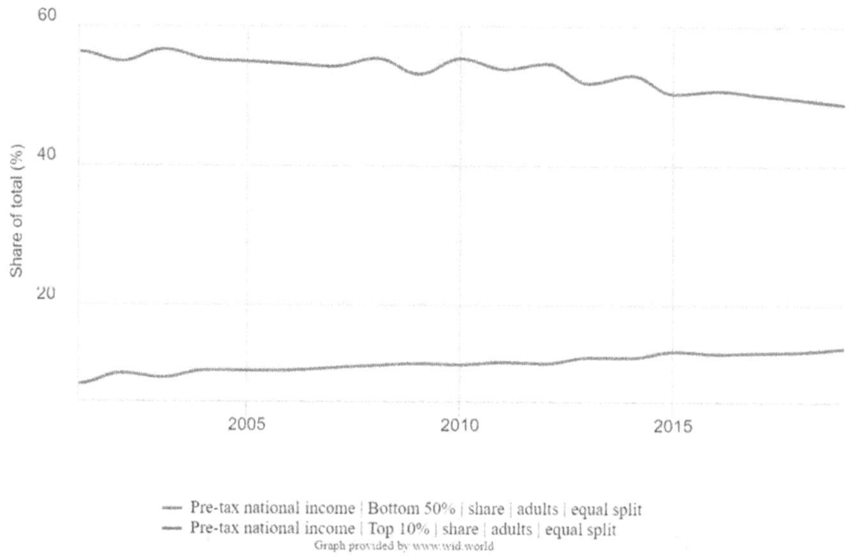

Figure 8. Income inequality in Philippines, 1980-2021 (https://wid.world/)

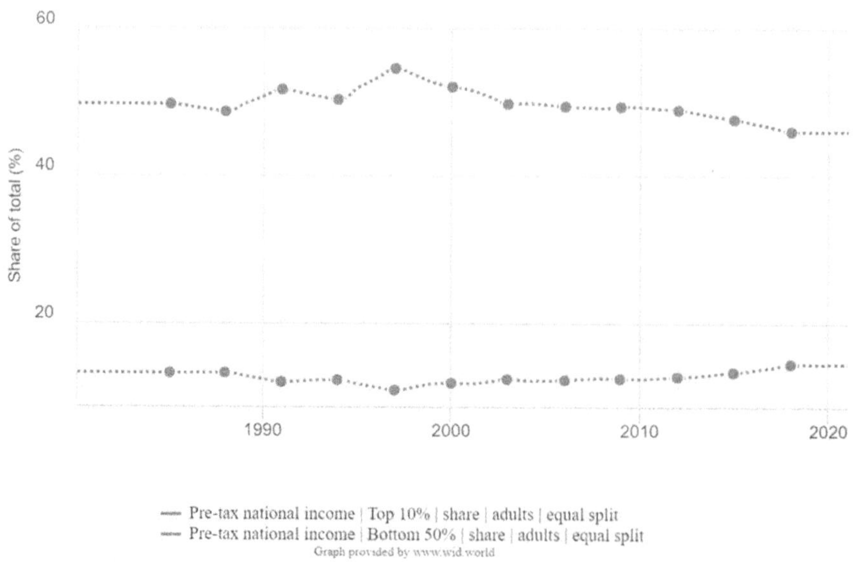

Figure 9. Increasing inequality in emerging and developing countries due to COVID 19 (IMFBlog)

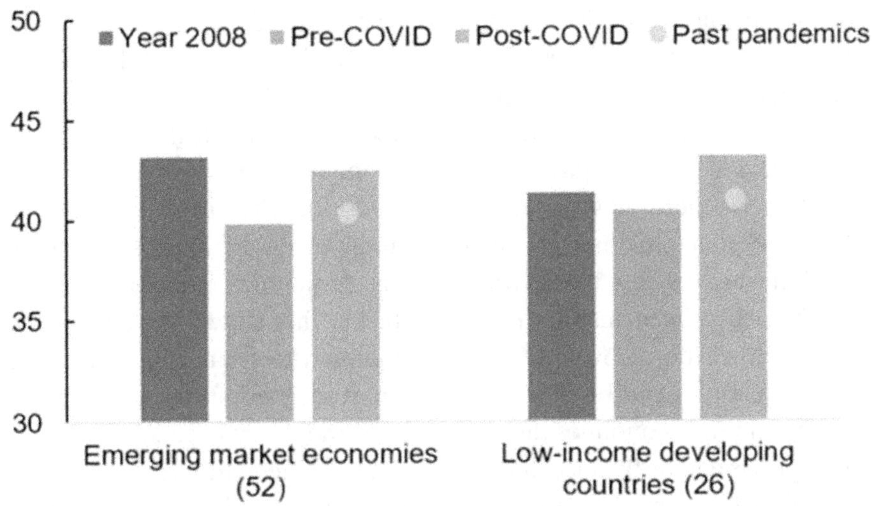

1997 in the Philippines as 54.6% of income was owned by the top 10%, and the bottom 50% owned only 10.7%. However, it has been declining steadily thereafter. Some of the main reasons for increasing inequality in Thailand could be widening differences between skilled and less educated workforce and the concentration of economic activities in particular regions at the expense of excluding others (Ahuja et al., 1997). Instead, in the time span of 18 years, it has meagerly declined. In 2001, the top 10% owned 56.2% of the income, declining steadily to 49.5% in 2018 (see figure 7). Inequality has increased in Indonesia over the last 25 years, which has resulted in slower poverty reduction. It could be the result of government measures like petroleum subsidy that benefit the richer sections more than the poorer ones (Hill, 2021). In Korea, the inequality has been widening due to the income differences between large family businesses and small and medium enterprises (Ishikawa & Vorranikulkij, 2019). In 1976, only 28.3% of the income was owned by the top 10%, which increased to 46.6% in 2010 and has stagnated thereafter (see figure 6). The New Economic Policy can be complemented with specific other policies, like a gradual increase in the minimum wage, labor productivity, and competitiveness in small and medium enterprises, to reduce the inequality in Korea (Ishikawa & Vorranikulkij, 2019).

The pandemics, from Black Death to COVID 19, have disproportionately affected the poor. The economic and social insecurities that follow the pandemic spread make the poor's lives further miserable and vulnerable. COVID 19 has been widening the gap between the rich and the poor more than the past pandemics (Furceri et al., 2020; Ahmed et al., 2020; Patel et al., 2020). The emerging and developing economies grew well before the COVID 19 pandemic hit. It is anticipated that the progress made in poverty and inequality reduction will be reversed due to the pandemic that will cause widening inequalities (Cugat & Narita, 2020). Hence, the COVID 19 pandemic has been called an inequality virus (McGreal, 2020). Since the low-income households could not avail the facility of work from home, it increased their risk of getting infected with the virus. They also cannot isolate themselves in case of infection, thereby increasing the chances of spreading the virus (Ali et al., 2020). The COVID 19 pandemic has also caused supply chain disruptions and a decline in demand, further causing the slowdown in the economies. The governments and central banks have been making efforts to tackle this slowdown and increasing inequalities. However, the recent Global Economic Prospects anticipates that this increased inequality cannot be alleviated in the short and medium term. The increasing inflation rates in the economies due to fiscal and monetary expansions and supply chain disruptions can further accelerate the economic inequality levels. Provision of specific welfare measures like more accessible access to quality education and health care services at affordable rates, cash transfers to the needy for the stipulated time period, unemployment benefits, and skill up-gradation with changing times to name a few, to the affected sectors can enable the economies to come out of the crises and get closer towards sustainable development (Sanchez-Paramo & Malgioglio, 2022).

DISCUSSION AND SUMMARY

In this chapter the inter relationship between economic crises and inequalities has been discussed. The major crises like the Great Depression, East Asian Economic Crisis, Great Recession, and COVID 19 have shattered the economies badly. Hence, analyzing its influence on economic inequalities enables policy makers to design policies for reducing the inequalities.

During the Great Depression era, inequality was reducing in USA. It would be worth analyzing further what are the factors that have caused this decline amidst the depression. The inequality has been increasing in USA after 1970s and it widened during the Great Recession. The East Asian Economic Crisis has caused alarming increase in inequality mainly in Malaysia, the Philippines, and Indonesia. It also widened in Korea and Thailand. There are factors, other than the economic crisis, that have contributed to the changes in inequality which are elaborated in this study. Like the previous crises, spread of COVID 19 has also resulted into reversal of progress made in reducing poverty and inequality across the countries. The governing authorities, Non-Government Organizations (NGOs), and international organizations have been gearing up to help the economies to overcome the crisis. However, the gap between haves and have nots may widen further due to the lingering effect of COVID 19, global supply chain disruptions, increased prices, geopolitical tensions, recessionary trends, and growing automation. The opportunity of re skilling can help the people to remain employed and not experience growing disparities. There is a need to design context specific policies to tackle the pressing economic problems and achieve more economic equality in the long run.

LIMITATIONS AND FUTURE RESEARCH DIRECTION

The East Asian Financial Crisis also impacted some other East Asian countries like Vietnam, Hong Kong, China, and other developing countries. Hence, it would be interesting to analyze what happened to the inequality levels in those countries. This study mainly discusses the extent of income inequality during the crises. However, it would be essential to estimate the influence of crises on other forms of inequality like gender, racial, wealth, health, and education, to name a few. The within-country inequality is also more alarming in several countries, and it has intensified after the spread of COVID 19. Hence, the extent of inequality within the countries post-COVID 19 can be studied along with the measures being taken by local and state governments to reduce it. Such studies can enable us to take corrective actions to reduce the inequalities and achieve SDG 10 by 2030.

REFERENCES

Ahmed, F., Ahmed, N. E., Pissarides, C., & Stiglitz, J. (2020). Why inequality could spread COVID-19. *The Lancet. Public Health*, *5*(5), e240. doi:10.1016/S2468-2667(20)30085-2 PMID:32247329

Ahuja, V., Bidani, B., Ferreira, F., & Walton, M. (Eds.). (1997). *Everyone's Miracle? Revisiting poverty and inequality in East Asia*. World Bank Publications. doi:10.1596/0-8213-3979-6

Ali, S., Asaria, M., & Stranges, S. (2020). COVID-19 and inequality: Are we all in this together? *Canadian Journal of Public Health*, *111*(3), 415–416. doi:10.1726941997-020-00351-0 PMID:32578185

Champernowne, D. G., & Cowell, F. A. (1998). *Economic inequality and income distribution*. Cambridge University Press.

Chancel, L., Piketty, T., Saez, E., Zucman, G., Duflo, E., & Banerjee, A. (2021). *World Inequality Report 2022*. World Inequality Lab.

Cugat, G., & Narita, F. (2020). How COVID-19 will increase inequality in emerging markets and developing economies. *IMFBlog*. Retrieved from https://blogs.imf.org/2020/10/29/how-covid-19-will-increase-inequality-in-emerging-markets-and-developing-economies/

Cynamon, B. Z., & Fazzari, S. M. (2016). Inequality, the Great Recession and slow recovery. *Cambridge Journal of Economics*, *40*(2), 373–399. doi:10.1093/cje/bev016

Deaton, A. (2021). *Covid-19 and global income inequality*. NBER working paper no. w28392. National Bureau of Economic Research. Retrieved from https://www.nber.org/system/files/working_papers/w28392/w28392.pdf

Ferreira, F. (2019). *Inequality of opportunity: New measurements reveal the consequences of unequal life chances*. The World Bank. Retrieved from https://www.worldbank.org/en/news/feature/2019/03/28/inequality-of-opportunity-new-measurements-reveal-the-consequences-of-unequal-life-chances

Furceri, D., Loungani, P., Ostry, J. D., & Pizzuto, P. (2020). Will Covid-19 affect inequality? Evidence from past pandemics. *Covid Economics*, *12*(1), 138–157.

Goldin, I., & Muggah, R. (2020). *COVID-19 is increasing multiple kinds of inequality. Here's what we can do about it*. World Economic Forum. Retrieved from https://www.weforum.org/agenda/2020/10/covid-19-is-increasing-multiple-kinds-of-inequality-here-s-what-we-can-do-about-it/

Hill, H. (2021). What's Happened to Poverty and Inequality in Indonesia over Half a Century? *Asian Development Review*, *38*(1), 68–97. doi:10.1162/adev_a_00158

International Monetary Fund. (1998). The Asian Crisis: Causes and Cures. *Finance & Development*, *35*(2).

International Monetary Fund. (2022). *The IMF and income inequality: Introduction to inequality*. Retrieved from https://www.imf.org/en/Topics/Inequality/introduction-to-inequality

Ishikawa, S., & Vorranikulkij, W. (2019). Korea: Tackling inequality with new economic policy for inclusive growth. *AMRO*. Retrieved from https://www.amro-asia.org/korea-tackling-inequality-with-new-economic-policy-for-inclusive-growth/

Kang, S. (2016). Inequality and crime revisited: Effects of local inequality and economic segregation on crime. *Journal of Population Economics*, *29*(2), 593–626. doi:10.100700148-015-0579-3

Koh, S. (2019). Inequality. In A. Kobayashi (Ed.), *International encyclopedia of human geography*. Elsevier.

Kuper, S. (2020). This economist has a radical plan to solve wealth inequality. *Wired*. Retrieved from https://www.wired.co.uk/article/thomas-piketty-capital-ideology

Kuznets, S. (1955). Economic growth and income inequality. *The American Economic Review*, *45*(1), 1–28.

Maloney, C. B., & Schumer, C. E. (2010). *Income inequality and the great recession*. US Congress Joint Economic Committee.

McGreal, C. (2020). The inequality virus: how the pandemic hit America's poorest. *The Guardian*. Retrieved from https://www.theguardian.com/world/2020/apr/09/america-inequality-laid-bare-coronavirus

Meyer, B. D., & Sullivan, J. X. (2013). Consumption and income inequality and the great recession. *The American Economic Review*, *103*(3), 178–183. doi:10.1257/aer.103.3.178

O'Brien, M. (2015). This chart explains everything you need to know about inequality. *The Washington Post*. Retrieved from https://www.washingtonpost.com/news/wonk/wp/2015/04/20/this-chart-explains-everything-you-need-to-know-about-inequality/

Patel, J. A., Nielsen, F. B. H., Badiani, A. A., Assi, S., Unadkat, V. A., Patel, B., Ravindrane, R., & Wardle, H. (2020). Poverty, inequality and COVID-19: The forgotten vulnerable. *Public Health*, *183*, 110–111. doi:10.1016/j.puhe.2020.05.006 PMID:32502699

Perri, F., & Steinberg, J. (2012). Inequality and redistribution during the Great Recession. *Economic Policy Paper*, 1.

Piketty, T., & Saez, E. (2003). Income inequality in the United States, 1913–1998. *The Quarterly Journal of Economics*, *118*(1), 1–41. doi:10.1162/00335530360535135

Rao, V. B. (1999). East Asian economies: Trends in poverty and income inequality. *Economic and Political Weekly*, 1029–1039.

Sanchez-Paramo, C., & Malgioglio, S. (2022). *Here's a remedy for COVID's legacy of growing inequality*. The World Bank. Retrieved from https://blogs.worldbank.org/voices/heres-remedy-covids-legacy-growing-inequality

Sander, F. (2015). *How can Malaysia reduce inequality?* World Economic Forum. Retrieved from https://www.weforum.org/agenda/2015/02/how-can-malaysia-reduce-inequality/

Schmitt, J. (2009). Inequality as policy. *Real Word Economics Review*, *51*(1), 2–9.

Sen, A. K. (1997). From income inequality to economic inequality. *Southern Economic Journal*, *64*(2), 384–401. doi:10.1002/j.2325-8012.1997.tb00063.x

Stiglitz, J. (2020). *Conquering the great divide.* International Monetary Fund. Retrieved from https://www.imf.org/Publications/fandd/issues/2020/09/COVID19-and-global-inequality-joseph-stiglitz

The World Bank. (1998). What effect will East Asia's crisis have on developing countries? *PREM Notes*, (1).

Thompson, J. P., & Smeeding, T. M. T. (2013). *Inequality and poverty in the United States: the aftermath of the Great Recession.* FEDS Working paper no. 2013-51. doi:10.2139/ssrn.2340665

Thorbecke, E., & Charumilind, C. (2002). Economic inequality and its socioeconomic impact. *World Development*, *30*(9), 1477–1495. doi:10.1016/S0305-750X(02)00052-9

WID. (n.d.). Retrieved August 30, 2022, from https://wid.world

World Bank. (n.d.). *Overview*. Retrieved August 30, 2022, from https://www.worldbank.org/en/country/malaysia/overview#1

Yonzan, N., Lakner, C., & Mahler, D. (2021). *Is COVID-19 increasing global inequality?* World Bank. Retrieved from https://blogs.worldbank.org/opendata/covid-19-increasing-global-inequality

Chapter 2
Rejuvenating Life, Livelihood on Economic Inequality Amidst the Global Crisis

Gayathri R.
https://orcid.org/0000-0001-9406-0191
SASTRA University (Deemed), India

Vijayabanu C.
https://orcid.org/0000-0002-0125-4534
SASTRA University (Deemed), India

Karthikeyan S.
SASTRA University (Deemed), India

ABSTRACT

Trade plays an important aspect in broadening the aperture to international merchandise and services; for instance, it allows nations to handle distress by changing suppliers when domestic or international links are disrupted. The COVID-19 pandemic's health and economic catastrophe has been a tremendous pressure for every national system, causing unparalleled distress to universal supply networks and trade associations. In nominal dollar terms, the global GDP fell by 3.3% worldwide, and trade in goods and services declined by 9.6% in 2020, ensuing in the most terrible recession since World War II. Countries that share boundaries with many other countries are predominantly susceptible to interruption in the delivery of crucial provisions due to transportation problem. The purpose of this chapter is to focus on the prevalent inequalities across all countries amidst diverse segments.

DOI: 10.4018/978-1-6684-5289-9.ch002

INTRODUCTION

The future is already here, it's just not evenly distributed.

- William Gibson

The pandemic has laid bare deep divisions, but it's not too late to change course.

- Joseph Stiglitz

Inequality arises when there is no equal opportunity provided to people across various aspects of life. Many countries face the difficulty of inequality in varied dimensions such as healthcare, education, wealth, income, employment opportunities, socio economic status etc. Deforestation, intensive farming, and climate change are all examples of environmental problems that can be aggravated by business. Trade may not be the main source of pollution but it does contribute to emissions through transportation and increasing output. These emanations contribute to environmental tumult and to the danger of climate-related natural catastrophe in the dearth of effective climate change policies are ardent.

A few perceived perils may arise in the form of pandemic, natural disasters, terrorist attacks, financial crisis, banking frauds, globalization, political instability etc. Covid 19 has destructively impacted the communities and the economies worldwide and has broadened the inequality among nations and distorted the combined aim of attaining the United Nations Sustainable Development Goals.

The Global Preparedness Monitoring Board (2019), highlighted that the pandemic associated diseases such as SARS, influenza and Ebola that are typically difficult to handle as the possibility of a pandemic spreading over the world is exceedingly rigorous due to the perspective of poor sanitation, unsafe drinking water, climatic conditions, transport, health care, migration, economic upheaval, unmitigated conflicts, fragile states etc.

According to the 2021 reports of World Health Organization, the COVID-19 virus has affected 156 million public and killed 3.25 million people over the world after its outbreak in China (Dec 2019) (World Health Organization,). and the numbers are still trailing as new-fangled version of the virus such as Delta, Omicron are highly rampant. The degree of inequality across various segments hinders the economic well being of the people and the advancement of the country. The disruptive impact of the worldwide health crises has clearly proven that the aim set to tackle the crisis are secondary objectives that are entirely devoid of social, ecological, and economical consequences. Some of the world's most vulnerable population has been disproportionately affected by this catastrophe. For instance, the COVID-19 disaster has caused a three-year setback in the struggle against poverty, which is one of the objectives of the United Nations Sustainable Development Goals (UNSDGs). According to the World Bank, if 9.2% global populace (689 million people) resided in severe paucity in 2017, as COVID-19 catastrophe have unnerved between 88 and 115 million of the people into extreme poverty, prolonging the struggle against poverty by three years[1].

Inequality may further intensify as a consequence of the pandemic, as business organizations seek to protect themselves by outsourcing duties that were previously undertaken by low-wage employees. The shift to online education have affected millions of people worldwide who survive in diminutive homes and have limited access to internet, cell phones, and other electronic equipment. Many small businesses were closed due to the severity and length of the lockdowns, which augmented the domination of bigger firms in many businesses. The problem has impacted all generations and groups: the elderly are the most vulnerable to the epidemic, while youth confront new impediments to social mobility, mental health challenges, uncertain economic prospects, and continuous environmental degradation. Climate change continues to be disastrous, and no one is immune to it, nor can the globe be vaccinated against it. Inequalities endure in a country due to the nature of political structure and on the society's choice on how they respond to the policies of the government in the country.

The current chapter examines the relationship of diverse aspects of inequality that hinders the advancement of the country amidst the pandemic. The information from different countries is examined. The purpose of this chapter is to highlight the widespread inequalities that exist amongst countries across many segments. The current chapter investigates the relationship between various forms of inequality that impede economic progress in the face of the pandemic and offers recommendations for policymakers around the world.

A SCRUTINY ON THE REVIEW OF LITERATURE

Lincon et al. (1981) investigated the behavioral antecedents related to higher female mortality than male mortality from birth to reproductive years in a rural area in Bangladesh. A paradigm was developed that hypothesized the intermediate variables during which sex-biased beliefs and behaviors would affect health, nutrition, and mortality. Malnutrition was much more common in female children than it was in male children even after accounting for nutrient necessities owing to pregnancy, erratic body weight, lactation, and physical activity levels. In-depth dietary surveys indicated that males every time absorbed more calories and proteins than females at all stages. Male preferences for health care at a free treatment center were evident, despite the fact that child infection rates were equivalent between the sexes.

Cockburn's (1983) research into the impact of technological development in the newspaper printing sector in the United Kingdom found that talented men and their sturdy trade union affiliations systematically marginalized women folk. Cockburn (1983) works with the concept of capitalist patriarchy, which connects capitalism to a sex/gender relations system.

Connell (1987) coined the term "gender regime" to describe gender subjugation in all institutions, including the home, the state, and the street. She emphasizes that institutions were investigated throughout the time she was writing as though gender played no role at all. Gender blindness is evident in the majority of articles on classic social science topics such as state, migration, and so on. Gender relations, on the other hand, are prevalent in all sorts of organizations and constitute a major structure in the majority of them. The "gender regime" of an organization refers to the institution's patterning of gender relations, particularly the ongoing pattern that provides the structural backdrop for specific interactions and individual practices. (Connell, 1987, pp. 6 in Connell, 2010).

Rather than studying wider social dynamics related to gender, Acker (1990) attempted to elucidate gender inequality by focusing on organizational practice and symbols within business organizations. In some aspects, this differs with Marxist-influenced perspectives like Elson and Pearson's (1981) and Weberian methods, with the latter highlighting the organization's bureaucracy. According to Acker, organizations are gendered, not gender neutral or asexual. To say that a corporate organization, or whichever analytic unit, is gendered is to say that it is patterned on a dichotomy between male and female, masculine and feminine, benefits and downsides, development and control, action and emotion, meaning and identity.

Hewamanne and Brow (1997) conducted interviews with workers in the Katunayake FTZ, examining the tensions and convergences between "neo-traditional cultural values" and "capitalist work culture."

One of the most important criteria in the debate over a country's long-term success, according to McMichael et al. (2004), should be the health of its population. A good human capital health status is also regarded to have a significant impact on economic life (Mihalache, 2017) and to be a representative feature of countries (Mihalache, 2019) (Madsen, 2016). This could explain why so many researches (Bloom, 2004, Sevilla, 2004; Weil, Husain, French, 2007) had paid attention on the association between national health and socio - economic outcomes. According to the research undertaken, it revealed that improved population health leads to bigger economic gains in the form of improved production and long-term income (Monterubbianesi, Granes; Dabus, 2017).

Furthermore, improvements in mortality diminution may result in potential financial investments, as measured by the number of years of life saved in the population (Boisclair, Decarie, Laliberte-Auger, Michaud & Vincent, 2018). The findings of a study on unjustified population fatalities by Alkire et al. (Alkire, Peters, Shrime, M.G, Meara, 2018) revealed that the unjustifiable character of these deaths results in economic fatalities in the form of countries' GDP decline. All these information illustrate that health outcome have a financial impact, but the economic impact of healthiness and inequities must also be considered.

The WHO Commission on Social Determinants of Health (CSDH), Marmot M, et al, (2008) advocated for even further study concerning health inequalities. This committee underlined the necessity of thoroughly examining the relevance of social inequalities, particularly living conditions, for health.

Finally, Piette et al., (2012) undertook a major investigation in order to obtain information on the implications of eHealth on healthiness outcomes and expenses. Although big eHealth implementation and research programs are being implemented and researched in many small- and middle-income countries, more evidence on the effects of eHealth on benefits and expenses in these contexts are still needed.

McInnes et al., (2013) investigated the homeless's access to and use of digital technologies. They observed that, based on the technological expertise (cellular, computer, or access to a public computer), the use ranged from 24% to 84 percent, and that this technology could help enhance the wellbeing of this population.

Managers allow internal, individualized voice channels for communicating employee issues, according to Gunawardene (2014). Managers employ some voice strategies to address disagreements, absenteeism, and other issues, according to her. Women share their problems and complaints with their direct superiors first, and if they aren't resolved, they are escalated to higher levels. She also analyses how social relationships, such as esteem instilled in hierarchies, limit women's authority in formal contexts as a consequence of socialization inside a patriarchal social order.

Gender stereotypes cause barriers for women in the workplace in a variety of ways, according to Madeline et al. (2015). These difficulties are numerous and troubling, with descriptive gender prejudices preventing women from being perceived as professional and compositional gender stereotypes hindering them from being regarded as appealing. Women are still regarded to lack the qualities required to be successful in male-dominated fields, and they are frequently rejected for acting in ways that contradict gender norms.

Brammer et al., (2020) has pointed out that the timeline of the existing worldwide health crisis connected to the COVID 19 seems to have been uncertain since the start of the pandemic. While a global vaccination campaign has been currently in progress since January 2021, the repercussions of the pandemic have been proved to be severe, including bereavement, unemployment, bankruptcies, mounting debts, kaput supply networks, psychological and health issues related to lockdown policies, to name a few.

Barbera et al., (2020) believe that additional studies on the effects of comprehensive global disaster on individuals, companies, and society are urgently needed, as they have remained largely unexplored in accounting and management research.

Thomasson et al., (2020) has highlighted the need to act in response to "grand challenges" plus "wicked problems" for instance environment changes, political insecurity, poverty and worldwide healthiness; upgrading has become increasingly emphasized in research across different discipline including public administration management business.

The work by Ahrens and Ferry (2021) examines the government of United Kingdom use of accounting standards and responsibility in reaction to COVID-19 using Foucault's concept of "apparatuses of Security." The study demonstrates how the government of United Kingdom managed the covid pandemic using accounting and statistical calculative procedures (including epidemiology and healthcare), while balancing numerous constraints and goals. As a result, the government faced higher budget deficits due to low income and higher spending.

A study by Ahn and Wickremasinghe's (2021) examined the community ramifications of calculative behavior, with an emphasis on the usage of large statistics in South Korea. They demonstrate how the epidemic endows with the setting for the establishment of a monitoring grouping to regulate and hold citizens responsible. It was made probable by the combined "desires": the government wanted to increase its authenticity and endorsement rating by controlling the pandemic, while residents wanted to keep their wellbeing and safety. At the similar time, this encroached on individual privacy, as residents were held responsible for their whereabouts and health conditions by the surveillance apparatus.

The political system, government policies, environmental changes, technological development, trade policy, poverty, unemployment, gender bias, health, income, wealth, Covid 19 pandemic etc are some of the prominent factors determining inequalities that have been scrutinized by researchers around the world.

WHAT IS ROUSING GLOBAL INEQUALITY?

Inequalities endure in a country due to the nature of political structure and on the society's choice on how they respond to the policies of the government in the country.

Inter-country and intra-country influences drive global income trends. Inter- and intra-country factors play a role in wealth inequality. Transition economies have had rapid economic development and widespread privatization and this has accelerated the accumulation of private wealth in large emerging economies compared to rich countries. This has the effect of reducing global wealth disparities between the developing and developed worlds.

The rise in *wealth inequality* inside countries, however, negated the effect. Several reasons contribute to increased wealth disparity within countries, as well as rising income inequality exacerbated by disparities in savings and return rates across diverse affluent categories. Across the globe, we see that the prosperous people save more and earn higher rates of return on their investments than the poor. The snowballing consequence of capital accumulation refers to the fact that the more one has now, the more one can have tomorrow.

Financial deregulation and modernization, which widened the disparity in rates of return for diverse sizes of financial portfolio, is another important factor driving rising wealth inequality at the top (Bauluz, 2021a).

In industrialized economies, *tax policy* is one of the most significant determinants of inequality levels. In the last 50 years, taxation in the United States and many other wealthy countries has been less progressive, implying that people with the greatest incomes have fewer tax obligations. Top earnings used to be taxed at substantially higher rates than they are now. Top incomes have risen faster as a result of less progressive taxes (Peterson Institute for International Economics, 2020).

The poorest people are the ones who are most affected by *climate change*. Climate change-related extreme weather patterns are expanding the gap between rich and poor. Low-income people are more vulnerable to severe flooding, hurricanes, and warmer temperatures, and they live in towns with ineffective disaster relief plans. Furthermore, some policy measures aimed at limiting the climate problem may adversely impact low-wage employees.

The changing *distribution of income* throughout the world's many social groupings results in a new power balance and new conflicts between these groups. In parallel to the literature on class politics in national countries, these issues raise fresh discussions concerning global distributive politics.

Why Bother About Inequality?

The most obvious argument for eliminating inequality is that everyone should have an equal opportunity to success. On the other hand, some renowned economists have long argued that there is a tradeoff between equality and growth—that increasing inequality is an unavoidable result of increased output—but this viewpoint is divisive. Some social scientists believe that inequality is acceptable if people are also raised out of poverty (regardless of whether others become extremely wealthy). Others argue that inequality is unavoidable as a result of variations in talent, as well as the critical role of individual choice. They claim that an overabundance of attention to inequality is unwarranted.

Recent studies have found evidence that inequality stifles a country's economic growth, and policymakers are beginning to agree. Jason Furman (PIIE, 2018) warns that generalizing about the causal relationship between inequality and growth is problematic, but policymakers don't have to pick because well-known "win-win" solutions, such as strengthening elementary education, are available (PIIE,).

Experts have linked rising inequality to a global surge of populism and authoritarianism, in which rulers exploit economic distress by appealing to "ordinary folks" in opposition to "power elite" accused of discriminating against foreigners, immigrants, and minorities in the workforce.

How Do We Measure Inequalities Among Countries?

In most high-income economies, the Gini coefficient—a common indicator of income distribution across population segments—increased. The discrepancy shows a rise in incomes for the wealthiest population groups for example USA, as well as stagnant or even declining incomes for the poorest, especially during difficult economic times.

The International Comparison Programme (ICP) brings together more than 190 countries' leading international statistics organizations and statistical administrations to undertake review to obtain price and the spending intensity for various products and services consumed worldwide.

For tracking global inequality, Market Exchange Rates (MER) can be relevant. While Purchasing Power Parity (PPP) data provide a more realistic view of worldwide inequality from the perspective of people who splurge their salaries in their home countries, MER numbers may be further illuminating regarding inequality in a future where on earth people can spend their money wherever they wish. This is especially true when considering the prosperity of global multimillionaires and billionaires, who can conveniently purchase commodities and services anywhere on the earth.

Furthermore, inequality indices like the T10/B50 income gap or the Gini coefficient do not allow for additive disintegrations, therefore the global Theil index is exactly equal to the total of intra-country and inter-country comparisons. Further, Theil index is used to focus emphasis on dissimilarity indicator based on revenue ratios because income ratios are more instinctive and simpler to understand.

Divergent policies among countries have influenced their gaps in inequality and growth. Nature has bestowed diverse resources unequally among all the countries worldwide. The accessibility of natural resources, the process of technological transition, the maturity of the society, the political and economy policies related to taxation, inflation, subsidies, GDP, exchange rates etc. have a tremendous impact on how the income and wealth is redistributed across different countries.

Comprehending Global Inequality Across the World

The COVID-19 outbreak exemplifies a conundrum: globalization has made the world more vulnerable to catastrophes while also making it more adaptable. On the one hand, economic integration makes us more reliant on global trade networks and more vulnerable to risk and shock spirals. Economic integration, on the other hand, empowers us to diversify our vendors, pool resources, and share knowledge and experience. The same characteristics that make the global economy vulnerable to crises – accessibility, interconnectivity, and networked technology – also make it resilient, creative, and better equipped to weather crises when they occur.

The total income earned by individuals of a country during a financial year is the national income of a country. An individual rewarded for his toil, is his income in terms of salary /wages and the income derived from dividends and other investments form the individual wealth. The worth of all the assets of an individual of a country comprises the national wealth.

According to the World Inequality Report 2022, the wealthiest 1% of India's population received more than one-fifth of the country's total national income (21.7%) in 2021, while the poorest 50% earned only 13.1%. According to this report, the top ten percent of the population held up to 57 percent of the country's national Income.

The lower half of the world's inhabitants receives only 8% of global revenue. This means that the bottom half of the people earned lesser than a fifth of the worldwide average, or €2,800 a year or €230 per month. The worldwide middle-income group which accounts to 40 percent earns 39 percent of the total, with an annual income of €16,500 or €1,375 a month, which is very close to the global average. The top ten percent of the global population receives 52% of the sum, which is to some extent more than five times the overall average. The average adult income is €87,200 per year, or €7,300 per month.

The concentration of worldwide wealth appears to be much more unequal than the proportion of worldwide revenue. The wealthy half of the population owns 98 percent of the world's wealth, while the poorest half owns only 2 percent. On an average, the lowest half of the population has Euro €2,900 in assets, which are typically in the form of cash, land, houses, deposits, and other financial instruments. 40 percent of the world's middle population owns only 22% of total wealth (on an average of €40,900 per adult), while the top 10% possesses 76 percent (on an average of €550,900 per adult, with a larger percentage of monetary wealth in the form of bonds and equities) (WID).

The worldwide income is expected to reach €86 trillion ($122 trillion) in 2021, while international net worth is expected to reach €510 trillion. In 2021, the global average adult monthly earnings will be €16,700 or PPP €1,390 ($23,380 and $1,950, respectively), with an average net worth of €98,600 ($139,000)[2]. This clearly indicates high level of inequalities in terms of income and wealth among various countries and people.

Through economic, financial, logistics and digital linkages, trade can enhance a country's vulnerability and exposure to hazards, as well as make it easier for those hazards to spread. In tandem, trade, as a chief driver of productivity and economic growth, assists countries in generating the requisite resources required to avoid risks and prepare them to face such turmoil.

Inequalities in Public Revenue and Spending Among Emerging Economies Since 1980's

During the previous four decades, many developing countries' expenditure and taxes have increased, though to a far lesser extent than in the West during the twentieth century - in fact, government income in many low-income countries has stagnated or decreased. In 1980, the government revenue in China and India accounted for 10-15% of national income, which was similar to the level in developed countries 60 years earlier. Government tax revenue has increased to 15-20% of gross domestic product in these nations since 1980. While this is a significant growth, it has occurred at a far slower rate than the enhancement seen in affluent countries during 1920 and 1960s. (where government income raised from 10-15 percent to 30-35 percent of national earnings). After the breakup of the Soviet Union in the mid-1990s, revenue in Russia and Central Asia fell from 35 percent to 30 percent today. Over the same time period, tax revenue in Sub-Saharan Africa fell from a little more than 19 percent to 15 percent. Investing on and education often follows the broader prototype of tax income: when tax earnings rise, expenditure in these areas rises as well. Between 1980 and 2020, rising countries such as China and Brazil boosted their public spending (from around 1 percent to 4 percent of national income). This increase undoubtedly aided in the fight against severe poverty, the reduction of inequality, and the creation of new income development prospects in many countries[3].

Spending increased across the majority of Latin America during the same time period, but it was substantially more restricted in South East Asia. In India, it climbed from 1% to some extent over 1% percent of national revenue, whereas in Indonesia, it increased from 1% to 1.8 percent of national GDP. Overall, public healthcare expenditure in low-income nations has declined from roughly 1.3 percent to 1 percent of national income since 2000[4].

Since 1980, global tax revenue has remained constant, fluctuating at 25% of global income from 1980 to the present. Global investments in education have remained stable (at around 5% of global income), whereas healthcare costs have only increased somewhat (from 3 percent in 1980 to about 5 percent of global income at present) Due to the massive expansion of high-income countries, global social expenditure has been getting popular in a different direction for the past four decades than it was between the 1950s and 1980s, and further between the 1920s and 1980s, while worldwide tax income and social expenditure both increased significantly[5].

Development aid (whether from foreign governments or individuals) has received a lot of attention in emerging and developing countries as a way to improve access to healthcare and learning. Foreign help, on the other hand, has frequently come at the expense of poor countries' ability to generate long-term tax revenue. Currently, universal development assistance account for lesser than 0.2 percent of worldwide GDP (and a mere 0.03 percent for emergency aid). To put the figures in context, climate change consequences in impoverished amount to several percentage points of GDP. Money outflows, in the form of global profits, are significantly greater to public aid inflows in the majority of nations getting development aid, whether in Africa, South Asia, or other regions. Between 1970 and 2012, capital proceeds surging from African countries to the remaining parts of the world accounted for three times the quantity of international aid pouring into African countries, according to government figures, and the situation has not altered considerably since then.

To put it another way, affluent countries claim to help impoverished countries, but they in fact benefit from how financial flows between the "core" and the "periphery" are organized. Developmental assistance in the form of extra tax revenues could likely help strengthen government actors, but overseas aid granted in the perspective of government weakness is unlikely to be of use (Piketty, 2014).

Gender Disparity in Workforce Participation and Wages

In the labor market, gender segregation of professions is still a persistent tendency. The current COVID-19 pandemic has thrown fresh barriers in the way of developing inclusive, successful economies and communities. Despite the fact that women have been at the forefront of crisis management as decisive employees, pre-existing gender imbalances have exacerbated the crisis in an odd way linking men and women. Women's sectors have been hit the worst by lockdowns and rapid digitization. The problem has hampered advancement toward gender parity in a array of countries and industry segments, particularly when combined with the additional duties of caring for the family at home.

Women's labor income share is characterized by two parameters: women labor force participation in contrast to male on one side, and the gender wages ratio on the other. The Global Gender Gap Report (2021) illustrates that income gaps between men and women continue to be enormous today, both within countries and globally, not only due to large wage disparities but also due to differences in types of occupation. In population-weighted averages, nearly 80% of men in the age of 15–64 are employed, compared to only 52.6 percent of women in the similar age group, mainly elucidating on the gender gap prevalent in labor force which remains above 35 percent. As a result, eliminating legal impediments to women's advancement and employment remains a top concern for governments and businesses in all countries (World Economic Forum, 2021).

Inequalities Leading to Poverty

COVID-19 had the deepest impact on people who lacked equal access to services, public goods, quality healthcare systems, and robust social protection for generations, making it more difficult to cope with any distress. The informal economy employs 1.6 billion people, whose livelihoods were jeopardized by the crisis. Furthermore, the efforts taken to contain the pandemic often pushed them farther into poverty, as the informal sector, which allows many poor people to live, was effectively shut down in many nations.

For the first time in nearly two decades, the worldwide extreme poverty rate grew in 2020. Several millions of people have been thrust back into poverty and acute hunger. Beyond the infection itself, the COVID-19 pandemic has disrupted more critical health care services and caused significant health risks. The virus had a greater likelihood of affecting the poor and disadvantaged people, who suffered the brunt of the economic repercussions.

According to the United Nations Sustainable Goals Report 2021, prior to the COVID-19 epidemic, the percentage of the world's population suffering from poverty had decreased from 10% in 2015 to 9.3% in 2017. The number of individuals living on very little than $1.90 per day fell from 741 million to 689 million. However, between 2015 and 2017, the annual percentage of decrease fell to less than half a percentage point, compared to one percentage point between 1990 and 2015. Conflict and climate change have both posed threats to progress, and the epidemic has added to them. Worldwide, there are informal employees who are left out of the social safety net, there are indeed 4 billion people who are yet to be covered by any social protection procedures and according to the estimates, between 119 million to 124 million people will be poor in the world by 2020, with 60 percent of them living in Southern Asia. The present forecasts draw attention to the fact, that the global poverty rate will then be 7% (approximately 600 million people) in 2030, lacking in terms of the goal of eradicating poverty (United Nations, 2021).

Inequalities Amongst Countries

Focusing on the disparity between government and private sector net worth is one way to understand these discrepancies. Countries have been much wealthier over the last four decades, while governments have turned out to be considerably poorer.

In successful countries, the proportion of money owned by public actors is nearly zero or negative, implying that private actors hold all wealth. During the Covid crisis, governments borrowed an equivalent of 10-20 percent of GDP, largely from the private sector, has accelerated this trend.

The existing little possessions of the governments have significant consequences for state capacities to address future inequality, over and above the crucial 21st century concerns such as climate change. Within countries and globally, there are disparities. Over the last three decades, global multimillionaires have reaped an inconsistent amount of global wealth growth: the top 1% has taken 38 percent of all additional wealth produced ever since the mid1990s, while the lowest 50% have taken only 2%.

This disparity arises from significant disparities in development between the topmost and the bottom most quartiles of the assets allocation. Since 1995, the affluence of the world's wealthiest people has expanded at a rate of 6 to 9% each year, while average wealth has grown at 3.2 percent per year. The percentage of global wealth held by billionaires has increased from 1% to over 3% since 1995. During the COVID epidemic, this rise was accelerated. In reality, the global billionaires' proportion of wealth increased at its fastest rate on record in 2020.

Between the early twentieth century and the 1980s, wealth disparity in Western countries was greatly reduced, although the poorer half of the populace in these countries has at all times possessed very little, between 2% and 7% of the total. In the other region, the contribution of the lowest half of the population is significantly smaller. These findings demonstrate that there is still considerable work to be completed in every county of the world if severe wealth disparities are to be reduced.

An organization's lifeblood is finance. Financial markets and intermediation are designed to aid in the flow of resources to where it is required, hence boosting global national incomes. Over the last few decades, financialization has a vital role in the global expansion of private capital. In practice, modern economies' financialization can have disastrous consequences for the reason that it makes them more susceptible to financial crises, which can spread globally due to financial integration (for example, the 2008-09 financial crisis began with the subprime loans in the United States and then stretched globally). Financial intermediation also has the effect of separating investment decisions about capital allocation and use from where economic growth really occurs. Investors from Singapore who choose to invest in the United States have distinct motivations than laborers and owners of capital in the United States. As a result, financial intermediation creates significant governance and regulatory concerns.

While financialization has risen dramatically in nations such as France and Japan in recent decades, some countries have resisted the trend. Financial liability to national income in Germany increased from 400 percent in 1980 to 800 percent in 2005 before falling to 700 percent, indicating that financialization has little to do with general financial achievement.

Financial wealth is increasingly held by foreigners as a result of the rise of financialization. Foreign liabilities account for 25-30% of domestic financial obligations in France and Germany (and other European countries in common), up from fewer than 10% in the beginning of 1980s and increasing significantly in the 2000s. In the United States, foreign financial liabilities have climbed as well, although at 17%, they are still far smaller than in Europe. The profiles of China and Japan are quite distinct. Their international financial liabilities account for 5% of their domestic financial liabilities in China and 10% in Japan, respectively. East Asian economic behemoths are far less receptive to global financial investment than their Western counterparts. The Chinese dynamics are fascinating to see. Foreign financial ownership in China grew quickly between 1978 and the mid-1990s, gaining ground with that of the United States. Their paths diverged after the mid-1990s, when China tightened its control over foreign money flows. Part of the rationale for the stark contrasts between European countries and others is their size: since European countries are diminutive than the United States, Japan, and China, the rest of the globe would only hold approximately 15-20 percent of European wealth if ownership were pooled at the European level (similar to US levels). Nonetheless, certain Asian countries, like as Japan and China, are more resistant to foreign ownership than European and North American ones. It's too soon to say whether the current US and European Union declarations aimed at restricting foreign ownership (particularly by China) would have a substantial impact on foreign asset ownership in these nations.

From the perspective of those who don't travel around the world and spend the most of their money in their own nations, Purchasing Power Parity provides a more accurate picture of global disparity. Though Market Exchange Rates (MER) may be a better way to reveal the level of inequality in a society where people are free to spend their money anyway they desire. At prevailing market exchange rates, the poorest half of the population, or 50% of the population, owns only 1% of global wealth, while the top 10% owns roughly 3%. PPP is frequently used to study global income disparities, but it is less frequently employed to discuss wealth inequality. When discussing wealth, though, both PPP and MER may be significant depending on the subject.

While focusing on the bottom of the global wealth distribution, it makes appropriate to utilize PPP values: €3,000 (at the existing market determined exchange rates) is a significant quantity of money in Ghana, yet €3,000 (at current market determined exchange rates) is a pittance in Germany. PPP aids us in comprehending these distinctions: Given the dissimilarity in the cost of commodities and services in the two countries, €3,000 in Ghana is worth slightly more than €9,000 in Germany. PPP is less useful in the case of international multimillionaires and billionaires, whereas Market Exchange Rates are further useful. Individuals with a billion dollars, whether in Ghana or Germany, use up a greater portion of their earnings and assets worldwide rather than just in their home country.

As a result, it is further logical to investigate the income of the very affluent and its consequences in terms of tax levy and redistribution, for example, using Market Exchange Rates (Bauluz, 2021b).

Inequalities in Carbon Emissions

Inequalities in worldwide revenue and prosperity are inextricably linked to inequalities in ecological and climate change. Fossil fuel combustion, certain manufacturing operations (such as cement manufacture), agricultural output (for example, cows discharge more of greenhouse gases), deforestation and waste management all contribute to carbon dioxide emissions. Carbon dioxide ($CO2$), in addition to other greenhouse gases including methane ($CH4$) and nitrous oxides, are produced as a result of these processes (NOx).

All of these gases contribute to global warming in distinct ways: one ton of methane equals 30 tons of CO2 released, while one ton of nitrous oxide equals 280 tons of CO2. Humans produce 6.6 tons of carbon dioxide (CO2) per capita per year on average. The new data related to inequalities in carbon emission indicates significant global disparity in CO2 emissions: the top 10% of emitters account for almost half of all emissions, while the poorest 50% account for only 12% of total emissions.

It demonstrates that inequalities aren't merely a matter of rich vs. poor countries. High emitters are found in lower- and middle-income countries, while low emitters are found in wealthy nations. The bottom half of Europe's people emit roughly five tons per person per year; the bottom half of East Asia emits approximately three tons, and the bottom half of North America emits around ten tons. This is in stark contrast to the emissions of the richest ten percent of the population in these areas (29 tons in Europe, 39 in East Asia, and 73 in North America). When these goals are presented on a per capita basis, the poorest half of the inhabitants in affluent countries is already at (or near) the 2030 climate objective established by rich countries, according to this analysis. For the upper half of the population, this is not the case.

Large disparities in emissions indicate that climate strategies should concentrate more on the richest polluters. Climatic regulations, for instance carbon taxes, have unreasonably impacted low and middle-income groups while excluding the utilization behavior of the wealthiest sectors untouched (Chancel, 2021).

Financial Inequalities

Regardless of the recent statements concerning the end of tax evasion and financial secrecy, the global financial system continues to be decidedly opaque in the twenty-first century. In practice, researchers, journalists, people, and government officials continue to face significant challenges in tracking global income and wealth transfers. Let us state right once that this predicament is the result of governmental decisions and is not unavoidable. Inequality is pervasive in the digital age, although it is frequently absent from public data. It's ironic, for example, that fortune magazines are frequently used by tax administration and the common public around the globe to be acquainted about the echelon of wealth disparity. In general, tax administrators should gather and circulate data on how diverse wealth groups operate in the international and nationwide economies, starting with the richest of the population to the poorest[6].

Housing Inequalities Globally

The rise in housing disparity highlights one of capitalism's basic inconsistencies in today's increasingly urbanized form. The concentration of intellect, industry, investment, and other economic assets in limited areas of cities and metropolitan areas is both the fundamental driver of economic growth and the most significant source of inequality. Much more than income or any other source of revenue, the capacity to buy and hold housing is a crucial role in the rising disparities between the economy's winners and losers.

The Global House Price Index monitors changes in average household prices in 56 nations and territories throughout the world. In local currencies, the index tracks nominal and actual price growth. Globally, house prices are continuing to grow. In the year leading up to Q3 2021, the average home's value climbed by 9.4%, up from 9.2% the previous quarter. Only Malaysia and Morocco defied the trend, with prices rising year over year in 54 of the 56 countries and territories examined by the index. Moreover, the proportion of property markets experiencing yearly price growth of more than 10% has increased to 48%, up from 13% at the start of the epidemic. With a 2.1 percent increase in rates during the year, India is ranked 51st in annual home price appreciation during Q4 2021 .

In nominal terms, Turkey has the highest house price index, with prices rising 59.6% in Q4 2021.When you take out Turkish inflation, which was 36 percent at the end of 2021 (and 54 percent by the end of February), Australia comes out on top in actual terms, with a 17.5 percent increase in prices. Turkey, New Zealand (22.6 percent), Czech Republic (22.1 percent), Slovakia (22.1 percent), and Australia (22.1 percent) are the top five performers, regardless of whether nominal or real prices are being tracked.

In 2021, just three markets – Malaysia (0.7%), Malta (3.1%), and Morocco – had price declines (6.3 percent). The 10 markets where house prices have raised the most since the epidemic began are mostly developed markets where governments have intervened to bolster economies and, in some cases, property markets through holidays packages or government subsidies[7].

Inequalities in Education

From a gender standpoint, the educational landscape in 1995 was considerably different. The blatant discrimination against millions of girls and women exposed in various parts of the world had consequences that are still with us today: directly, in the form of a sharply rising proportion of women in the total population of illiterate adults, and indirectly, with women bearing the consequences of having no support in matters of reproductive success or inclusion in business, socioeconomic, and political processes.

One aspect of exclusion in educational systems is gender discrepancy and inequality. Girls are fewer likely to have the right to use, participate in, and finish education in many, usually poorer nations, whereas boys are most likely to be disconnected from education in other countries, mostly richer ones. Girls and boys, as well as women and men, are not all the same. Their educational experiences are molded not only by gender, but furthermore by an amalgamation of economic, political, cultural and social elements that influence individual prospects as well as communal institutions. As a result, it's critical to include both micro-level events like personal identity formation and interpersonal interactions, as well as macro-level issues like educational policies and practices (Grant & Zweir, 2017).

In 2018, girls and boys enrolled in elementary and secondary education in similar proportions around the world, compared to roughly 90 females for every 100 boys in 1995; this growth was fueled by huge increases in Southern Asia, particularly India. Girls' primary school achievement rates enhanced more rapidly than boys' in the 56 nations having data from 2000 to 2018. Girls were more likely than boys to complete elementary education in one-third of the 86 nations having 2013–18 data.

Regardless of the progress made in school enrollment across the globe, ICT skills are becoming more disparate. Women are less probable to have utilized a fundamental mathematics formula in a worksheet in the seven poorest countries, whereas parity prevails in the three richest countries, according to a study of ten low- and middle-income countries with thorough data. Three-quarters of primary school-aged youngsters who may never attend school are girls around the world. In 2018, there were fewer than 90 females for every 100 boys in elementary, lower secondary, and upper secondary education in seven nations. In four nations, fewer than 80 girls completed primary school, 15 countries completed lower secondary, and 22 countries completed upper secondary.

Almost no deprived rural young woman completes higher secondary school in at least 20 countries, while over 70% of poor boys do not meet the minimal reading competency level in 24 countries participating in PISA 2018. In terms of literacy skills, the most marginalized women are even further behind. Women in the age group of 15 to 49 from the poorest household are four times more likely than those from the wealthiest households to be illiterate in 59 countries.

Over two-thirds of countries have less than 25% of females studying engineering, manufacturing, or construction, or ICT. Girls' professional choices are hampered by gender segregation by field of study. Only 14% of top-performing girls in science or math anticipated to work in science or engineering in OECD countries, compared to 26% of top-performing guys. In Silicon Valley, women make up less than 1% of the application group for technological positions in Data analytics and Artificial Intelligence (UNESCO, 2020).

HOW CAN WE REDUCE INEQUALITY?

"Doing the right things at the right time is the rope which binds the wealth, making it boundless."– Thirukkural, Chapter 49, Verse 482.

Over the last four decades, the growth of social spending and redistribution in developing and rising countries have been relatively sluggish. Hundreds of millions of natives have been pulled out of tremendous poverty, yet hundreds of millions more are still struggling to make ends meet. The Welfare State's fragility in numerous parts of the world raises serious concerns at a time when large investments in education, healthcare and infrastructure are essential to meet the dynamic challenges of the twenty-first century[8].

The Global Preparedness Monitoring Board published their third Annual report in October 2021; 'From Worlds Apart to a World Prepared' claimed that the Covid 19 pandemic was caused by inaction and disparity among the countries. The onus is on the governments of every country to reduce the inequalities that persist and enhance opportunities for growth and development. However, the role of the government is crucial in reducing these effects.

Some governments have made requests to change production destinations, encourage self-reliance, and unravel trade integration in order to establish a more "resilient" economy as a result of pandemic-related economic difficulties.

Appropriate economic policies intended at the overall welfare of the people can definitely reduce the problem of inequality across all countries. Tax aid, income support or transfers from the government programs such as welfare measures for all sections of the society, reducing the cost on education, free health care universally, subsidies, distribution of essential commodities at lesser cost, progressive taxation, corporate regulations, public private partnership in disaster management, social security measures etc are a few examples of policies that governments might use to reduce inequality. A prudent tax policy aimed at reducing income and wealth disparities in all countries might pave the way for true equality.

Mobility, on the other hand, provides answers since it permits for rapid information transmission, promoting research that can lead to the discovery of remedies for communicable diseases in the shorter duration and the intensification of wellbeing in the long run. Universal healthcare coverage at a reasonable cost for all segments of the population to safeguard them from unanticipated health complications and pandemics.

The education system alone will not be able to achieve gender parity in education. Gender bias in education is a result of lingering negative gender standards in society, which influence instructors' attitude, subject and professional choices, and women's prospects later in life.

Countries must rework to make schools all-encompassing of children, regardless of their origin, abilities, or identities. This necessitates improved sanitation in schools, a stronger focus on gender-based violence in schools, particularly online, and policies that encourage girls to return to school. At a point in time when COVID-19 has worsened inequality, the message of inclusiveness is powerful.

Universal preschool education and childcare sponsored by the government could bring financial advantages to lesser skilled and low-income individuals while also assisting women in remaining in the workforce. Primary education for all children worldwide at zero cost, improving edification quality, and introducing additional skill training initiatives at the school level.

Because many working women have left the workforce to take on care duties, the COVID-19 problem has highlighted the need for sustained, expanded public investment in childcare. Investing in and expanding publicly financed childcare is another approach to generate non-automated jobs.

The fundamental concepts of globalization need to be reexamined. It is acceptable to presume that every country in the globe should encompass equivalent rights to growth, in the sense that every person should, at the very least, have equivalent access to basic education and healthcare facilities. The query of how to support such essential services is largely political, relying on the norms and institution established by the societies all over the world. The transfer of international aid to low-income countries might then resume. However, this would be on top of the significant increased tax revenue that growing countries already generate (Mann, 2015).

While the WTO has already made a significant contribution to economic resilience, it can and must do more as we face an increasing number of natural and man-made hazards and disasters in the future. The trading system, on the other hand, has shown to be more resilient than numerous forecasts at the start of the crisis. Even though the epidemic first affected international economic stream, supply chains quickly changed, products sustained to flow across borders, and many economies began to recover steadily.

CONCLUSION

Globalization in reality has abridged the inequality across countries and has paved way for progress and development, but the growth is not consistently spread across countries. The advancement of computers and internet led to the emergence of technically sophisticated companies that deliberated the trail to conduct business much more efficiently. Tapping the global markets brought in a plethora of opportunities for the manufacturers as well as the consumers in varied dimensions. Automation and trade reforms have dramatically altered labor markets in industrialized countries, delivering disproportionate benefits to highly educated and skilled individuals. Inequality between the world's poorest and wealthiest people has reduced significantly in recent decades.

"If we could change ourselves, the tendencies in the world would also change. As a man changes his own nature, so does the attitude of the world change towards him. We need not wait to see what others do." - Mahatma Gandhi

The best change can happen only when we change, a lot of research reports have given us an idea of the prevalent level of inequality across continents, and the onus does not lie only with the policy makers, economists, the government, corporate leaders etc. to implement new policies, but it lies with each one of us who desire the world as a better place to inhabit. Blending of thoughts towards enhanced sustainable development and collaborating with the various stakeholders will definitely pave way to equality. Cooperation and harmony across all communities and countries would undoubtedly improve the quality of life of the people in the world.

REFERENCES

Acker, J. (1990). Hierarchies, jobs, bodies: A theory of gendered organizations. *Gender & Society*, *4*(2), 139–158. doi:10.1177/089124390004002002

Ahn, P. D., & Wickramasinghe, D. (2021). Pushing the limits of accountability: Big data analytics containing and controlling COVID-19 in South Korea. *Accounting, Auditing & Accountability Journal, 34*(6), 1320–1331. doi:10.1108/AAAJ-08-2020-4829

Ahrens, T., & Ferry, L. (2021). Accounting and accountability practices in times of crisis: A Foucauldian perspective on the UK government's response to COVID-19 for England. *Accounting, Auditing & Accountability Journal, 34*(6), 1332–1344. doi:10.1108/AAAJ-07-2020-4659

Alkire, B. C., Peters, A. W., Shrime, M. G., & Meara, J. G. (2018). The economic consequences of mortality amenable to high-quality health care in low-and middle-income countries. *Health Affairs, 37*(6), 988–996. doi:10.1377/hlthaff.2017.1233 PMID:29863936

Alvaredo, Chancel, Piketty, Saez, & Zucman. (2018). *World Inequality Report 2018*. Harvard University Press. https://www.hup.harvard.edu/catalog.php?isbn=9780674984554

Bajard & Chancel. (2021). *Global wealth inequality on WID.world: Estimates and imputations*. WID World Technical Note 2021/02.

Barbera, C., Guarini, E., & Steccolini, I. (2020). How do governments cope with austerity? The roles of accounting in shaping governmental financial resilience. *Accounting, Auditing & Accountability Journal, 33*(3), 529–558. doi:10.1108/AAAJ-11-2018-3739

Bauluz. (2021a). https://wid.world/methodology,%20Bauluz%20et%20al.%20(2021)%20and%20updates

Bauluz. (2021b). https://wir2022.wid.world/methodology/

Blanchet, Sodano, & Toledano. (2021). Estimation of Global Wealth Aggregates in WID. World: Methodology. WID World Working Paper 2021/22.

Bloom, D. E., Canning, D., & Sevilla, J. (2004). The effect of health on economic growth: A production function approach. *World Development, 32*(1), 1–13. doi:10.1016/j.worlddev.2003.07.002

Boisclair, D., Decarie, Y., Laliberte-Auger, F., Michaud, P. C., & Vincent, C. (2018). The economic benefits of reducing cardiovascular disease mortality in Quebec, Canada. *PLoS One, 13*(1), e0190538. doi:10.1371/journal.pone.0190538 PMID:29300783

Brammer, S., Branicki, L., & Linnenluecke, M. K. (2020). COVID-19, societalization, and the future of business in society. *The Academy of Management Perspectives*, *34*(4), 493–507. doi:10.5465/amp.2019.0053

Chancel. (2021). https://wir2022.wid.world/

Chen, L. C., Huq, E., & d'Souza, S. (1981). Sex bias in the family allocation of food and health care in rural Bangladesh. *Population and Development Review*, *7*(1), 55–70. doi:10.2307/1972764

Cockburn, C. (1983). *Brothers: Male dominance and technological change*. Pluto.

Connell, R. W. (1987). *Gender and power*. Polity.

French, D. (2012). Causation between health and income: A need to panic. *Empirical Economics*, *42*(2), 583–601. doi:10.100700181-011-0541-5

Gayathri, R., & Vijayabanu, C. (2021). Upshot of Gender Inequalities Towards Labor Markets: A Macro Level Perspective. In *Women Empowerment and Well-Being for Inclusive Economic Growth* (pp. 73–88). IGI Global.

Grant, C. A., & Zwier, E. (2017). *Intersectionality and education*. Oxford University Press. doi:10.1093/obo/9780199756810-0188

Gunawardana, S. J. (2014). Reframing employee voice: A case study in Sri Lanka's export processing zones. *Work, Employment and Society*, *28*(3), 452–468. doi:10.1177/0950017013491451

Heilman, M. E., & Caleo, S. (2018). *Gender discrimination in the workplace*. Academic Press.

Hewamanne, S. (1999). If They Allow Us We Will Fight": Strains of Consciousness Among Women Workers in the Katunayake Free Trade Zone. *Anthropology of Work Review*, *19*(3), 8–13. doi:10.1525/awr.1999.19.3.8

Husain, M. J. (2010). Contribution of health to economic development: A survey and overview. *Economics, 4*(1).

Madsen, J. B. (2016). Health, human capital formation and knowledge production: Two centuries of international evidence. *Macroeconomic Dynamics*, *20*(4), 909–953. doi:10.1017/S1365100514000650

Mann, G. (2015). *From Empires to NGOs in the West African Sahel* (Vol. 129). Cambridge University Press. https://www.cambridge.org/core/books/from-empires-to-ngos-in-the-west-african-sahel/A091DE71429912E256C6A1E093CD7274

Marmot, M., Friel, S., Bell, R., Houweling, T. A., & Taylor, S. (2008). Closing the gap in a generation: Health equity through action on the social determinants of health. *Lancet*, *372*(9650), 1661–1669. doi:10.1016/S0140-6736(08)61690-6 PMID:18994664

McInnes, D. K., Li, A. E., & Hogan, T. P. (2013). Opportunities for engaging low-income, vulnerable populations in health care: A systematic review of homeless persons' access to and use of information technologies. *American Journal of Public Health*, *103*(S2), e11–e24. doi:10.2105/AJPH.2013.301623 PMID:24148036

McMichael, A. J., McKee, M., Shkolnikov, V., & Valkonen, T. (2004). Mortality trends and setbacks: Global convergence or divergence? *Lancet*, *363*(9415), 1155–1159. doi:10.1016/S0140-6736(04)15902-3 PMID:15064037

Mihalache, I. C. (2019). Health state of human capital in the economic theory. *Postmodern Openings*, *10*(4), 182–192. doi:10.18662/po/102

Monterubbianesi, P. D., Grandes, M., & Dabús, C. (2017). New evidence of the health status and economic growth relationship. *Panoeconomicus*, *64*(4), 439–459. doi:10.2298/PAN150505020M

OECD. (n.d.). https://www.oecd-ilibrary.org/economics/a-contribution-to-the-purchasing-power-parity-vs-market-exchange-rates-for-use-in-long-term-scenarios-discussion_oecd_papers-v6-art9-en#:~:text=Market%20Exchange%20Rates%20(MER)%20balance,and%20services%20in%20different%20countries

Peterson Institute for International Economics. (2020). https://www.piie.com/research/piie-charts/how-governments-tax-reduces-inequality-more-how-theyspend%20%C2%A9%202020%20Peterson%20Institute%20for%20International%20Economics

Piette, J. D., Lun, K. C., Moura, L. A. Jr, Fraser, H. S., Mechael, P. N., Powell, J., & Khoja, S. R. (2012). Impacts of e-health on the outcomes of care in low-and middle-income countries: Where do we go from here? *Bulletin of the World Health Organization*, *90*(5), 365–372. doi:10.2471/BLT.11.099069 PMID:22589570

PIIE. (n.d.). https://www.piie.com/commentary/op-eds/right-question-about-inequality-and-growth

Piketty, T. (2014). *Capital in the 21st century*. Harvard University Press. https://www.hup.harvard.edu/catalog.php?isbn=9780674430006

Thomasson, A., Lapsley, I., & Steccolini, I. (2020). "Managing" wicked problems: Uncovering the roles of budgets, financial systems, and collaboration. *Financial Accountability & Management, 36*(2), 113–116. doi:10.1111/faam.12246

UNESCO. (2020). *Global education monitoring report gender report 2020*. https://en.unesco.org/gem-report/gender-reviews

United Nations [UN]. (2021). *The UN Sustainable Goals Development Report 2021*. https://unstats.un.org/sdgs/report/2021/The-Sustainable-Development-Goals-Report-2021.pdf

Well, D. N. (2007). Accounting for the effect of health on economic growth. *The Quarterly Journal of Economics, 122*(3), 1265–1306. doi:10.1162/qjec.122.3.1265

WHO Commission on Social Determinants of Health & World Health Organization. (2008). *Closing the gap in a generation: health equity through action on the social determinants of health: Commission on Social Determinants of Health final report*. World Health Organization.

Wir2022. (n.d.). https://wir2022.wid.world/chapter-10/

WID. (n.d.). https://wir2022.wid.world/www-site/uploads/2021/12/wir2022-full-report-english.pdf

World Bank. (2020). *Poverty and Shared Prosperity 2020: Reversals of Fortune*. Washington, DC: World Bank. https://www.worldbank.org/en/publication/poverty-and-shared-prosperity/

World Bank. (n.d.a). https://datahelpdesk.worldbank.org/knowledgebase/articles/906519-world-bank-country-and-lending-groups

World Bank. (n.d.b). https://www.worldbank.org/en/topic/poverty/overview

World Economic Forum. (2021). *Global Gender Gap Report 2021*. https://www3.weforum.org/docs/WEF_GGGR_2021

World Health Organization. (n.d.). https://covid19.who.int/

KEY TERMS AND DEFINITIONS

Gini Co-Efficient: It is used to measure the distribution of income across various sections of the population in a country.

Global House Price Index (GHPI): An index that measures the housing prices in 56 countries using official statistics.

Market Exchange Rate (MER): It refers to the market exchange rate used for trade by different countries.

Purchasing Power Parity (PPP): It is used to compare the standard of living of people in different countries by examining the price level of common commodities.

Theil Index: It is used to measure the prevailing economic inequality of the population.

ENDNOTES

1 For more data on poverty, see World Bank (2020).

2 This value is expressed at PPP. At Market Exchange Rates (MER), global wealth is equal to €392 trillion. At MER, EUR1= USD1.2 = CNY7. Global net wealth is the sum of global net private wealth and global net public wealth. Global net private wealth is equal to the sum of all financial and non-financial assets, net of debts, held by the private sector (OECD, n.d.).

3 For more in depth discussion of inequality dynamics in China and Brazil, see Alvaredo et al. (2018).

4 Low-income countries as per World Bank definition, i.e. per capita Gross national income less than $1,045 (World Bank, n.d.a).

5 We estimate global tax revenues at around 5% of global income in 1900, 20% in 1950 and 25-27% in 1980 (Wir2022, n.d.).

6 This chapter is based on data from Blanchet et al. (2021) and from Bajard and Chancel. (2021).

7 Knight Frank Research Reports are available at https://www.knightfrank.com/research

8 The number of global extreme poor (living with less than $1.9 per day) decreased from 1.9 billion in 1990 to 730 million in 2020 according to the World Bank (n.d.b).

Chapter 3
Post-Pandemic Global Inequalities:
Causes and Measures

Neelima K.
https://orcid.org/0000-0002-4296-3273
Sree Vidyanikethan Engineering College, India

Subhas Chennapalli
JNTUA College of Engineering, Kalikiri, India

ABSTRACT

The global spread of COVID-19 in the post-pandemic situation had a very drastic impact on various aspects of livelihood. The deaths have risen to more than 3.1 million wherein majorly the aged people remained in danger. The other aspects include the inequalities in sectors like unequal income, prices, opportunity, vaccine access, global recovery, extreme poverty, rising debt levels, etc. The major causes of these are regional trends, migration of skilled workers, the impact of policy, climate mitigation, and adoption policies, etc. Due to sudden switching of teaching in online mode, the education levels have drastically fallen causing learning poverty too. The extreme increase in basic commodities and fuel prices is seen in post-pandemic situations. The climate conditions are also drastically affected causing the people to migrate from one place to another place globally or locally. This chapter details the various causes of post-pandemic situations and the measures to overcome them for eradicating global inequalities.

DOI: 10.4018/978-1-6684-5289-9.ch003

INTRODUCTION

The COVID-19 pandemic had affected lives in many aspects (Bick Alexander, 2020). The age group balances mismatched due to inequalities over gender, ethnic races, economy etc. The policymakers had to rapidly adjust their responses in the effort to "flatten the recession curve". The major causes of inequality being at economic, social, environmental, etc. levels. This chapter projects the impact of inequality around technological innovation, climate change, urbanization and international migration. Technological change provokes growth in economy by enhancing possibilities in the fields of education, health care, communication and productivity (Gourinchas PO, 2020). But still it affects absurdly with wage inequality and displace workers. The climate change accelerates the suffering of the poorest countries and groups living in rural areas. Urbanization provides unmatched opportunities for wealth but allows glaring of high and growing levels of inequality. International migration of people for seeking new opportunities helps in reduction of global disparities (Chen Sophia, 2020). The inequality and crisis trend is as shown in figure 1.

The wealth inequality reported by World Bank is as shown in figure 2. Nearly 50% of the population owns only 2% of the total wealth while 1% of the population owns 38% among 10% of population owning 75% of the total wealth.

The wealth and health of richer countries in spite of their advantages have shown a larger loss in life years due to the pandemic than many poorer countries as shown in figure 3.

The major focus is on

Inequality

Inequality i.e., as of now where we stand. The 2030 Agenda aims at ensuring equal opportunity and draws attention to attributes and circumstances that affect access to opportunity, namely age, sex, disability, race, ethnicity, origin, religion and economic or other status. While high- and growing-income inequality is fueling polarized political debates around the globe, a consensus has indeed emerged that all should enjoy equal access to opportunity – that one's chances to succeed in life should not be determined by circumstances beyond an individual's control.

The Technological Revolution: Winners and Losers –

The world being ready for rapid, revolutionary and often disruptive technological breakthroughs. Advances in biology and genetics, robotics and artificial intelligence, 3D printing, and other digital technologies are transforming economies and societies, with unfolding and often unforeseen consequences. For all its promise, technological

Figure 1. Inequality and crisis (Ruth Hill, 2021)

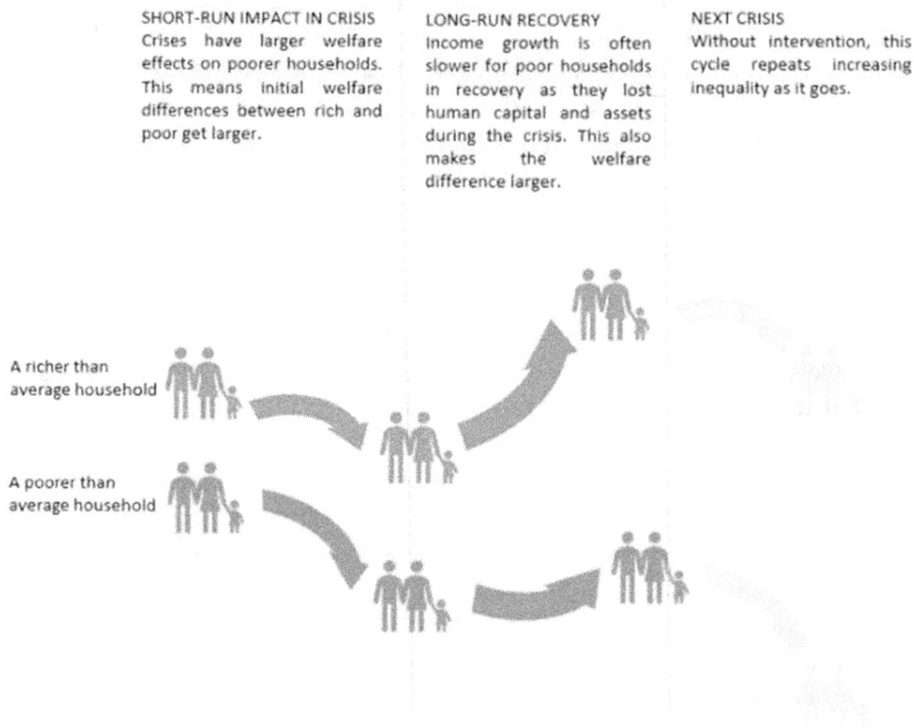

Figure 2. Wealth Inequality report by World Bank during 2022

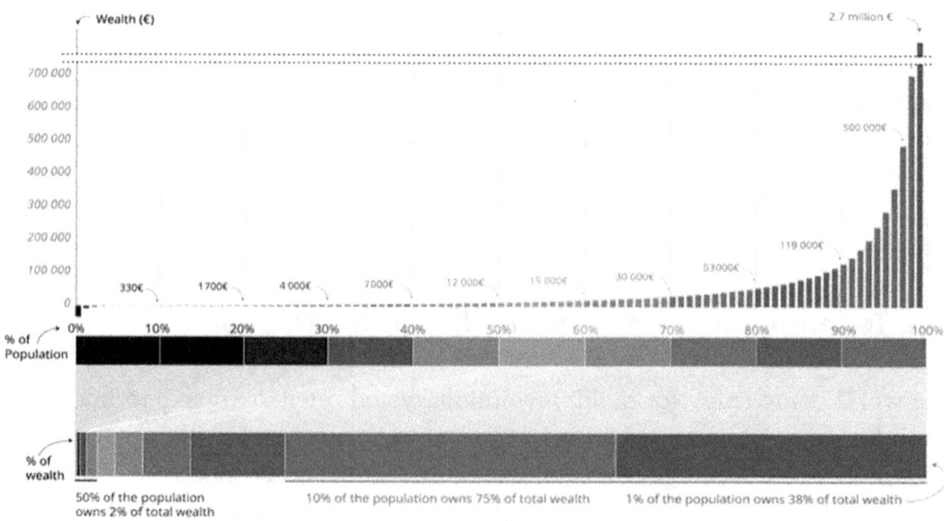

Figure 3. Purchasing Power Parity as mentioned by Ferreira and others (2021)

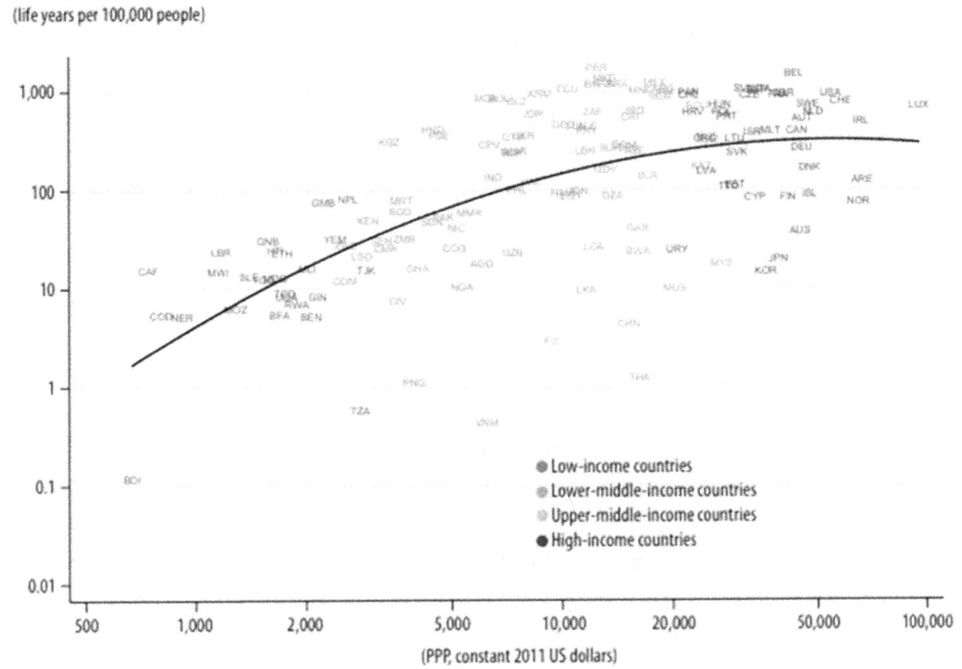

change tends to create winners and losers. And its current pace brings new and urgent policy challenges for navigating uncharted territories. Much depends on how these policies play out, especially on the degree to which Governments and international institutions address distributional effects and maximize the benefits and opportunities that new technologies can bring. In the world of work, emphasis has focused largely on the potential implications of technological change for job destruction. Yet technologies usually replace specific tasks, rather than entire jobs. Often ignored is the fact that new technologies also generate new jobs and tasks, including those necessary to use, test, supervise and market new products and services (Autor D., 2020).

Climate Change: Exacerbating Poverty and Inequality

Climate change accelerates environmental degradation and increasing the frequency and intensity of extreme weather events, among other impacts. The effects of both gradual environmental degradation and sudden shocks, such as hurricanes and floods, disproportionately affect vulnerable populations. Whether they impinge on infrastructure, livelihoods, resources, health or even the loss of lives and homes, these impacts are by no means uniform across countries or population groups. Rising temperatures have adversely affected economic growth in countries located in the tropics, which tend to be poorer than countries located in more temperate climate zones. They have made the world's poorest countries poorer. The ratio between the income of the richest and poorest 10 per cent of the global population is 25 per cent larger than it would be in a world without global warming. Unaddressed, changes in climate can reverse current progress in reducing inequality among countries (Baarsch, 2019).

Urbanization

Expanding Opportunities but Deeper Divides - Geography matters i.e., where a person are born and live has a lasting influence on their opportunities in life. Access to safe drinking water, electricity, health care, good schools, decent work and other goals envisioned in the 2030 Agenda have a clear spatial dimension. Regional inequalities within countries are often larger than inequalities among countries. Disparities between rural and urban areas stand out. The rural-urban divide is closing in some countries but widening in others. The gap in levels of stunting among children, for instance, has declined in 35 out of 53 developing countries with data – and has increased in the remaining 18 – since the 1990s. The difference between the percentage of urban and rural residents that have access to electricity has increased in 23 out of 55 countries with data.

International Migration

A Force for Equality under the Right Conditions - International migration is a powerful symbol of global inequality, whether in terms of wages, opportunities or lifestyles. Millions of people move each year across countries and continents to seek better job opportunities, study, marry, reunite with family members or flee conflict or natural disasters. Migration does not arise only from inequality or failed development: middle-income countries send more migrants abroad than low-income countries (Clemens, 2019). In general, migration takes off once countries have started to grow economically and develop. Industrialization and urbanization have long been associated with massive displacements of people, mostly from rural to urban areas, but also across countries. As countries develop, more people have the economic means to migrate. Improvements in education and access to ideas, information and affordable transportation often increase the desire and opportunities to migrate. International migration generally benefits most migrants and their countries of origin and destination. Yet its costs and benefits are not shared evenly across countries or within countries (Republic of Kiribati, 2019).

Promoting Equality and Social Justice in a Changing World

The 2030 Agenda recognizes the challenges are interrelated and overcome them integrated solutions are required. Also addressing inequalities may now seize opportunities presented by the transformative changes for the world as a whole.

Causes for Inequality

The major causes for inequality (Carvalho Vasco M, 2020) are

1. Unequal vaccine access – a need for COVID-19 vaccines shared in fair and broad access to save lives so as to strengthen recovery of global economy (Cicala Steve, 2020).
2. Lack of infrastructure to deploy vaccines – many countries still require good infrastructure to ensure delivery and distribution of vaccines successfully.
3. Unequal global recovery – due to economic gaps i.e., white collar workers worked from home but low collar workers in services like nursing, policing, teaching, cleaning, etc had to live in contact with infected people. Low paid workers in sectors like hotels, restaurants, tourism services, etc had suspended activities which caused economic gaps and income losses for the poorest increased by 40% as shown in figure 4.

4. Trade disruptions at global and local levels so if provided with persistent foreign exports demand along with assurance for the availability of intermediate imported products and services.
5. Rising debt levels amid the pandemic – as per global economic prospects, the expansion of fastest and broadest world debt levels were experienced. It was acute in low-income countries that have led to debt distress during pandemic. The complexity of debt reporting as shown in figure 5.

As per debt transparency report of developing countries, large gaps of 30% of low-income countries was seen due to differing definitions and standards locally and internationally. This can be overcome by greater debt transparency to facilitate high quality investments with reduced corruption.

6. Increased learning poverty – 70% of low- and middle-income countries had experienced devastating impacts on the poor and vulnerable to inequalities in education due to prolonged closure of schools with poor learning outcomes as shown in Figure 6.

Figure 4. GDP Growth Rate during 2018-2021 (Venkata Gopala Krishnan, World Bank 2021 from Global Economic Prospects June 2021)

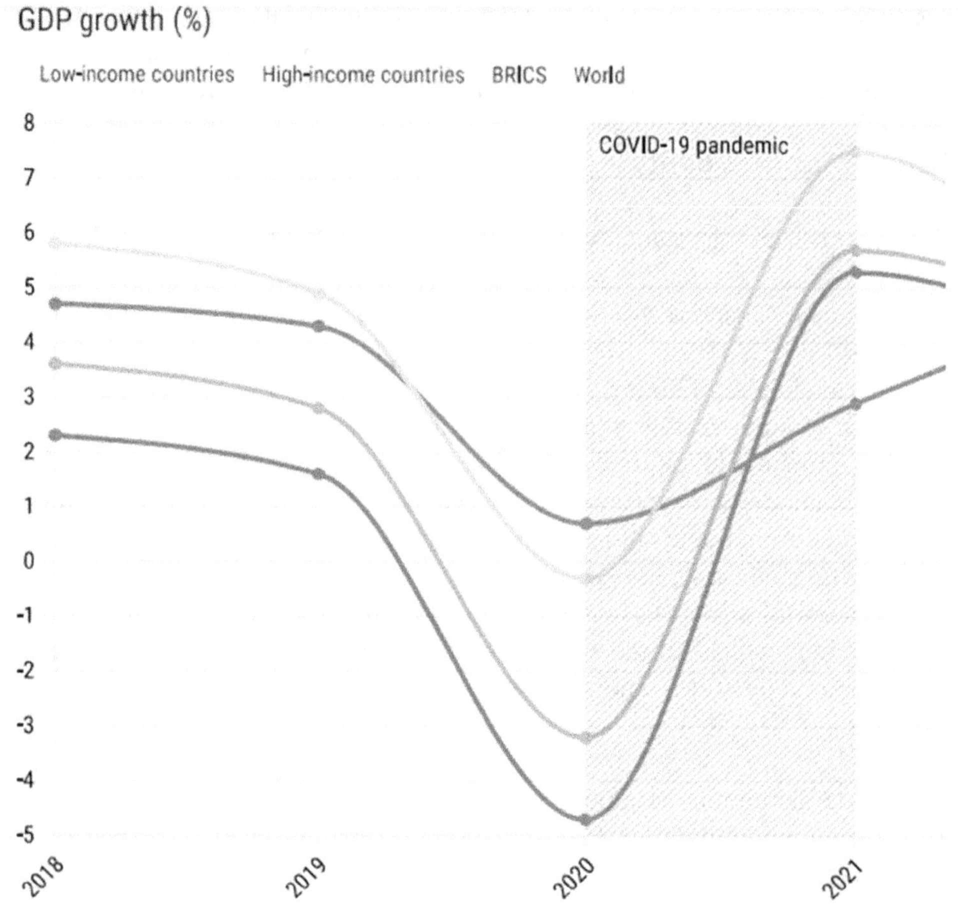

7. Rise in fuel and commodity costs – energy prices hiked by 80% higher in 2021 which exacerbated food insecurity in developing countries.
8. Challenging climate crisis – with natural calamities like flooding and vector borne diseases also impede alleviating extreme poverty.
9. Increased induced internal migrants could be reduced significantly if greenhouse gas emissions are reduced.
10. The gender and ethnic inequality also increased as poor, women, disabled, elderly and migrant populations have burnt of the fallout from the pandemic. As services like catering, hospitality were shut down (Ian Goldin, 2020). Many had to face job losses. The pandemic hotspots had concentrated more in poorer neighborhood. In New Orleans, people living on streets had probability

Figure 5. direct and indirect reporting of debt (Venkat Gopal krishnan, 2021)

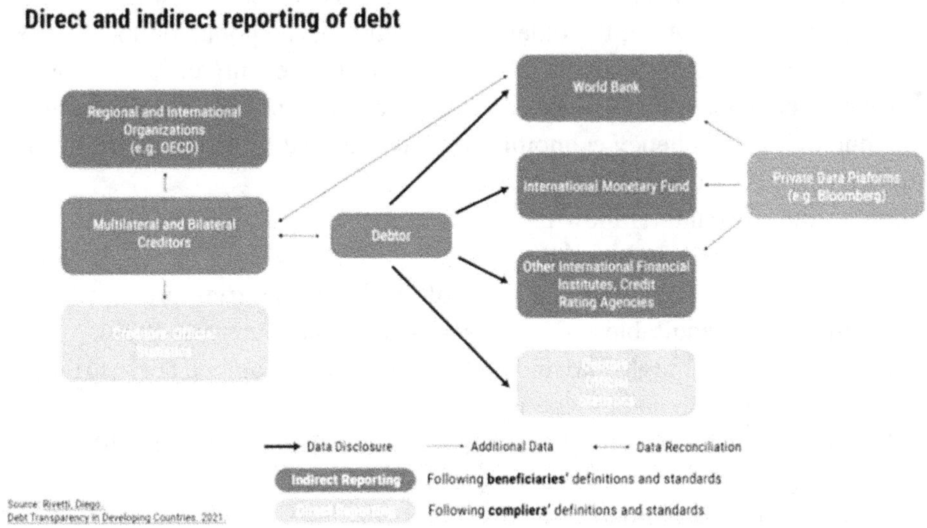

of black people 2 to 3 times more likely to die from COVID-19 than white people. The inequality is measured by parameters like the Gini coefficient, the Theil index, and the income share of the wealthiest in society which are sensitive to distribution and ranking (Francisco H.G. Ferreira, 2021) (Clark, 2020).

Using the concept of life years lost to the disease, the ages at death were estimated along with the residual life expectancies to find the mortality burden of the pandemic

Figure 6. Learning Poverty due to closure of schools

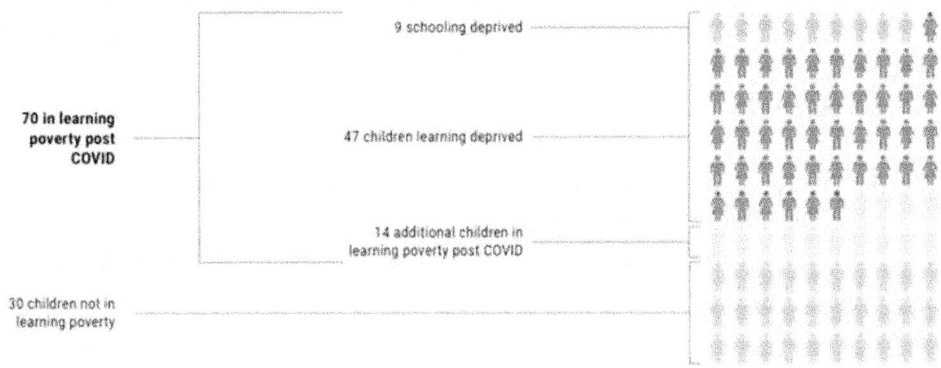

that has been positively correlated with national per capita income, despite good health conditions and public prevention systems enforced in richer countries (Deaton, 2021) (Ferreira, 2021). Also, the older age structure of the population and illness or lethality is highly age selective. Higher life expectancies, urbanization, and the spread of pandemic played a major role in trade. Inequality persists among low wage earners due to high frequency economic indicators in real time, large effect of the shutdown (Oriol Aspachs, 2021).

These studies reveal the following:

- 86% of public in 27 high- and middle-income countries preferred more sustainable and equitable economic status (António Guterres, 2020).
- 64% of public in 11 high- and middle-income countries agreed fair distribution of country's wealth and prosperity.
- 8/10 SMEs supported a wealth tax in Argentina (Esmé Berkhout, 2021).
- 71% of Europeans supported universal basic income.
- In the UK, 70% supported wage cap limits.
- In several countries, including India, Mexico, China, Brazil and South Africa, [3]80% supported for green economic recovery (UN, 2020).

Also, the prediction of impact was seriously assessed based on global poverty levels was at least by 2% points after pandemic for a period of decade as shown in figure 7.

POSSIBLE SOLUTIONS

Policymaking should be under an equality lens to reduce inequalities. As we can't allow growth in technological changes, urbanization or migration, their effects need to be managed to encourage sustainable societies (Kristalina Georgieva, 2020). Climate changes can be irreversible and significant. The countries can transit to green economies by adopting migration policies based on social considerations (P. Espinoza Revollo, 2021).

Make policies such that

1. Boost investments in health and education to prevent dropouts and provide learning support.
2. Level active labor market policies and training to enable re-entry of unemployed women and youth into jobs.

Figure 7. Prediction of Inequality Impact on Global Poverty Levels in the Decade after Pandemic (Oxfam International January 2021)

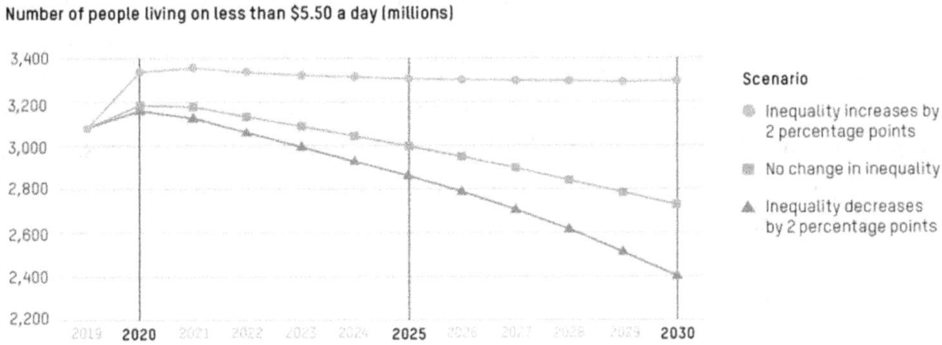

3. Enhance access to technological financial services provided for low cost with an access to digital infrastructure which helps micro and small firms to remain active and competitive.
4. Invest in social insurance to protect against loss of human and physical assets (Ruth Hill, 2021).

World Bank can boost support for climate adaptation to enable building of green economy i.e., climate smart economies with low carbon and resilient transition (Venkat Gopalkrishnan, 2021).

A world with equality as a measure that matters by a way of sustained reduction in inequality. Governments can set concrete, time-bound targets to reduce inequality by focusing on Gross Domestic Product (GDP). We can fight inequality including gender and racial by efforts for economic rescue and recovery (Chetty Raj, 2020).

The world and governments care for people by rejecting brutal and unsustainable austerity which ensure peoples' wealth, gender or race to not dictate their health or education. The future investment must be in free universal healthcare, education and other public services which lay foundation for free and fair societies with unparalleled power to reduce inequality. Also, they close or reduce the gap between rich and poor, women and men, etc. with unpaid care (Godoy, 2019).

The world without exploitation and income security by allowing businesses to be redesigned to prioritize society rather than greater payouts to rich stakeholders. Guaranteed income and maximum wages can be introduced as the billionaires with extreme wealth may become a cause of economic failure (Banerjee, Abhijit, 2019).

Motivate the richest to pay their fair share of tax for their increased wealth, financial transactions, etc. so as to put an end to tax dodging. This progressive taxation from the richest members of society can enable equitable recovery from the crisis and can serve as an investment for green and equitable future.

The climate safety and breakdown is the biggest threat to human existence which had destroyed the livelihoods and lives of poorest, economically excluded and historically oppressed communities. Especially women are affected most from these communities. Thus, the governments should initiate green economy that prevents further degradation of our planet. Also, the subsides for fossil fuels and its corporations must end so as to end rich shareholders making profits from government bailouts.

Final Motivation

A strong motivation needs to be appraised for

a. Reducing Inequality Within Countries:

Rethinking of strategies call countries to reduce inequalities within countries. Hence a single set of policies may or may not be applicable to all countries in all contexts.

b. Promote Equal Access to Opportunities

Universal access to quality education is capable of expanding opportunities and encouraging a more equal distribution of capabilities. The educational system has to serve as a medium to reinforce inequalities. The supporting people must realize their potential to promote full employment and decent work. The looming and transformative changes in work, the Governments and the international community need to manage them. The governments can increase investments in labor market institutions and policies, support new forms of collective representation, ensure that non-standard employment contracts or outside the formal sector also have a voice of opinion.

c. Institute a Macroeconomic Policy Environment

Greater equity can be obtained from Fiscal and monetary policies. With a direct impact on income distribution, the resources can be mobilized for social policies which in addition include social protection. The social contract can be adjusted by allocating taxes and expenditures appropriately.

Universal access of social protection reduces poverty and inequality. The social protection systems provide unemployment benefits, disability benefits, child benefits, old-age pensions, access to health care, etc. offer security of income at all stages of the life cycle and minimize the risk of poverty.

d. Tackle Prejudice and Discrimination to Enable Participation of Disadvantaged Groups in Economic, Social and Political Life

Social and economic policies still need reforms on the basis of ethnicity, race, gender or other characteristics to reduce inequality. Ending prejudice and discrimination requires reforming institutions, influencing social norms and behaviors. The changes in constitution, revision of laws and policies, framing of new laws to prevent discrimination, promoting the well-being of excluded groups can lay the groundwork for greater fairness. But still these measures are likely to encounter resistance and tend to challenge the status quo.

The lack of sound technical advice or adequate capacity along with the political constraints need to reduce inequality and devising ways to overcome them. The universal policy frameworks need broader support to focus on addressing inequality issues.

e. Reducing Inequality in an Interconnected World

Governments and other national stakeholders can modify the gaps in well-being and opportunities within and among countries as a national and global problem, which demand integrated, multilateral solutions. The decisions or actions of one country on climate change or international migration might affect costs and benefits for other countries. The issues of imbalance between top greenhouse gas-emitting countries and those suffering from the impacts of climate change can be addressed unilaterally. The concerted, coordinated and multilateral action is needed to address challenges that impact inequality like tax evasion, cross-border financial flows, transnational crime, international trade, intellectual property rights, etc.

The multilateral system needs to strengthen rather than dismissing the current global challenges. By restoring trust in international problem-solving needs multilateral institutions that give adequate voice to regions and countries with growing influence in the global economy.

Hence it is clear that reducing inequalities strengthens social front, economic and environmental dimensions for sustainable development. However, the growing inequalities and overreliance on the market threatens social justice and contract.

CONCLUSION

The COVID-19 pandemic exposed inequalities in terms of wealth, gender and race. Also, this crisis has led to destructive aspects in terms of global economy, unequal income, prices, opportunity, vaccine access, global recovery, extreme poverty, rising debt levels, etc. The majority of the causes whirl around regional trends, migration of skilled workers, the impact of policy, climate mitigation and adoption policies, etc. The various measures to overcome them can be strict policies, green economy adaptation, cooperation among humankind, etc at local and global levels.

REFERENCES

Alexander, B., & Adam, B. (2020). *Real time labor market estimates during the 2020 coronavirus outbreak*. Technical report, Arizona State University. https://papers.ssrn.com/sol3/papers.cfm?abstract_id=3692425

Aspachs, O., Durante, R., Graziano, A., Mestres, J., Reynal-Querol, M., & Montalvo, J. G. (2021, March 31). Tracking the impact of COVID-19 on economic inequality at high frequency. *PLoS One, 16*(3), e0249121. Advance online publication. doi:10.1371/journal.pone.0249121 PMID:33788886

Autor, D., Cho, D., Crane, L., Goldar, M., Lutz, B., & Montes, J. (2020, July). *An evaluation of the paycheck protection program using administrative payroll microdata*. Technical report, MIT WP. https://blueprintlabs.mit.edu/research/an-evaluation-of-the-paycheck-protection-program-using-administrative-payroll-microdata/

Baarsch, F., Granadillos, J. R., Hare, W., Knaus, M., Krapp, M., Schaeffer, M., & Lotze-Campen, H. (2020). The impact of climate change on incomes and convergence in Africa. *World Development, 126*, 104699. https://doi.org/10.1016/j.worlddev.2019.104699

Banerjee, A., Niehaus, P., & Suri, T. (2019). *Universal basic income in the developing world*. NBER Working Paper No. 25598. National Bureau of Economic Research. https://www.nber.org/system/files/working_papers/w25598/w25598.pdf

Berkhout, E., Galasso, N., Lawson, M., Pablo, A. R. M., Taneja, A., & Diego, A. V. P. (2021, January). *The Inequality Virus*. OXFAM Briefing Paper. https://www.oxfam.org/en/research/inequality-virus

Carvalho, V. M., Stephen, H., Alvaro, O., Ramon, G. J., Tomasa, R., & Rodriguez, M. S. (2020). Tracking the covid-19 crisis with high-resolution transaction data, Technical report. *CEPR, DP14642*. Advance online publication. doi:10.1098/rsos.210218

Clark, A., D'Ambrosio, C., & Lepinteur, A. (2020). *The Fall in Income Inequality during COVID-19 in Five European Countries. ECINEQ Working Paper 2020-565*. Society for the Study of Economic Inequality. http://www.ecineq.org/milano/WP/ECINEQ2020-565.pdf

Clemens, M. A., & Pritchett, L. (2019, May). The new economic cases for migration restrictions: An assessment. *Journal of Development Economics, 138*, 153–164. https://doi.org/10.1016/j.jdeveco.2018.12.003

Deaton, A. (2021). *COVID-19 and Global Income Inequality. NBER Working Paper 28392*. National Bureau of Economic Research. https://www.nber.org/papers/w28392

Espinoza Revollo, P. (2021). *The Inequality Virus: Methodology note*. Oxfam. https://oxfamilibrary.openrepository.com/bitstream/handle/10546/621149/bp-the-inequality-virus-summ-250121-en.pdf

Ferreira, F., Sterck, O., Mahler, D., & Decerf, B. (2021). Death and Destitution: The Global Distribution of Welfare Losses from the COVID-19 Pandemic, LSE Public. *Policy Review, 1*(4), 2. http://hdl.handle.net/10986/35634

Ferreira, F. H. G. (2021, June). Inequality in the time of COVID-19. *Finance & Development*, 20–23. https://www.imf.org/external/pubs/ft/fandd/2021/06/inequality-and-covid-19-ferreira.htm

Georgieva, K. (2020). No lost generation: can poor countries avoid the Covid trap? *The Guardian*. https://www.theguardian.com/business/2020/sep/29/covid-pandemic-imf-kristalina-georgieva

Godoy, A., & Reich, M. (2019, July). *Minimum wage effects in low-wage areas*. Institute for Research on Labour and Employment Working Paper No. 106-19. https://irle.berkeley.edu/files/2019/07/Godoy-Reich.pdf

Goldin, I., & Muggah, R. (2020, October 9). *COVID-19 is increasing multiple kinds of inequality*. Word Economic Forum. https://www.weforum.org/agenda/2020/10/covid-19-is-increasing-multiple-kinds-of-inequality-here-s-what-we-can-do-about-it/

Gopalkrishnan, V., Wadhwa, D., Haddad, S., & Blake, P. (2021, December 21). *2021 Year in Review in 11 charts: The Inequality Pandemic, Feature Story*. https://www.worldbank.org/en/news/feature/2021/12/20/year-2021-in-review-the-inequality-pandemic

Gourinchas, P. O. (Ed.). (2020). *Flattening the Pandemic and Recession Curves in Mitigating the COVID Economic Crisis: Act Fast and Do Whatever.* CEPR Press. https://voxeu.org/content/mitigating-covid-economic-crisis-act-fast-and-do-whatever-it-takes

Guterres. (2020). *World Social Report 2020: Inequality in a Rapidly Changing World.* United Nations Publication.

Hill, R., & Narayan, A. (2021, January 7). *What COVID-19 can mean for long term inequality in developing countries.* Voices. https://blogs.worldbank.org/voices/what-covid-19-can-mean-long-term-inequality-developing-countries

Raj, C., Friedman, J. N., Nathaniel, H., & Michael, S. (2020). *Real-time economics: A new platform to track the impacts of covid-19 on people, businesses, and communities using private sector data*. Technical report, NBER WP 27431. https://opportunityinsights.org/wp-content/uploads/2020/06/Short_Covid_Paper.pdf

Republic of Kiribati. (2019, May 1). *Tebunginako Village*. Office of the President. https://www.climate.gov.ki/case-studies/abaiang/

Sophia, C., Deniz, I., Nicola, P., & Presbitero, A. F. (2020). *Tracking the economic impact of covid-19 and mitigation policies in Europe and the United States.* Technical report, IMF WP/20/125. https://www.imf.org/en/Publications/WP/Issues/2020/07/10/Tracking-the-Economic-Impact-of-COVID-19-and-Mitigation-Policies-in-Europe-and-the-United-49553

Steve, C. (2020). *Early economic impacts of covid-19 in europe: A view from the grid.* Technical report, University of Chicago. https://epic.uchicago.edu/research/early-economic-impacts-of-covid-19-in-europe-a-view-from-the-grid/

UN. (2020). *Tackling the Inequality Pandemic: A New Social Contract for a New Era.* UN Secretary - General's Lecture for Nelson Mandela's International Day. https://www.un.org/sg/en/content/sg/statement/2020-07-18/secretary-generals-nelson-mandela-lecture-%E2%80%9Ctackling-the-inequality-pandemic-new-social-contract-for-new-era%E2%80%9D-delivered

KEY TERMS AND DEFINITIONS

Climate Calamity: Climate calamity refers to natural events in weather cycles such as floods, droughts, storms, heat waves, etc.

COVID-19: Coronavirus disease (COVID-19) is an infectious disease caused by the SARS-CoV-2 virus. Most people infected with the virus will experience mild to moderate respiratory illness and recover without requiring special treatment.

Debt Levels: Debt level is a measure of how much debt is outstanding where debt is used to finance household consumptions, businesses, and government spendings.

Economic Crisis: Economic crisis is a period in an economic cycle in which an economy faces difficulties for a long time.

Global Recovery: Global recovery is the recovery in a country's economy which happens or affects all parts of the world.

Inequality: Inequality refers to the phenomenon of unequal and/or unjust distribution of resources and opportunities among members of a given society.

Migration: Migration refers to the process of the process of moving or being moved from one place to another.

Online Teaching: Online teaching is the process of educating others via the internet from any location (home, coffee shop, co-working space) using various methods such as one-on-one video calls, group video calls, and webinars, by enrolling students from various backgrounds and geographical areas.

Opportunity: Opportunity is an occasion or situation that makes it possible to do something that you want to do or have to do, or the possibility of doing something.

Pandemic: Pandemic refers to a disease outbreak that spreads across countries or continents which affects more people and takes more lives than an epidemic.

Policymaking: Policymaking is the act of creating laws or setting standards for a government or business.

Poverty: Poverty is a state or condition in which a person or community lacks the financial resources due to low-income level and essentials for a minimum standard of living like having proper housing, clean water, healthy food and medical attention.

Regional Trends: Regional trends refer to a trend pertaining to a region of considerable extent.

Trade: Trade is the activity of buying and selling, or exchanging, goods and/or services between people or countries.

Vaccine: Vaccine is a substance used to stimulate the production of antibodies and provide immunity against one or several diseases, prepared from the causative agent of a disease, its products, or a synthetic substitute, treated to act as an antigen without inducing the disease.

Section 2
Sectorial Inequalities

Chapter 4
Economic Impacts and Management of the COVID-19 Global Crisis:
A Study of the Tourism Industry

Fatma Feyza Gündüz
Adana Alparslan Türkeş Science and Technology University, Turkey

Güneş Akgül
https://orcid.org/0000-0002-9076-8915
Adana Alparslan Türkeş Science and Technology University, Turkey

ABSTRACT

The tourism industry has been one of the fastest growing sectors of the world economy since the second half of the 20th century. Along with the COVID-19 global crisis, the sector has suffered a great destruction in a process where the tourism sector is gaining momentum. This chapter was carried out on the measurement and management of the economic effects of the COVID-19 global crisis on the tourism sector. A survey was conducted with 322 participants working as managers in different units in various travel agencies operating in Turkey. The construct validity of the scales was carried out by exploratory factor analysis. In the chapter, it was seen that crisis management practices were gathered under four dimensions. In results of the data, the total variance explanation rate for the marketing factor was 57.291%, for the human resources was 10.132%, for the government support was 7.937%, and for the maintenance was 5.286%.

DOI: 10.4018/978-1-6684-5289-9.ch004

Table 1. Number of destinations with complete border closure April 2020-February2021. Source: UNWTO (2020)

Date	27.04.2020	18.05.2020	19.07.2020	01.09.2020	01.11.2020	01.02.2021
Number of Destinations	156	165	117	93	59	69

INTRODUCTION

The world has struggled with many global epidemics throughout the history, and as a result, it has faced major crises that affect human life and the world economy. In these outbreaks, three of them stand out, which also affect the Eastern Mediterranean-Middle East region. The Plague of Justinian, which started in the 6th century BC and lasted in waves until the 8th century, the Black Plague, which began in the middle of the 14th century and returned frequently until the second quarter of the 19th century, and the Spanish Flu, which started in the last year of the First World War and spread all over the world. Each of these three global epidemics has led to the death of tens of millions of people. As today, global epidemics in the past have had important economic consequences besides the loss of life (Pamuk, 2020).

The coronavirus (Covid-19), an epidemic disease of the last century, first appeared on December 2019 in Wuhan, the capital of the Hubei region of China, and has affected the whole world. The World Health Organization (WHO) declared Covid-19 as a pandemic on February 11, 2020. Due to this epidemic, more and more people have been affected and infected every day or have had to change their normal lives. With the emergence of the Covid-19 global epidemic, many sectors, especially the service sector, have been negatively affected by this situation; one of the main ones is tourism and the aviation sector, to which it is directly related. In recent years, while people prefer air transportation primarily due to the advantages of air transportation, many countries have suspended their flights to many countries, especially with Republic of China, and closed their borders, considering that the Covid-19 virus is transmitted faster by contact and respiration (Akca, 2020).

The table 1 shows the number of countries that closed their borders between 27 April 2020 and 1 February 2021. As it is known, the tourism sector is one of the sectors that contribute the most to the world economy. Although all these practices are carried out by considering public health and with the idea of returning the whole world to normal life as soon as possible, it has brought economic negativities, which is one of the biggest destructions of the epidemic.

Figure 1. Tourism Statistics of Turkey. Source: TUIK (2020)

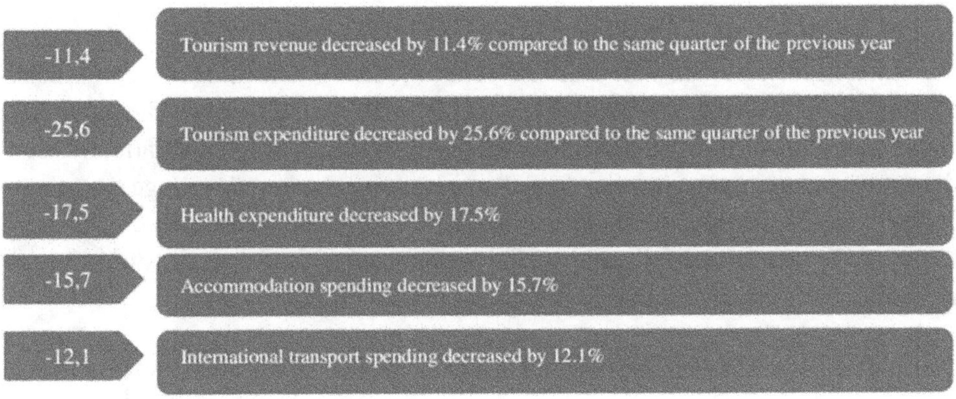

The aim of this study is to measure and manage the economic effects of the Covid-19 global crisis, which emerged in December 2019 and spread all over the world, on travel agencies, which are an important part of the tourism sector in Turkey.

The first Covid-19 case in Turkey was detected on March 10, 2020, and immediately after that, in order to prevent the spread of cases, the country decided to close its borders. Turkey closed its borders with 21 countries firstly. These countries are United Arab Emirates, China, Iran, Italy, Iraq, Germany, France, South Korea, Spain, Norway, Denmark, Sweden, England, Netherlands, Austria, Belgium, Azerbaijan, Egypt, Saudi Arabia, Switzerland and Ireland (Erdem, 2020).

During the peak periods of the epidemic, serious warnings were made for people to stay at home and not to go out unless necessary, and those who did not comply with these rules were punished with fines. Programs have been made to raise awareness of the public about Covid-19 viruses, and restrictions have been applied in all areas of life. ''Stay at Home'' practice was implemented, religious activities, social activities and intercity travels (with exceptions) were suspended. The rule of wearing masks in closed and open areas was introduced, and the distance education model from home was continued instead of face-to-face education in schools (Turan and Çelikyay, 2020).

Figure 1 reflects the tourism statistics for the period January-March 2020 in Turkey. Turkey has become a preferred country for cultural and nature tourism activities with its cultural, natural and archaeological values. Tourism revenues, which were at high values until the last month of 2019, came to a standstill with the sudden, unexpected emergence of the Covid-19 global epidemic. Especially with the spread of the epidemic all over the world and the implementation of travel restrictions, tourism mobility has been hit. Tourism revenues contracted, tourism-based health expenditures, accommodation expenditures, international transportation expenditures contracted.

Considering the contributions of the study, in addition to its contributions to the literature, its reflections on the tourism sector, which is one of the most economically affected sectors during the Covid-19 pandemic, will be understood. The difficulties encountered by the tourism agencies, which constitute the implementation phase of the study, and the strategies they follow to overcome these and manage the process correctly constitute the theme of the study. It is thought that it will contribute in terms of the ways to be followed by the tourism sector and the measures that can be taken in possible global crisis situations in the future.

Tourism and Its Economic Effects

Tourism is one of the fastest growing sectors in the world. The increase in disposable incomes, the acceleration of technology and the development of transportation networks have encouraged people to participate in more tourism movements. The tourism sector also has a great advantage in terms of providing intense employment. Tourism is derived from the word "tournus", which means to move, to go around, and its origin is based on Latin. The words "tourner" and "tour", which mean to return in French, continue to be used today (Aydın, 2012). The first definition of tourism was made by Guyer Feuler in 1905. According to Feuler, tourism is; 'A phenomenon unique to modern time which is dependent on the people's increasing need for a change and relaxing, the wish of recognizing the beauties of nature and art and the belief that nature gives happiness to human beings and which helps nations and communities' approaching to each other thanks to the developments in commerce and industry and the communication and transportation tools' becoming excellent." According to the definition made by the World Tourism Organization, tourism; includes the activities of persons traveling to and staying in places outside their normal environment for not more than one year in a row for vacation, business and other purposes (World Tourism Organization, 1985). Tourism means a holiday that human beings take for purposes such as leaving their routines and exploring different places, resting, having fun, and getting rid of their problems, and people who perform this process are called 'tourists' (Demir and Demirel, 2019).

Turkey has started to implement state-supported tourism policies since the 1960s. The basis of tourism policies can be listed as; ensuring the growth and development of the country's economy, protecting cultural and natural assets, increasing economic diversity, spreading employment in tourism throughout the year, and making positive contributions to the balance of payments between countries (Özbey, 2003).

Since tourism is both a consumption and a production tool, it is linked to economic science. As a result of all expenditures and consumptions made for tourism purposes,

Table 2. Distribution of foreign visitors to Turkey by years and months. Source: T.R. Ministry of Culture and Tourism (2022)

	January	**February**	*March*	*April*	*May*	*June*	*July*	*August*	*September*	*October*	*November*	*December*
2019	1.539.496	1.670.238	2.232.358	3.293.176	4.022.254	5.318.984	6.617.380	6.307.508	5.426.818	4.291.574	2.190.622	2.147.878
2020	1.787.435	1.733.112	718.097	24.238	29.829	214.768	932.927	1.814.701	2.203.482	1.742.303	833.991	699.330
2021	509.787	537.976	905.323	790.687	936.282	2.047.596	4.360.952	3.982.168	3.513.453	3.471.540	1.763.982	1.892.520

Table 3. Top 10 countries sending the most visitors to Turkey in January-August 2021. Source: TURSAB (August 2021)

Countries	Russia	Germany	Ukraine	Bulgaria	Iranian	Iraq	France	Holland	Poland	Romania
Number of Visitors	2.460.537	1.871.801	1.441.708	642.408	556.035	479.849	417.214	409.253	377. 590	341. 526

the relevant countries earn income. Tourism is among the service sectors, the services provided in this sector have an abstract concept, tourism is directly or indirectly related to many economic sectors. In order for tourism to exist, it is expected that a country should have natural, historical or cultural characteristics. In order for tourism activities to be carried out, it is required that those countries be free from terror and a war; because in the tourism service sector, the safety of people's life and property should be at the highest level (Bilgiçli and Altınkaynak, 2016).

Turkey has attracted the attention of domestic and foreign tourists for years in terms of its location and natural beauties. This intense interest has led to an increase in investments in the tourism sector. Tourism activities in Turkey showed a great development especially after 1980s and played an important role in eliminating external deficits and increasing employment by providing foreign currency inflows during the times when the country was in economic difficulties (Çımat and Bahar,

Figure 2. Number of visitors to Istanbul in the January-August period. Source: TURSAB (2021)

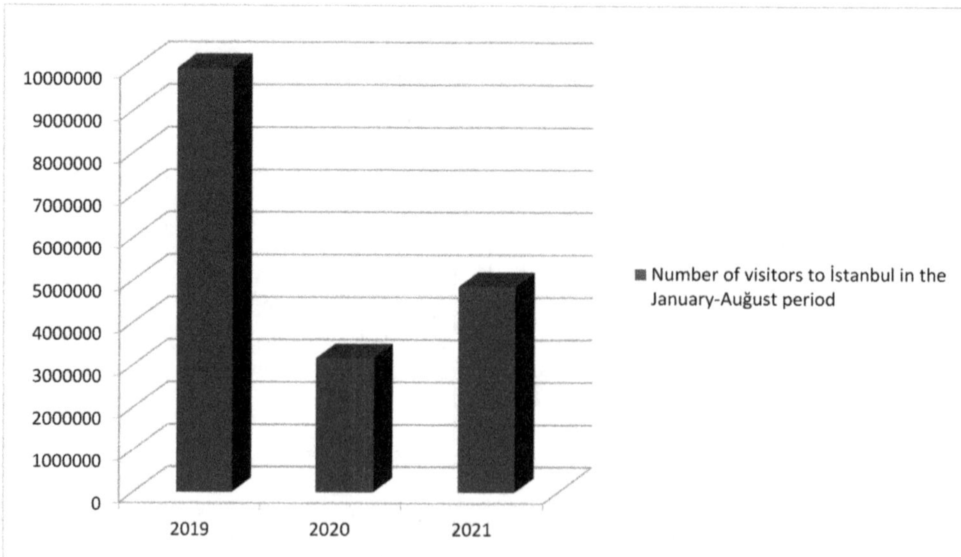

Figure 3. Top 10 countries sending the most visitors to Istanbul. Source: TURSAB (2021)

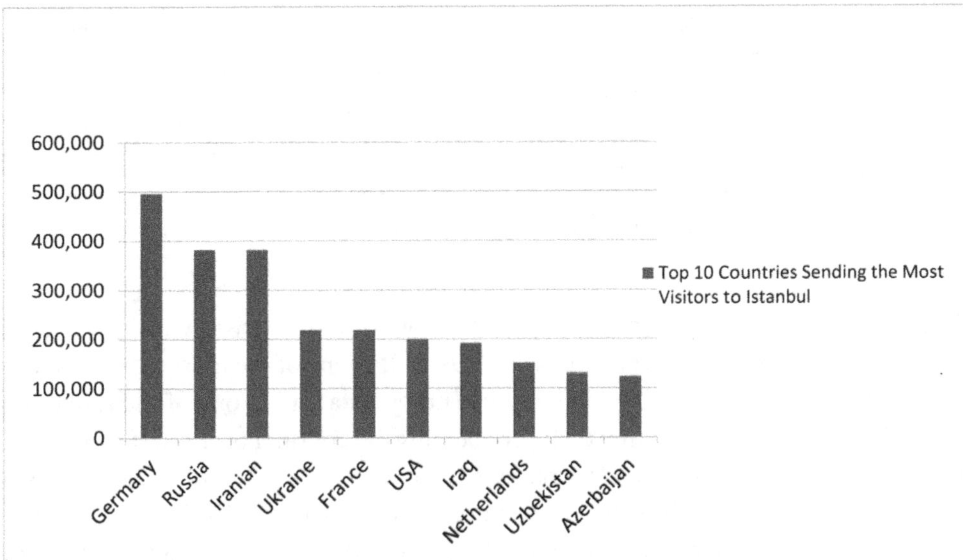

2003). Turkey has hosted many tourism activities in recent years with its geographical location, natural beauties, and development in the field of health services. Since the 1990s, more environmentally and economically sustainable types of tourism have developed. New tourism types such as eco-tourism, adventure tourism, trekking, nature tourism, conference tourism, health tourism, religious tourism have become the rising trends of recent years (Soyak, 2013).

The table 2 shows the distribution of foreign visitors coming to Turkey by years and months. With the month of March 2020, there was a sharp decrease in the number of visitors to Turkey. Visitor data obtained for the first two months of 2022 were 1.281.666 people for January and 1.541.393 people for February. The total number of foreign tourists visiting Turkey in the first two months of 2022 is 2. 823.059, and the data for 2022 are provisional. It is seen that there is a great decrease in the number of foreign visitors coming to Turkey in March, April, May and June of 2020. These sudden decreases indicate that the cases of Covid-19 have increased and therefore the travel restrictions that have been relaxed in some periods have started again.

The table 3 shows, the countries sending the most visitors to Turkey in January-August 2021. In line with the information covering the first 8 months of 2021, Turkey received the most visitors from Russia.

Istanbul is Turkey's one of the most populous cities. It is a city that welcomes tourists from all over the world with its two big airports, transportation network, and

Table 4. Tourism income, distribution of average expenditure by years share of tourism revenues in GDP. Source: T.R. Ministry of Culture and Tourism (2021)

Years	Tourism Income (1000$)	Average Spend ($)	Share of Tourism Revenues in GDP (%)
2018	29512 926	647	3.8
2019	34520 332	666	4.6
2020	12 059 320	762	1.7
2021	16 850 958	830	-

5-star hotels. Istanbul has become the capital of cultural tourism with its cultural, natural and archaeological values (Aydin, 1997). It is one of the most crowded cities in the world and the most crowded city in Turkey. Istanbul is one of the rare cities located on two continents in the world, connecting the continents of Asia and Europe. It is full of cultural richness as it contains many cultures. Istanbul, a city that was the capital of many empires, has been important for both the Christian world and the Islamic world. There are many churches, city walls, baths, mosques and palace ruins from the Byzantine, Roman and Ottoman periods in the city (İçellioğlu, 2014).

When Figure 2 is examined, the number of visitors to Istanbul, which is one of the most visited cities in Turkey, in the first eight months of 2021 reached 4 million 854 thousand 4 people with an increase of 53.6 percent compared to the same period of the previous year. In the talk period, the number of foreign visitors to Istanbul decreased by 51.3 percent compared to the same period of 2019, which was a record year.

The top 10 countries that sent the most visitors to Istanbul in the eight periods of 2021 are listed as follows: Germany, Russia, Iran, Ukraine, France, USA, Iraq, Netherlands, Uzbekistan and Azerbaijan.

Tourism is considered to be one of the service-intensive sectors that enable a country to earn income in economic, social and cultural areas. In studies on developed and developing countries, it has been understood that tourism is one of the most important sources of economic growth and development. Today, tourism stands out as a sector that contributes to the economies of countries with its features

Table 5. Losses of Turkey's competitors in tourism. Source: UNWTO (2020)

Country	Spain	Italy	Greece	Croatia	Portugal	Egypt
Loss of Visitors %	-76	-43	-81	-53	-40	-82

such as increasing foreign currency inflow and reducing unemployment by creating employment, increasing international cultural and social communication, and making great contributions to the preservation of world peace. Tourism, which is one of the indispensable values of the Turkish economy, is an issue that governments that seek solutions to inflation and unemployment emphasize (Çoban and Özcan, 2013).

According to the information obtained from Table 4, between the years 2018-2021 (the data for 2021 covers the months from January to September), Turkey earned the highest income in the field of tourism in 2019. With the emergence of the Covid-19 global crisis towards the last months of 2019, there has been a great decrease in these revenues.

In 2020, when the pandemic emerged and spread rapidly, tourism destinations around the world suffered great losses. This year, Turkey's competitors hit bottom levels. According to the data of the United Nations World Tourism Organization (UNWTO), Spain, one of Turkey's leading competitors in tourism, decreased by 76 percent in the first 8 months, while Greece experienced a decline of 81 percent in the first 7 months. While the loss experienced by Italy in tourism in the first 7 months of the year was 43 percent, Croatia, one of the rising destinations of the Mediterranean basin in recent years, experienced a loss of 53 percent in the 8-month period. In Portugal, another important destination in the Mediterranean basin, the loss in the 8-month period was 40 percent, and the loss in Egypt was 82 percent.

TRAVEL AGENCIES

Travel agencies, which are the most important part of the tourism sector, are at the top of the business areas most affected by the Covid-19 global epidemic. Travel agencies have faced with a difficult process economically and have tried to implement the right crisis management strategies in order to survive with the cessation of the tourism sector.

According to the definition made by the Ministry of Culture and Tourism, Travel Agencies are commercial establishments that provide information to local or foreign tourists about tourism, create and sell package or daily tours, provide accommodation, transportation, excursion, sports and entertainment services for tourism purposes and earn profit in return (Ministry of Culture and Tourism, 2022).

Travel agencies are commercial enterprises established to meet and mediate the touristic needs of individuals participating in tourism activities. Travel agencies offer tours prepared by tour operators for sale, and they play an important role in the decision-making processes of individuals who benefit from these services (Alaeddinoğlu and Can, 2007). According to the law numbered 1618 to which travel agencies are subject; "Travel agencies are commercial establishments that provide

Table 6. Number of travel agencies and branches by group. Source: TURSAB, Tourism Statistics (2020)

Group	Headquarters	Branch office	Total
A	9653	2445	12098
B	50	3	53
C	100	18	118
TOTAL	9803	2466	12269

transportation, accommodation, sightseeing and entertainment opportunities to tourists for profit, provide them with tourism-related information, provide all services related to this issue, and contribute to the tourism economy and generally the balance of payments." Travel agencies are commercial organizations that meet all the needs of people who want to participate in travel activities. Tour organizations, transfer, information, congress and conference organization, touristic trip organization, car rental, ticket sales, selling the products of travel companies, selling touristic information and promotional materials are among the activities carried out by travel agencies (Dönmez and Çevik, 2010).

Travel agencies in Turkey are affiliated with TÜRSAB (Association of Turkish Travel Agencies), which was established on September 28, 1972, with the law numbered 1618. TÜRSAB is an institution that is authorized for all transactions of all travel agencies (establishment procedures, obtaining documents, canceling documents, etc.). Travel agencies in Turkey are divided into 3 groups according to the types of activities they do; "A" group travel agencies; they can do all their travel activities. "B" group travel agencies; reservation and ticket sales services of all transportation vehicles, as well as reservation and sale of tickets for tours organized by "A" group travel agencies. "C" group travel agencies; promotes, produces, markets or sells domestic tours for Turkish citizens only. In addition, "B" and "C" group travel agencies perform the services provided by "A" group travel agencies and promote, market or sell the products of these agencies. The task that a group "A" travel agency will assign to a "B" or "C" travel agency must be documented in a letter or contract. This task cannot be as a package tour or the entire tour is organized by a group B or C travel agency (TÜRSAB; Association of Turkish Travel Agencies, 2020).

In the table 6, the total number of certified travel agencies in Turkey as headquarters and branches is given according to their groups.

Travel agencies in Turkey are also structurally divided into classes. Those can be listed as; retail travel agencies, wholesale travel agencies and chain travel agencies. Retail travel agencies, they are the most common type of travel agency, they are

Table 7. Number of travel agencies in Turkey by years. Source: TURSAB, Tourism Statistics (2020)

Year	2014	2015	2016	2017	2018	2019	2020
Number of Travel Agencies	7987	8717	9316	9795	10305	11410	12269

operated with commissions from activities such as car rental and tour sales. Wholesale travel agencies, it is a type of agency activity that buys package tours offered by tour operators with great discounts in advance and sells them to retail agencies. Chain travel agencies, they are agencies with more than one branch throughout the country and they cooperate with tour operators. Also functionally, travel agencies are called as incoming and outgoing agents (Tourism and Hospitality Portal, 2008).

In order to be able to operate as a travel agency in Turkey, certain guarantees must be paid to the ministry culture and tourism. These guarantees differ according to each agency class. While the fee to be paid as a guarantee for a group “A” travel agency for the year 2022 is 7000 TL (Turkish Liras). This amount is 6000 TL for “B” group travel agencies and 5000 TL for “C” group agencies. Member registration amounts for 2022 are 101,761.32 TL for all groups. Travel agencies in Turkey must have at least one qualified employee in their headquarters or branches. These people can be tour guides, information officers, tourism school graduates. It is sufficient for the person who will operate a “C” group travel agency to have an information officer certificate, and there is no foreign language requirement in this group (TÜRSAB, Association of Turkish Travel Agencies, 2022).

One of the most important professions in cooperation with travel agencies in Turkey is the tourist guide profession. The tourist guiding profession has been given the status of a profession since 2012 and it has an important place in terms of tourism in Turkey. According to the official definition made by the Ministry of Culture and Tourism in Turkey, the tourist guiding profession is a profession for individuals who have a good command of speaking at least one foreign language that they have chosen during their education, provided that they are not directly engaged in travel agency activities, in terms of the country’s culture, tourism, history, environment, nature, social or similar values in line with cultural and tourism policies, or to manage the tours organized by travel agencies as defined in the written documents of the travel agency and sold to the consumer and managed on behalf of the agency (Ministry of Culture and Tourism, 2022).

As of 31.12.2020, travel agencies services are determined by laws. The activities that can be done by companies that are evaluated within the scope of travel agency are the promotion and sale of domestic or international tours or package tours, reservation and sales of transportation vehicles and transfer activities. Sports activities, excursions and entertainment tours, accommodation activities, congress organizations are also counted among the activities that travel agencies can do to make a profit (Ministry of Culture and Tourism, 2022).

Duties of travel agencies; it can be listed as providing professional discipline, maintaining professional development activities, solving the problems that travel agencies encounter and/or may encounter, sharing the problems encountered in the tourism service sector with the public and informing the relevant institutions and authorities on this issue. Travel agencies are the members of the World Tourism Organization, the International Federation of Travel Agencies Associations and the Travel Agencies and Tour Operators Associations Group (Wikipedia, 2020).

The table 7 gives the number of travel agencies which are established in Turkey between the years 2014-2020. The number of agencies, which was 7987 in 2014, was recorded as 12,269 in 2020. It is understood that the establishment of a travel agency continues in the Covid-19 period.

Some of the travel agencies, which had the most negative impact on the Turkish economy during the global crisis, had to close their agencies and branches because they could not meet their costs. Looking at the data of the Association of Turkey Travel Agencies (2022), the number of travel agencies that had to close in the 2019-2022 period is as follows: 61 travel agencies in 2019, 51 travel agencies in 2020, 45 travel agencies in 2021 and 15 travel agencies in 2022.

LITERATURE REVIEW

In the literature review, the economic effects faced by Turkey and the world during the Covid-19 epidemic and its effects on the tourism sector, as well as the difficulties and negative effects of travel agencies, one of the most important intermediary institutions in the sector, were examined and studies were mentioned.

In the study conducted by Avcı and Küçükusta (2013), research was conducted on the problems faced by travel agencies, which are an integral part of tourism, during crisis periods and how appropriate and sufficient the measures taken against these problems are. The importance of a flexible management approach that adapts to difficult conditions in times of crisis was emphasized. As a result of the study, it includes suggestions by the representatives of the sector to predict the negativity before the crisis occurs, to take the necessary precautions, and to make the necessary planning. In the study conducted by Acar (2020), the effects of the coronavirus epidemic, which emerged in Wuhan, China in December 2019, on the tourism sector were investigated. As a result of the study, it has been concluded that the negative effects of the Covid-19 virus, which has taken the world under its influence, on the country's economies and the tourism sector can continue for a long time.

Atay (2020), conducted the study which is called the Covid-19 epidemic and its effects on tourism, stated that the tourism sector, one of the pioneers of the service sector, was most affected by the crisis, and as a result, thousands of people were left unemployed. According to the study the crisis affected the provinces whose economy depends on tourism the most in Turkey. These can be listed as Antalya, Muğla and Nevşehir. Author stated that after the crisis, travel agencies could transfer the products they sell to digital environments and therefore individuals who use social media and technology effectively would be more advantageous.

In the study conducted by Alaeddinoğlu and Rol (2020), it was discovered that how people's holiday understanding is shaped during epidemic periods. The decisions taken during epidemic periods are more psychological than economic ones, and there are significant changes in people's desire to take a holiday. For the sustainability of the sector, which has come to the point of collapse due to the epidemic, it is envisaged to include packages that support the participation of vaccinated individuals in travel activities, with the implementation of fairer practices and the acceleration of vaccination studies.

Demir, Günaydın and Demir Ş. (2020), presented the research which includes interviews with senior executives in these companies in order to measure and analyze the effects of the coronavirus epidemic on tourism stakeholders such as tour operators, travel agencies, food and beverage businesses, airline businesses, yacht and boat businesses. As a result of the study, the necessity of complying with the Covid-19 epidemic measures for people who benefit from tourism services, the expansion of personal transfers instead of transfers in groups, the implementation of more isolated systems instead of the all-inclusive system applied in accommodation facilities, the need for airline companies and transfer providers to continue their services with less capacity.

Doğancılı (2020), examined the measures taken by institutions to accelerate the Turkish tourism sector. In the study, it was seen that the most comprehensive regulations were made in the accommodation sector. With the "Health Tourism Certificate Program" implemented by the Ministry of Culture and Tourism, the health of many employees and visitors is guaranteed. The findings obtained as a result of the study suggest that these regulations are limited to the accommodation sector, and that similar applications should be made for travel agencies and professional tourist guides, who are the stakeholders of tourism.

İbiş (2020), evaluate the effects of the Covid-19 epidemic on travel agencies and to make suggestions about the future of the sector, stated that the tourism sector and travel agencies, one of the important institutions of tourism, were adversely affected by this crisis and epidemic. As a result of the study, it was concluded that although travel agencies had no income during the epidemic period, their fixed expenses continued and travel agencies needed more government support. In the study which conducted by Kıvılcım (2020), it was stated that the sector went to digitalization to a large extent after the epidemic and the technology would be used more. It has been mentioned that social distance will be at a high level, contactless transactions will increase and even a transition will be made to a period in which robots will be used a lot, all-inclusive systems can be replaced by individual tourism and health tourism activities can be the most preferred tourism area.

In the study, which conducted by Bakar and Rosbi (2020), stated that with the emergence of the Covid-19 epidemic, people's participation in tourism activities decreased significantly. In the study, they used the supply and demand curve to explain this effect in the tourism industry. As a result of the study, they stated that governments should take urgent measures, otherwise there may be a long-term collapse in the tourism sector. Urfa, Can and Yüceol (2021), examined the crisis situations in the tourism sector throughout Turkey during the Covid 19 epidemic. The aim of the study is to present suggestions and opportunities about how sector stakeholders are affected by this crisis and recession environment and how to get out of this situation. As a result of the study, in which SWOT analysis was used, suggestions were made to adapt to the epidemic by keeping Turkey's features (geographical location, climate, cultural values, etc.) in the foreground.

Khalid, Okafor and Burzynska (2021), emphasized that the Covid 19 epidemic negatively affected tourism activities all over the world, countries restricted travel activities to prevent the spread of the epidemic, and incentive packages provided by countries. The study was conducted to investigate whether the size of the tourism sector influences the economic policy response to the Covid-19 pandemic using data from 136 countries. As a result of the study, it was seen that the size of the tourism sector was positively related to the monetary policy responses to the pandemic.

METHODOLOGY

This study was carried out on the measurement and management of the economic effects of the Covid-19 global crisis on the tourism sector. Based on the subject of the study, a questionnaire was applied to the participants. The data obtained from the questionnaire were analyzed with the IBM SPSS 24.0 (Statistical Package for the Social Sciences) package program. When the collected questionnaires were checked, it was determined that all of them were filled in completely and without errors, and the quality of the data coded into the analysis program was examined before the analysis was carried out. In order to ensure this situation, error-free control was ensured by looking at the frequency distributions, mean and standard deviations of the data, and the reliability and validity results were prevented from being affected. In addition, the problems that may occur due to errors that may occur in data entry, not responding to questions or incorrect coding by marking more than one option were examined and no errors were found in the data set as a result of the control. The factor construct validity of the scale was carried out by factor analysis. Then, the reliability of the data was tested with Cronbach's Alpha. Finally, ShapiroWilk and Kolmogorov Smirnov tests were applied to examine whether the data showed a normal distribution. Now, factor analysis and applied tests will be briefly mentioned.

Exploratory and Confirmatory Factor Analysis

Factor analyses are divided into two as Exploratory Factor Analysis (EFA) and Confirmatory Factor Analysis (CFA). The purpose of Explanatory Factor Analysis (EFA) is to explain the simple structure that underlies the set of variables and consists of unknown number of factors and is exploratory in nature. EFA assumes that any variable can be associated with any factor. CFA, on the other hand, is used to test the proposed model and to make a priori theory-based assumptions about which factor theories or models are most appropriate (Henson et al., 2006, Thompson, 2004). CFA differs from EFA in that it is based on a theoretical foundation (Bryne, 2010). In CFA, performing the necessary analysis on a model is based on 3 basic stages. The first of these is the determination of the number of factors. The second, constructing the loads of the observed set of variables. The third is the determination of the relations of the factors (Bollen, 1989; Brown, 2015). Prior to the extraction of the factors, several tests should be used to assess the suitability of the respondent data for factor analysis. These tests include Kaiser-Meyer-Olkin (KMO) Measure of Sampling Adequacy (Kaiser, 1970), Bartlett's Test of Sphericity (Barlett, 1950). In particular the KMO index is recommended when the cases to variable ratio are less than 1:5. The KMO index varies between 0 and 1, and a value of 0.50 is considered suitable for factor analysis ($p<.05$) for factor analysis to be suitable (Hair, et.al, 1995, Tabachnick and Fidell, 2007).

Data Set

The questionnaire part of the study consists of three parts. The questions in the first part cover demographic questions of travel agencies and participants (age, gender, career year, education level and the number of employees). In the second part, questions about the practices during the Covid-19 global crisis and in the third part, questions about the positive and negative effects were used. In the study, there are questions created by using Israeli and Reiche (2003), Israeli (2007), Israeli, Mohsin and Kumar (2011), Avcı and Küçükusta (2013) and Okumuş and Karamustafa

Table 8. Distribution regarding demographic characteristics of participants

Variables	Groups	Percentile	Variables	Groups	Percentile
Gender	Female	46,3			
	Male	53,7			
	≤ 20 ages	2,2			
	21-30	19,6		High school	23,3
Age	31-40	44,7	Education Level	Undergraduate	65,5
	41-50	19,9		Postgraduate	5,3
	≥ 50	13,7			
	< 1 year	1,9		1-5	50,6
	1-3 years	11,2		6-10	35,1
Career Year	4-6 years	23,3	Number of Employees	11-20	10,6
	7-9 years	26,4		≥ 21	3,7
	> 10 years	37,3			

(2005). It is aimed to measure and manage the economic effects of the Covid-19 global crisis on travel agencies by the participants who participated in the survey by using a 5-point Likert scale (1-Strongly Disagree, 5-Strongly Agree). A pilot study was conducted for trial purposes on a group of 50 people in order to test whether the survey items were understood correctly before the survey application was launched. Since the internal consistency values obtained from the study were within acceptable limits, the questionnaire was finalized thanks to the notifications. In the study, a survey was conducted with 322 participants working as managers in different units in various travel agencies operating in Turkey. While conducting the survey, data were collected through face-to-face and online survey applications.

As a result of the tests applied, it was seen that the data did not show a normal distribution, since the significance value was p=0.000. When the skewness and kurtosis values were examined, it was seen that they were in the range of ± 1 and it was decided to use parametric tests in the study, assuming that the data showed a normal distribution. In this context, first of all, Kaiser-Meyer-Olkin (KMO) sample adequacy test and Bartlett Sphericity test were applied to evaluate the suitability of the data set for factor analysis. As the KMO coefficient (KMO=0.90) and Bartlett Sphericity test ($p<0.000$) were found to be significant, it was determined that the data set was appropriate and explanatory factor analysis was applied. Then, the reliability of the data was tested with Cronbach's Alpha. The reliability coefficient (Cronbach's Alpha) of the scale used in the study was found to be, 951.

Table 9. Factor analysis table for crisis management practices variable

Factors	Items	Factor Loading Values				Eigenvalue	The explained variance %	Mean	Cronbach Alfa	F test	The level of significance
		1	2	3	4						
Marketing	Marketing to domestic tourists in joint campaigns with local merchants	,952				8,312	57,291	4,02	0,937	4,038	,000
	Marketing to domestic tourists with focus on specific attributes of the location	,942						4,04			
	Price drop on special offers	,771						4,10			
	Reducing list price	,749						4,09			
	Marketing to foreign tourists with specific focus on the location's distinctive features and relative safety	,648						4,12			
	Marketing and promoting new products or services (family events, catering)	,620						4,12			
Human Resources	Firing employees to reduce labor force		,863			1,824	10,132	3,93	0,892	20,654	,000
	Using unpaid vacation to reduce labor force		,929					3,95			
	Decreasing number of working days per week		,669					3,55			
	Freezing pay rates		,781					3,44			
	Replacing high-tenure employees with new employees		,808					2,15			
	Increased reliance on outsourcing		,537					4,06			
Government Support	Organized protest against the lack of government support			*,704*		1,429	7,937	4,30	0,948	8,688	,000
	Industry-wide demand for governmental assistance with current expense			,918				4,35			
	Industry-wide demand for a grace period on tax payments			,936				4,38			
	Extending credit or postponing scheduled payments			,926				4,43			
Maintenance	*Cost cuts by limiting hotel services*				,797	1,020	5,286	3,93	0,739	24,632	,000
	Cost cuts by postponing maintenance of the building				,752			3,94			

FINDINGS

When Table 8 is examined, it is seen that 65.5% of the participants are undergraduate graduates. This rate is important in terms of showing us that the personnel working

Table 10. Positive and negative effects of the crisis

Factors (Positive Effects)	Mean	Std. Deviation
The crisis let us decrease our costs	3,37	1,19
Introduced new management technique	3,58	1,08
We recognized some of our operational problems	3,80	1,21
Introduced a restructuring process	3,86	1,16
The crisis helped us to build our self-confidence	2,86	1,03
Government support to the industry increase	1,93	0,97
Factors (Negative Effects)	**Mean**	**Std. Deviation**
Domestic demand decreased	3,07	1,06
Faced difficulties in collecting loans	3,80	0,96
Postponed future investment projects	3,56	0,93
Experienced a stressful working environment	4,15	1,10
Delays in services from the local authorities	3,88	1,12
Faced difficulties paying our debts	4,01	1,08
Reduced our budget for training	3,51	0,96
Our costs increased	3,20	1,20

Scale values: 1 = strongly agree, 5 = strongly disagree

in the travel agency are trained professionals in their field. 44.7% are between the ages of 31-40, and the number of women and men is close to each other. The fact that the ratio of female and male employees is close to each other gives the impression that the female profile is effective in the tourism sector. In addition, it is seen that 37.3% of the participants have been in the profession for more than 10 years. It is seen that the number of people working in the agencies where the participants work is mostly between 1-5 people. The fact that the number of people working in the travel agency is mostly between 1-5 can be interpreted as the result of the large number of travel agency businesses.

The factor analysis results of the data are presented in Table 9. In the factor analysis, it is seen that the expressions are collected in four dimensions. The first factor was named as "marketing". The total variance explanation rate for the marketing factor is 57,291% and its eigenvalue is 8,312. The second factor obtained as a result of factor analysis was named as "human resources". The total variance explanation rate for the second factor is 10.132 and its eigenvalue is 1,824. The third factor was named as 'government support', and the rate of explaining the total variance for this factor was 7,937% and its eigenvalue was 1,429. For the fourth factor, maintenance, the total variance explanation rate was 5,286% and its eigenvalue was 1,020. The Covid-19 global crisis has caused great damage especially to developing countries whose economy is dependent on tourism. In particular, travel restrictions, the inability of countries to coordinate in the fight against Covid-19, the slowness in the recovery of airline flights can be listed as the factors that most affect economic mobility. In Table 8, the positive and negative aspects of the Covid-19 global crisis for travel agencies and their perceptions are given.

From the positive aspects of the crisis, it was seen that the most contribution was made in terms of restructuring processes, reviewing operational problems, and the implementation of new management techniques. Therefore, while the crises negatively affect businesses, sectors or individuals, it can be said that they experience restructuring and recovery by reviewing the effects of the whole process. Among the negative effects of the crisis, issues such as increased stress in business life, difficulties in payments and loan collection, and delay in services came to the fore. Reflections of negative effects on sectors or individuals can be directly proportional to the size of the effect. In addition to the tolerable negative effects, the irreversible negative effects of the crisis should never be ignored.

CONCLUSIONS AND POLICY RECOMMENDATIONS

The tourism sector is one of the most affected sectors in the world from the negative effects of the Covid-19 global crisis. The sector includes various and many business areas and there are dozens of employees in each business area. Therefore, all the negativity experienced in the economic sense in this process was reflected in all stages of the sector. The revival of the sector depends on the acceleration of the vaccination program, but there has been a loss of confidence in travel due to the limited access to the vaccine in poor countries, the constant change of travel restrictions in rich countries and the lack of intergovernmental coordination, and all these processes have affected the sector. This study was carried out to measure how travel agencies, one of the most important parts of the tourism sector in Turkey, managed this process and to what extent they were affected economically, together with the Covid-19 global crisis. In the study conducted with 322 participants, it was seen that crisis management practices were gathered under four dimensions: marketing, government support, human resources and maintenance. In the analysis results of the data, the total variance explanation rate for the marketing factor was 57,291%, the total variance explanation rate for the human resources was 10,132%, the total variance explanation rate for the third factor, government support, was 7,937%, and the total variance explanation rate for the fourth factor, maintenance, was 5,286%.

In the study, it is seen that the applications related to marketing emerged as the first factor. In parallel with the literature, the importance of marketing by highlighting local features for domestic tourists, organizing campaigns for domestic tourists, reducing prices in special packages, lowering list prices, and developing marketing strategies based on the different characteristics and reliability of the region for foreign tourists have come to the fore. Israeli and Reichel (2003) determined that the desire to create a marketing activity in domestic tourism is one of the most applied crisis management practices. Ayyıldız (2020) emphasized that hotel businesses were deeply affected by the Covid-19 epidemic and developed new marketing strategies. It has been determined that sales and marketing activities have also changed shape by emphasizing the security measures taken, and social media advertisements have been emphasized. It is among the remarkable findings that digitalization applications that require less contact and using QR code readers are also included and will be used more in the coming years. Israeli, Asad, and Kumar (2011) emphasized the importance they attach to the search for new markets within the scope of marketing new products and services in crisis management practices in luxury hotels in India.

When the human resources factor is examined, methods such as taking unpaid leave to reduce personnel costs, reducing the number of personnel, reducing the number of weekly working days, freezing wages, changing personnel are the last methods companies consider to apply during the crisis, but the effects of the Covid-19 crisis on the sector it is seen that undesirable methods have to be applied due to its severe effects. Vardarlıer (2016) emphasized that human resources management means being ready for any crisis with management and business continuity plans. Sorribes et al., (2020) noted that periods of recession and economic crisis create major challenges for companies that depend on job quality and human resources departments. The third factor, government support, includes applications such as demanding the cover of support to the entire sector, organizing to obtain government support, the demand for postponing taxes in the sector, and extending the maturity of loans. Turkey is one of the countries where the Covid-19 global crisis, which has affected the whole world, is best managed and arrangements are made to provide optimal benefits in terms of state facilities. Abate, Christidis and Purwanto (2020) evaluated government support measures for the air transport industry following the outbreak of the Covid-19 pandemic. The analysis shows that most governments place a high priority on maintaining air transport connectivity in aviation itself and related sectors such as tourism to protect economic activity and employment.

The biggest reason for some disruptions is that this crisis negatively affected not a single sector but all sectors and institutions. Under the maintenance factor, there are practices to reduce costs by reducing services and to reduce costs by postponing renewal investments. Although the innovations, investments and concept changes made by tourism enterprises for the new season before the Covid-19 epidemic were the reasons for preference for domestic and foreign tourists, the tourism sector, which almost stopped with travel restrictions after the Covid-19 epidemic, sought ways to keep the sector alive by reducing costs. Considering the economic positive and negative effects of the crisis, it was seen that the most positive aspects of the crisis were restructuring processes, reviewing operational problems, and applying new management techniques, respectively. Among the negative effects of the crisis, issues such as increased stress in business life, difficulties in payments and loan collection, and delay in services came to the fore.

When the study is evaluated in terms of policy recommendations, it is inevitable for the tourism sector and all other sectors to take joint decisions, ensure normalization and receive support from policy makers in this process in order to overcome this process in the easiest way. In the aforementioned process, it is necessary to determine the policies meticulously, and to implement practices that will provide the highest benefit, such as the rights of sector employees, financial losses, applied loans and supports, and innovations in the process management of employers. At this stage, it is necessary to give importance to the fact that the supports given by public institutions and organizations are followed by the companies and that the processes are carried out with great care. Considering the increasing risk and crisis management processes with Covid-19, addressing common problems, developing appropriate solution strategies, implementing them in line with the recommendations of the scientific committee and policy makers, and regularly evaluating and monitoring the developments are the most important steps to be taken for the proper management of this process.

This study has some contributions to both the literature and the industry. Although there are limitations in terms of time, feedback from the participants and evaluation processes in the implementation phase of the study, the contribution of the result to the literature is very important. Experience has been gained on the measures to be taken in possible crises in the future, and it is certain that more cautious steps will be taken. Again, earlier measures will be taken to avoid financial problems for the tourism sector and especially for travel agencies, and to minimize personnel restrictions. In addition, researchers who want to work in this field in the future can be recommended to evaluate the economic effects and management processes of the crises in terms of different components of the tourism sector.

As a result, considering the Covid-19 epidemic process, effects such as restructuring and developing new management strategies for the tourism sector are the biggest dynamites that keep the process alive. Campaigns organized by the agencies, new packages, being organized in a way that will overcome the process and the crisis in the most comfortable way are indispensable conditions for the tourism sector. Although the stress has increased in the sector and the employees of the sector due to the cessation of business life, economic difficulties arise and there are disruptions in services due to all these, it is very important to keep the sector alive with the motivation that this process is temporary, to motivate the employees and to manage the crisis correctly. Travel agencies, which are the most important step of the tourism sector, have succeeded and gained experience in managing this challenging process. With the gradual return to normal life in Turkey and all over the world, it is expected that there will be a great demand for the upcoming tourism seasons and the sector will reach its old pace again. At this point, it is foreseen that it will be an intense and exciting process for managers and employees in every unit of the tourism sector, especially travel agencies.

REFERENCES

Abate, M., Christidis, P., & Purwanto, A. J. (2020). Government support to airlines in the aftermath of the Covid-19 pandemic. *Journal of Air Transport Management, 89*, 101931. doi:10.1016/j.jairtraman.2020.101931 PMID:32952317

Acar, Y. (2020). The novel coronavirus (covid-19) outbreak and impact on tourism activities. *Journal of Contemporary Tourism Research, 4*(1), 7–21.

Akca, M. (2020). The impact of covid-19 on aviation sector. *Eurasian Journal of Researches in Social and Economics, 7*(4), 45–64.

Alaeddinoğlu, F., & Can, A. S. (2007). Tour operators and travel agencies in Turkish tourism sector. *Journal of Commerce & Tourism Education Faculty, 2*, 50–66.

Alaeddinoğlu, F., & Rol, S. (2020). Covid-19 pandemic and its effects on tourism. Van YYU the Journal of Social Sciences Institute.

Atay, L. (2020). Covid-19 salgını ve turizme etkileri [Epidemic and Its Effects on Tourism]. *Journal of Travel and Hospitality Management, 17*(1), 168–172.

Avcı, N., & Küçükusta, D. (2013). Effect of global economic crisis on travel agencies and crisis management practices in Turkey. *Dokuz Eylül University Journal of Graduate School of Social Sciences, 15*(4), 571–587.

Aydın, O. (2012). An alternative tourism in Turkey; Health tourism. *KMU Journal of Social and Economic Research, 2012*(2), 91–96.

Aydin, Ş. (1997). *Kongre turizmi ve Türkiye'nin kongre turizmi potansiyeli* [Congress Tourism and Turkey's Congress Tourism Potential] [Unpublished Master's thesis]. Çanakkale Onsekiz Mart University Social Sciences Institute.

Ayyıldız, A. Y. (2020). Marketing strategies of the hotels in covid-19 pandemic process: Kuşadası sample. *Business & Management Studies: An International Journal, 8*(3), 3328–3358.

Bakar, N. A., & Rosbi, S. (2020). Effect of coronavirus disease (COVID-19) to tourism industry. *International Journal of Advanced Engineering Research and Science*, *7*(4), 189–193. doi:10.22161/ijaers.74.23

Bartlett, M. S. (1950). Tests of significance in factor analysis. *British Journal of Psychology*, *3*, 77–85.

Bilgiçli, İ., & Altinkaynak, F. (2016). Importance and availability of tourism Industry in Turkey's economy; approach to economic paradigm. *Int. Journal of Management Economics and Business*, *12*(12), 560-580.

Bollen, K.A. (1989). *Structural equation with latent variables*. A Wiley-Interscience Publication.

Brown, T. A. (2015). *Confirmatory factor analysis for applied research*. The Guilford Press.

Byrne, B. M. (2010). *Structural equation modelling with AMOS: Basic concepts, applications and programming*. Taylor and Francis Group.

Çımat, A., & Bahar, O. (2003). An assessment of tourism sector and its significance in the Turkish economy. *Akdeniz IIBF Journal*, *3*(6), 1–19.

Çoban, O., & Özcan, C. C. (2013). The relationship between economic growth and tourism income of Turkey: A causality analysis (1963-2010). *Eskişehir Osmangazi University Journal of Economics and Administrative Sciences*, *8*(1), 243–261.

Demir, M., Günaydın, Y., & Demir, Ş. Ş. (2020). The evaluation of the antecedents, effects, and consequences of coronavirus (covid-19) pandemic on tourism in Turkey. *International Journal of Social Sciences and Education Research*, *6*(1), 80–107. doi:10.24289/ijsser.734263

Demir, S., & Demirel, E. Ü. (2019). What makes an experience memorable? A conceptual evaluation of memorable tourism experience. *Trakya University Journal of Social Science*, *21*(2), 661–682.

Doğancılı, O. S. (2020). Tourism supports after covid-19 outbreak. *Journal of Turkish Tourism Research*, *4*(3), 2808–2820.

Dönmez, D., & Çevik, İ. (2010). Stakeholder dialogues as source for innovation in businesses: A quantitative research on travel agencies. *The Journal of Selcuk University Social Sciences Institute*, (24), 189–202.

Erdem, İ. (2020). Quarantine and precaution policies of Turkey against coronavirus (covid-19). *Electronic Turkish Studies*, *15*(4), 377–388.

Guyer-Feuler, L. (1905). *Contributions to statistics of tourism*. Springer Vieweg.

Hair, J. F., Anderson, R. E., Tatham, R. L., & William, C. (1995). Black: multivariate data analysis with readings (4th ed.). Academic Press.

Hair, J. F., Black, W. C., Babin, B. J., Anderson, R. E., & Tatham, R. L. (2006). *Multivariate data analysis* (Vol. 6). Pearson Prentice Hall.

Henson, R. K., & Roberts, J. K. (2006). Use of exploratory factor analysis in published research: Common errors and some comment on improved practice. *Educational and Psychological Measurement*, *66*(3), 393–416. doi:10.1177/0013164405282485

İbiş, S. (2020). The effect of covid-19 outbreak on travel agencies. *Saffron Journal of Culture and Tourısm Researches*, *3*(1), 85–98.

İçellioğlu, C. Ş. (2014). Urban tourism and brand cities: Istanbul's swot analysis in terms of tourism potential. *Istanbul Journal of Social Sciences*, (1), 37–55.

Israeli, A. A. (2007). Crisis- Management Practices in the Restaurant Industry. *Hospital Management*, *26*(4), 807–823. doi:10.1016/j.ijhm.2006.07.005

Israeli, A. A., Mohsin, A., & Kumar, B. (2011). Hospitality crisis management practices: The case of Indian luxury hotels. *International Journal of Hospitality Management*, *30*(2), 367–374. doi:10.1016/j.ijhm.2010.06.009

Israeli, A. A., & Reichel, A. (2003). Hospitality Crisis Management Practices: The Israeli Case. *Hospital Management*, *22*(4), 353–372. doi:10.1016/S0278-4319(03)00070-7

Kaiser, H. (1970). A Second-Generation Little Jiffy. *Psychometrika*, *35*(4), 401–415. doi:10.1007/BF02291817

Khalid, U., Okafor, L. E., & Burzynska, K. (2021). Does the size of the tourism sector influence the economic policy response to the covid-19 pandemic? *Current Issues in Tourism*, *24*(19), 2801–2820. doi:10.1080/13683500.2021.1874311

Kıvılcım, B. (2020). Probable effects of covid-19 (new coronavirus) on tourism sector. *International Journal of Western Black Sea Social and Humanities Sciences*, *4*(1), 17–27.

Okumuş, F., & Karamustafa, K. (2005). Impact of an economic crisis evidence from Turkey. *Annals of Tourism Research*, *32*(4), 942–961. doi:10.1016/j.annals.2005.04.001 PMID:32572284

Özbey, F. R. (2003). *Türkiye 'de turizm politikası ve planlaması* [Tourism Policy and Planning in Turkey] [Unpublished master thesis]. Anadolu University Institute of Social Sciences.

Pamuk, Ş. (2020). Tarihte küresel salgınlar ve iktisadi sonuçları. *Sarkaç Bülten, 9.*

Republic of Turkey Ministry of Culture and Tourism. (2020). *General evaluation of tourism statistics.* https://yigm.ktb.gov.tr/Eklenti/81939,3103turizmistatistikleri2020-4pdf.pdf?0

Republic of Turkey Ministry of Culture and Tourism Board of Inspectors. (2022). *Travel agencies regulations.* https://teftis.ktb.gov.tr/TR-14578/seyahat-acentalari-yonetmeligi.html

Republic of Turkey Ministry of Culture and Tourism. (2022). *Tourism statistics.* https://yigm.ktb.gov.tr/TR-9851/turizm-istatistikleri.html

Republic of Turkey Ministry of Culture and Tourism. (2022). *Travel agency.* https://yigm.ktb.gov.tr/TR-9648/seyahat-acentasi.html

Republic of Turkey Ministry of Culture and Tourism. (2022). *Tourist guiding professional regulation.* https://teftis.ktb.gov.tr/TR-120445/turist-rehberligi-meslek-yonetmeligi.html

Sorribes, J., Celma, D., & Martínez-Garcia, E. (2021). Sustainable human resources management in crisis contexts: Interaction of socially responsible labour practices for the wellbeing of employees. *Corporate Social Responsibility and Environmental Management, 28*(2), 936–952. doi:10.1002/csr.2111

Soyak, M. (2013). The recent trends in the international tourism and the evolution of tourism policies in Turkey. *The Journal of Marmara Social Research*, (4), 1–18.

Tabachnick, B. G., Fidell, L. S., & Ullman, J. B. (2007). *Using multivariate statistics.* Pearson.

Thompson, B. (2004). *Exploratory and confirmatory factor analysis: Understanding concepts and applications.* Academic Press.

Tourism and Hospitality Portal. (2008). http://www.goktepe.net/turkiyede-seyehat-acenteleri-ve-gelisimi.html

Turan, A., & Çelikyay, H. H. (2020). Fight against covid-19 in Turkey: Policies and actors. *International Journal of Management Academy, 3*(1), 1–25.

Türkiye İstatistik Kurumu. (n.d.). Retrieved Jan 03, 2022, from https://www.tuik.gov.tr/

Türsab. (2021). *August statistics.* Association of Turkish Travel Agencies. https://www.tursab.org.tr/e-dergi?pdf=/assets/assets/uploads/turizm-istatistik/tursab-turizm-istatistik-r-agust.pdf

Türsab. (2022). *Association of Turkish travel agencies.* https://www.tursab.org.tr/acenta-kurulus-evraklari

Urfa, A. M., Can, E., & Yüceol, N. (2021). Swot analysıs of the tourısm industry in Turkey in the context of covıd-19 pandemic. *Journal of Travel and Tourism Research*, (18), 22–50.

Vardarlier, P. (2016). Strategic approach to human resources management during crisis. *Procedia: Social and Behavioral Sciences, 235*, 463–472. doi:10.1016/j.sbspro.2016.11.057

Wikipedia. (2020). *Association of Turkish travel agencies.* https://tr.wikipedia.org/wiki/T%C3%BCrkiye_Seyahat_Acentalar%C4%B1_Birli%C4%9Fi

World Tourism Organization. (n.d.). Retrieved August 8, 2022, from https://www.unwto.org/

KEY TERMS AND DEFINITIONS

China: It is the largest of all Asian countries and has the largest population of any country in the world.

COVID-19 Global Crisis: It is an unprecedented global health crisis that has caused massive and serious casualties.

Epidemic Disease: An unexpected increase in the number of disease cases in a specific geographical area.

Factor Analysis: A process in which the values of observed data are expressed as functions of a number of possible causes in order to find which are the most important.

Multivariate Analysis: A subdivision of statistics encompassing the simultaneous observation and analysis of more than one outcome variable.

Tourism Industry: The sum of all businesses that directly provide goods or services to facilitate social activities within the scope of work and leisure away from the home environment.

Travel Agencies: It is a private seller or public service that provides travel and tourism related services, outdoor activities, visa, airline, car rental, travel line, hotels, railroads, travel insurance and tour packages.

Turkey: Turkey is a transcontinental country located mainly on the Anatolian Peninsula in Western Asia, with a small portion on the Balkan Peninsula in Southeast Europe.

World Health Organization: An organization affiliated with the United Nations that conducts international studies on public health.

Wuhan: A sub-state city in the Hubei province of the People's Republic of China. It is the administrative center and largest city of Hubei. It is one of the largest metropolises in China and has been designated as the "National Center City."

Chapter 5 The COVID-19 Pandemic in the 4th Industrial Revolution: A Critical Review

Abdulrahman Abdurazzag Abu Raas
University of KwaZulu-Natal, South Africa

Abdurazzag Ali Aburas
University of KwaZulu-Natal, South Africa

ABSTRACT

In this research work, the concept of corporate entrepreneurship and the fourth industrial revolution were studied and analyzed in the context of the COVID-19 pandemic. The challenges brought by the COVID-19 pandemic forced businesses and organizations of all scales and across all sectors worldwide to react by introducing or updating their services and products and the way they were delivered to the consumer. A critical review was done to understand how corporate entrepreneurship could be used in the fourth industrial revolution, and it was found, through the numerous examples analyzed, that COVID-19 accelerated the use of both concepts by businesses to successfully turn challenges into entrepreneurial opportunities.

INTRODUCTION

Ever since the start of the coronavirus (COVID-19) pandemic, the entire population everywhere around the world has had to change the way they work, study, build, interact, and live. The virus created various issues and presented challenges affecting every sector of society on every continent. Everywhere around the world, countries

DOI: 10.4018/978-1-6684-5289-9.ch005

responded to the COVID-19 pandemic using imposing lockdowns to try and limit the virus' transmission. This, of course, proved successful in decreasing the virus' rate of transmission and infection (Belitski, Guenther, Kritikos & Thurik, 2021). Still, it came at a hefty cost for many countries and their populations, specifically, countries with fragile economies like many countries in Africa.

With lockdowns being imposed, people had to restrict their movement. This meant that shopping malls, shops, and entertainment venues like cinemas, gyms, and parks had to shut their doors to the public. Businesses of all sizes had to stop operating as offices were seen as super-spreaders of the virus (Belitski, Guenther, Kritikos & Thurik, 2021). The restaurant and the fast-food industry could not provide their services under these restrictions as fewer and fewer people went out to eat to stay safe from the virus.

Since the COVID-19 pandemic did not show any sign of slowing down even months after it had started. Some businesses and restaurants that could not cope with the challenges created by the pandemic went out of business. They had to lay off their employees, which resulted in many people losing their livelihoods. However, many other companies, restaurants, and shops strategically and swiftly made plans to cope with the current times. They try to find new, better ways to provide their products and services to stay afloat and persevere through the pandemic. All this caused the idea of entrepreneurship and corporate entrepreneurship to rise among the youth and corporations alike even more so than before.

Corporate entrepreneurship (also known as intrapreneurship), according to (Sakhdari, 2016), is any new activity, venture, product, service, or process created within an existing business or organization to generate new revenue or create value. (Kim, Trimi, Hong & Lim, 2020) stated that businesses and organizations taking input from consumers and outside factors to improve upon a product or service or create a new one entirely (which is the essence of the concept of corporate entrepreneurship) provides them with very positive results in their performance. It provides them with a significant strategic advantage. The research identified two primary and essential factors that play into an organization's ability to thrive using corporate entrepreneurship: visibility and flexibility.

Vision allows the organization to see challenges long before they put the organization at a disadvantage, and flexibility provides them the methods to quickly respond to the challenge. Businesses had to find new and creative ways to develop their products and deliver their services to people even with the pandemic still in full force. To do that, businesses decided to utilize the rise of the 4(fourth) Industrial Revolution (4IR). Klaus Schwab, the creator of the term "The Fourth Industrial Revolution" in his book: "The Fourth Industrial Revolution," states that 4IR is a new age where people around the world can move between the offline and digital realities. It is the combination and integration of technology of all types and advances of technology, including artificial intelligence. Internet of things, and 3D printing, among many others, with different disciplines (Schwab, 2018). With the tools that the fourth industrial revolution provides, businesses and organizations can tackle and face the challenges that the COVID-19 pandemic introduced. The result is new opportunities created from the circumstances through corporate entrepreneurship, which will revive businesses and make them flourish throughout the pandemic and beyond and improve their country's economy.

Another major problem the fourth industrial revolution can possibly tackle is the issue of inequality, especially in African countries such as South Africa. According to (Olaitan et al., 2021), the amount of inequality in Africa is large and still growing. 0.0001% own a little over one-third of all the wealth in Africa. In South Africa, over 50% of the youth are unemployed and the overall unemployment rate is extremely high reaching 29.1%. These issues all lead to a greater crime rate, an economic crisis, and a drastic decrease in the quality of life (Makamase, 2022). The fourth industrial revolution, if implemented and used correctly, can dramatically improve the issues of inequality that South Africa, and the African continent as a whole, face.

Objectives of the Chapter

Understanding how businesses and organizations in Africa and around the world were able to cope with the challenges that the COVID-19 pandemic created. Also, by making use of the idea of corporate entrepreneurship in the fourth industrial revolution to turn those challenges into entrepreneurial opportunities. Finally, how the fourth industrial revolution could be used as a solution to the lifelong issue of inequality.

BACKGROUND

(kafile, 2022) argued through research done on corporate entrepreneurship motivation in south Africa. The research was on the businesses and organizations which lack research departments with skilled researchers, do not have innovative policies in place, and resist new ideas due to their poor mindsets, minimal communication, and resistance to change. Because of these reasons, employees working in those businesses that come up with any new innovative ideas are not rewarded by their managers and bosses because of management's fear of the unknown and the possible failure that comes with change. All of this contributes to a reduction in the number of businesses that can adapt to challenging situations by employing the concept of corporate entrepreneurship to introduce new products and services to keep up with the times. So, it is important to encourage research and reward the research of new concepts and ideas for businesses of all scales to turn challenges into opportunities.

The covid-19 pandemic accelerated this, as many organizations had to accept change and innovation as a greater risk (being out of business) loomed upon many. that was what distinguished organizations that employed corporate entrepreneurship and the ones that did not. According to (lee & trimi, 2021), innovative convergence is pivotal for businesses to succeed and survive in the difficult and harsh market environments businesses operate in today. The researchers explain how change can be very difficult, complex, and a challenge in and of itself in today's competition which agrees with the research done by (kafile, 2022). In (Lee & trimi, 2021) continues to explain that for businesses to thrive in this environment. They require agility and be extremely dynamic to accept change and embrace it to flourish and grow, especially in unprecedented challenges like the covid-19 pandemic. This further proves the fact that businesses need to embrace the fourth industrial revolution if they are to turn the challenges into opportunities.

The (Lotz & van der Merwe, 2018) conducted a study to investigate how corporate entrepreneurship can alter the success of a business. The study was conducted in South Africa by sending managers in large and small businesses questionnaires to conduct the investigation, and a total of 533 questionnaires were analyzed. The results from (Lotz & van der Merwe, 2018) indicated that businesses with managers who offered employees flexibility and encouragement (through financial support and enticement for their ideas) and allowed them to perform their work freely without continuously supervising them. They have high organizational effectiveness and efficiency along with happy employees who are entirely committed to their place of employment. businesses with strict and unimaginative managers. On the other hand, were found not to have any of those benefits. This indicates that organizations with an emphasis on the corporate entrepreneurship ideology are more likely to succeed against unprecedented and unexpected challenges purely due to their creative, dynamic, and committed managers and employees. (Ravjee & Mamabolo, 2019) conducted a study on one of the leading South African banks and their management system to understand how support from management for creative and new ideas and rewards for those ideas contribute to the success of corporate entrepreneurship.

This study's results agree with the research done by (Lotz & van der Merwe, 2018). However, the results that (ravjee & mamabolo, 2019) obtained from the bank they analyzed showed that the pre-pandemic banking sector did not care much for change or providing new services and products as management saw no need for it. This study further confirms the fact that the covid-19 pandemic accelerated corporate entrepreneurship by making use of the fourth industrial revolution as newer research done in this paper will show.

(Sobrosa neto, Sobrosa Maia, de silva Neiva, Scalia & de Andrade Guerra, 2020) state that the disruption that the covid-19 pandemic had caused can be compared to the disruption that World War II caused. That is further confirmed by experts saying that the issues caused by covid-19's pandemic can be divided into two: health issues, and economic issues. Furthermore, (Subrosa Neto, Sobrosa Maia, de silva Neiva, Scalia & de Andrade Guerra, 2020) argues that to solve these issues the fourth industrial revolution must be used and further confirms the covid-19 pandemic as a catalyst for its introduction to many countries around the world. The research, however, did not show any evidence or real-world results from the above claims which leaves an open area for research to be done to understand how the covid-19 pandemic, was in fact, a catalyst for the fourth industrial revolution.

(Telukdarie, Buhulaiga, bag, Gupta & Luo, 2018) argues that integrating businesses with tools from the fourth industrial revolution provides exceptional value and offers great strategic and operating advantages. The research (which was simulation-based) concluded that businesses who push for this integration are rewarded with a reduction in uncertainties concerning supply and demand as they are making use of big data and analytics. It also provides them with valuable information on consumers and their requirements which is invaluable for any business in the complex, uncertain, and enigmatic environment organizations work. It was also found that managers benefit from this integration, as they can access data regarding all levels of the organization which can certainly increase the efficiency of the business and decrease costs.

(Gift Makgamatha & Maureen Makgato-khunou, 2021) stated that they used secondary data to see how African countries are utilizing the fourth industrial revolution and whether they are fully utilizing it or not. From the research done on the subject, it was concluded that African countries were not utilizing the fourth industrial revolution due to most countries in Africa being in the development stage. The research recommended that the governments should start proactively supporting the technology trends and make use of them to improve the economy. However, the research and its results generalized that those African countries did not make use of 4IR even though some countries have and still are utilizing it in invaluable ways to get over the challenges posed by covid-19. Because of this, the research also stated no real-world examples of how the different sectors in some countries in Africa did make use of the fourth industrial revolution and so left some uncovered areas for further future research to be done.

(gwagwa et al., 2021) states that through the research done on artificial intelligence in Africa. It was identified that there are both, opportunities to be explored and challenges and issues that might be faced by African countries to fully make use of artificial intelligence. Their focus, however, was on agriculture which is one sector/ discipline out of many other important sectors, and what applies to the agricultural sector might not apply to other sectors. Artificial intelligence is also still not the focus of many businesses in Africa. Their focus is mainly on other aspects of the fourth industrial revolution like the internet of things developments and improving the utilization of the cloud. (Onu & Mbohwa, 2021) states that the fourth industrial revolution has unlimited potential to ensure business and manufacturing sustainability. The researcher talks theoretically about how big data, artificial intelligence, the internet of things, and more innovations from the 4IR could be used. however, the research does not reveal where these tools were used or should be used, so more research is required to prove the point further.

(Sima, Georgiana Gheorghe, Subi´c & Nancu, 2020) states that according to their research, in which 160 research papers were analyzed relating to the fourth industrial revolution. It was found that the fourth industrial revolution will result in some jobs across different sectors slowly disappearing or transforming their profile and becoming significantly different than what it was before digitalization. However, it was also noted that even more jobs will be created across the education, delivery, and health sectors which will require employees to acquire new skills especially the digital, and online ones. Overall, this will improve the quality of life for all. The research also states that for this to occur, companies, and governments both need to continuously work on training and educating the employees. This is to ensure that the different sectors have the qualified staff required with the right skill set so that the fourth industrial revolution can continue to flourish and improve the economy.

(Van tonder, Schachtebeck, Nieuwenhuizen & Bossink, 2021) makes an interesting remark on business model innovation. The researchers state that businesses and organizations from all industries and sectors, and of all sizes, need to ensure that their business models are innovative enough and must constantly be monitored and updated accordingly. This offers countless renewal and transformation opportunities for any business that wants to stay competitive in its environment. It allows them to react and adapt to any challenge that the business could face and react accordingly, with speed and efficiency, to turn it into an opportunity, even if that means introducing a new product or service to achieve it. These business models allow the organizations to have a framework for how to manage the risks and mitigate them. The researchers state that for a business to achieve innovative business models, they require making use of the tools that the fourth industrial revolution provides such as artificial intelligence, big data modeling and analysis, the internet of things, and many other technologies that help in shaping the best model. The 4IR tools ensure that the new model can provide some form of futureproofing for businesses.

(vizitiu, agapie, paiusan, hadad & nastase, 2018) conducted a study about corporate entrepreneurship in Romania. The study made use of questionnaires to obtain information from various employees (175 Professionals) from different private sector companies. The study revealed that there are ten key factors for businesses. The must-haves for corporate entrepreneurship to work, namely: stress, vertical communication, sharing of knowledge, horizontal communication, time availability, decreasing formalization, support from higher-ups, strategy, delegation, and having a dynamic environment. These key factors found in the study conducted in Romania agree with the findings of the other study conducted by (lotz & van der merwe, 2018) and (ravjee & mamabolo, 2019) in South Africa. This indicates that corporate entrepreneurship does indeed work for businesses and organizations across the globe. However, there is a need for businesses to understand how it is implemented to make use of it and turn challenges into opportunities.

(mhlanga & moloi, 2020) conducted a study to see the covid-19 pandemic's influence to motivate a digital transformation across different sectors but mainly, the education sector. many countries had to shut down their education systems when the covid-19 pandemic started. some countries. However, used the fourth industrial revolution and the tools that it offered to transform the way the education sector functioned (mhlanga & moloi, 2020). Many countries across the world introduced online (remote) work as well as online teaching and learning as a new service. It does support the staff and learners with the internet, data, devices, and websites required for online teaching and learning to be successful. This form of corporate entrepreneurship offered universities and schools a way to keep thriving even through the pandemic. They in turn did not have a need to lay off their staff members and generated revenue that they otherwise would not have been able to generate if they did not offer the new online learning and teaching service (ogunlela & tengeh, 2021). It also saved students by offering them a way to keep studying and not waste time being unproductive.

METHODOLOGY AND DISCUSSION

The methodology used for this research was mainly questionnaires and surveys conducted by researchers around the world. A desktop study was done and many research papers were reviewed and analyzed to gain as much insight and data to support this research as possible.

South Africa

While South Africa is still considered to be behind the rest of the world when it comes to the fourth industrial revolution (gwagwa et al., 2021) and has many inequality issues (makamase, 2022). It still utilized it remarkably well. Especially after the covid-19 pandemic started, and it can be seen in many different sectors.

Many different businesses and organizations have improved or introduced a delivery service for their customer's safety, convenience, and satisfaction, which in turn profited the organization. Shoprite checker's, for example, one of the leading supermarkets in South Africa. They introduced their new online shopping and delivery service "sixty60" at the start of the pandemic. It allowed consumers to shop online and order their daily grocery needs from the safety and convenience of their homes and have the goods delivered to them within 60 minutes. This is a perfect example of how a business can take the lockdown challenge introduced by covid-19 and turn it into an opportunity by introducing a new service that generates income for the business. They utilized the fourth industrial revolution and made use of the internet of things concept to create a mobile application that enables consumers to do all their grocery shopping online. The mobile apps, however, have it delivered to them with zero human-to-human contact. It now operates in all nine provinces and still, to this day, generates checkers revenue and is in line with the covid-19 guideline restrictions (layton-matthews & landsberg, 2022).

Another example is the banking sector. Banks across South Africa immediately started digitalizing the banking process and started significantly shifting the focus of how the banks interacted with the consumer to a contactless online process. Every major bank like FNB, standard bank, Absa, and more all started using mobile applications that the banks developed for most, if not all, interactions. Virtual cards also became more mainstream as more and more consumers banked online.

Takealot, South Africa's leading online shopping retailer used by millions, introduced contactless delivery at the start of covid-19 as a new, improved service to stay functional during the covid-19 pandemic. (layton-matthews & landsberg, 2022). Pick n pay is another excellent example of a business using the fourth industrial revolution and corporate entrepreneurship. It introduced online shopping and delivery at the start of the pandemic in March. Although the delivery service was being used by pick n pay pre-pandemic, they only delivered alcohol using their application at the time. However, following the alcohol ban in March in South Africa (bashizi bashige murhula & nunlall, 2022), pick n pay immediately revamped the pick n pay asap software application to allow consumers to order from their stores online and get the goods delivered to them. They introduced a newly updated service to mitigate the risks and challenges the covid-19 pandemic brought and created a new revenue stream in these challenging times. This also increased the competitiveness as checkers were a step ahead as they introduced their online shopping and delivery service sooner. All the mentioned above were only possible due to the fourth industrial revolution (sobrosa neto, sobrosa maia, de silva neiva, scalia & de andrade guerra, 2020).

As the fourth industrial revolution continues to expand and reaches more and more South Africans, the issue of inequality can either improve or worsen. This depends on the government's efforts on ensuring that all South Africans get the proper training and education required for them to start making use of the tools of the fourth industrial revolution provides. When people are equipped with the knowledge and tools that the fourth industrial revolution provides, then they can create solutions to problems that will overcome the issue of inequality. Otherwise, the inequality gap will only increase as some will get access to and make use of those tools, while others will not (gray, 2017).

The United States and Europe

A good example that can be found in the United States is Pfizer. Pfizer, a pharmaceutical company that focused mainly on manufacturing medicine pre-pandemic, took it upon itself to introduce a new, very important product: the covid-19 vaccine. As soon as the pandemic started, Pfizer and other companies like johnson and johnson started focusing research and resources on developing a vaccine. They created a new product line because of the covid-19 pandemic. They made use of the advancements in the fourth industrial revolution in the United States by utilizing the advancements in biotechnology to create the vaccine in record time. This resulted in hundreds of millions of lives saved and generating income for the company through new investments and stakeholders (biontech, 2020). As covid-19 pressured companies to leave the concept of office work behind, millions worldwide began working remotely from home. The only way for businesses to move from office work to working remotely from home was by using the fourth industrial revolution through the tools it offered.

The internet of things allowed employees to connect to their workplace's network and communicate with one another using VoIP, emails, and many more methods of communication. The cloud and cloud storage concept also allowed businesses to securely store the data used by employees remotely using servers from google or Microsoft. This concept of remote work was seen in countries worldwide across all continents. (cserháti, 2020) stated that a survey was conducted in 2019. Two thousand five hundred remote working employees and their employers (from around

Table 1. Employer and employee responses to the survey. Source: (cserháti, 2020)

Employer response	Employees' response
91% support the concept of remote work	99% support the idea of remote work and found it very attractive.
31% of the organizations have worked fully remotely ever since the covid-19 pandemic started	40% found that the flexibility remote work offers (working from anywhere, spending more time with family members, and working at any time) were a great benefit.
40% of organizations made use of blended work (part remote and part worked from their workplace's offices)	Some employees found that complete remote work was isolating, and so preferred blended work.
The majority of employers do not pay for remote office costs.	The majority of employees did not mind the costs of remote office as other costs were removed (like transportation costs)

the world) were asked their opinion of online work. The responses can be found summarized in table 1 below.

The responses indicate positive reception of the concept of remote work. These responses show that remote work while being a new concept for many businesses. Implement, was necessary for businesses' productivity as the alternative was shutting down and laying off the employees.

Figures 1 and 2 below show a graph representing data collected from an online survey conducted across Europe by euro found (cserháti, 2020).

Figure 1. Pre-pandemic remote work by country (cserháti, 2020)

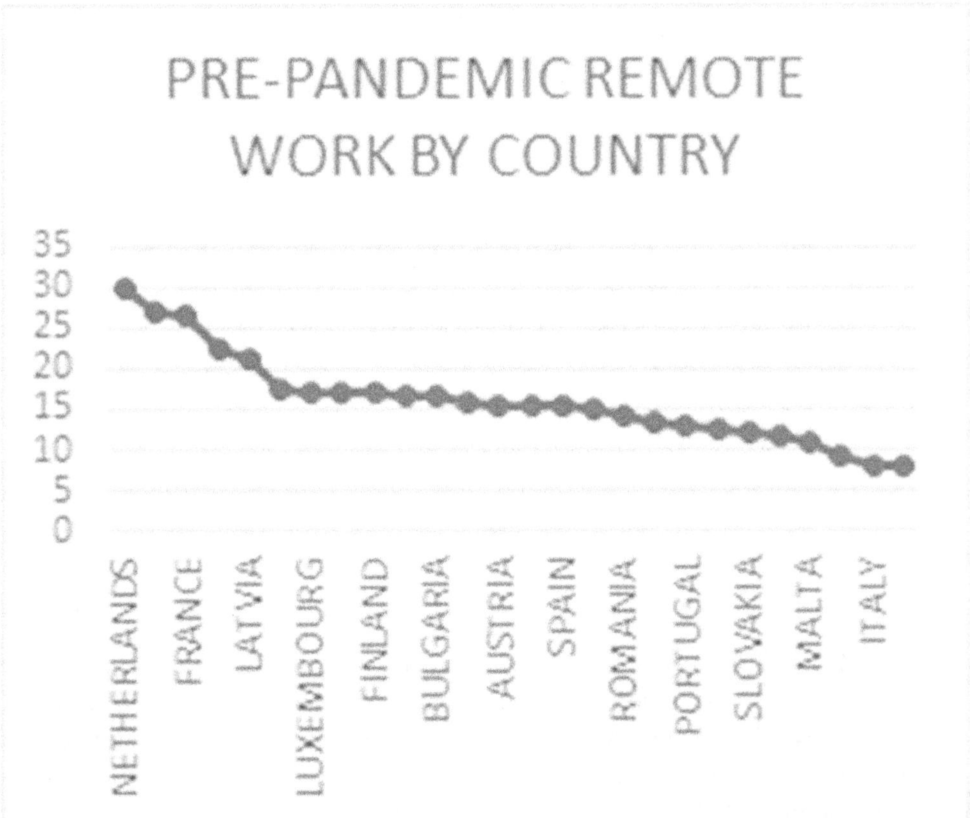

Figure 1 above shows the percentage of businesses and organizations using remote work and partial remote work before the covid-19 pandemic started. It can be noted that the highest rate was from the Netherlands, which reached the 30% mark. However, most countries in Europe did not even pass the 20% mark. It can be concluded that remote work was not popular in Europe before the pandemic hit.

Figure 2. Remote work percentages because of the covid-19 pandemic (cserháti, 2020)

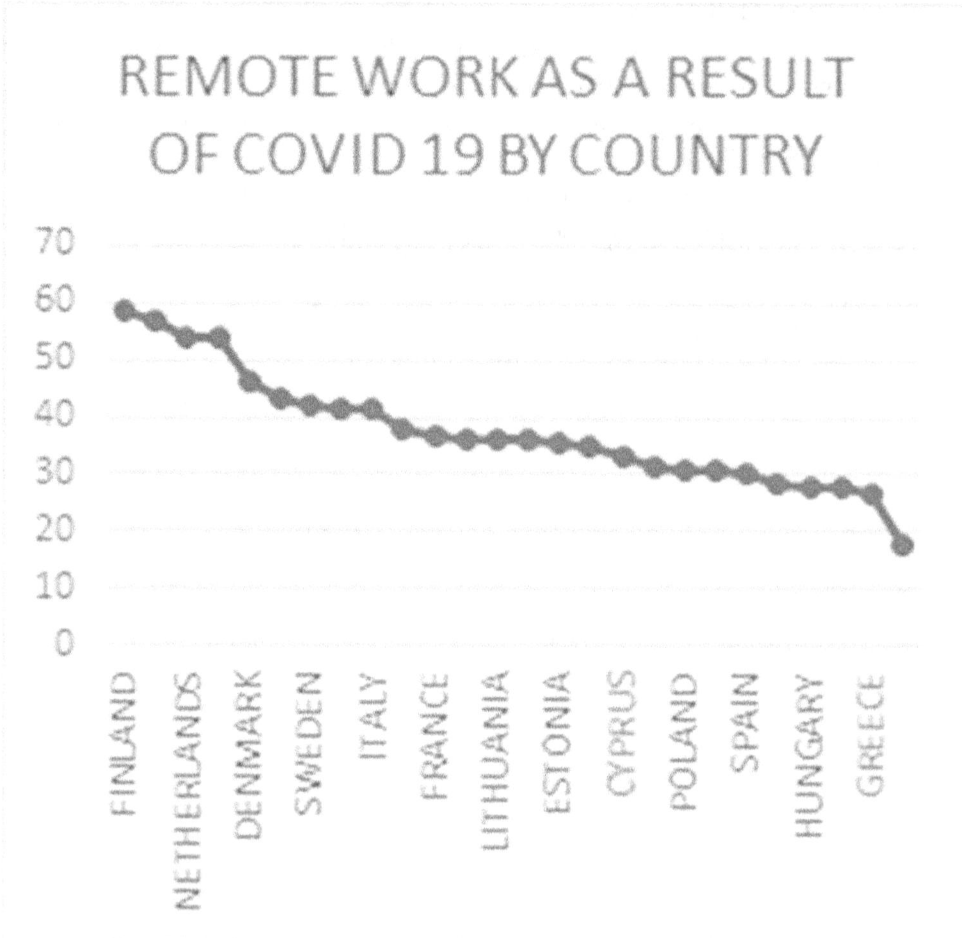

Figure 2 above shows the percentage of businesses and organizations that make use of remote work after the covid-19 pandemic. Compared with figure 1 above, most countries had a significant increase in remote work. This is evident from the fact that the highest percentage for remote work pre-pandemic was 30%, while it doubled to around 60% due to the covid-19 pandemic.

Notable mentions from the data above:

- Italy, which went from 8% of businesses and organizations using remote work to 40.3%
- Spain, which went from 15% to 30%
- Finland, which went from 16.9% to 58.8%

- Luxembourg, which went from 17.1% to 57%
- Greece, which went from 8% to 27%
- Belgium, which went from 22.4% to 53.6%
- Ireland, which went from 12.5% to 43.5%

By analyzing the above data, the percentages of businesses and organizations in European countries that made use of remote work doubled because of the covid-19 pandemic. This further proves how the covid-19 pandemic accelerated corporate entrepreneurship in the fourth industrial revolution. Corporate entrepreneurship and the use of the fourth industrial revolution can be found in the education sector as well. Universities worldwide started conducting their teaching and learning by making use of remote teaching and learning. Through new mediums and by providing new and updated services, many universities successfully used remote teaching and learning. It helped them retain their academic staff and ensured students did not miss what could be years lost due to the covid-19 pandemic (mhlanga & moloi, 2020).

From the above discussion, it can be stated that innovative businesses and organizations across the world took the challenges brought by the covid-19 pandemic. Therefore, the use of the fourth industrial revolution and corporate entrepreneurship turned them into tremendous opportunities that generated success. Finally, it allowed them to get through those challenges unscathed. The way businesses reacted to these challenges resulted in reducing the rate of unemployment by purely not shutting down and laying off their employees while also providing economic benefit to their countries. All this was possible through the innovation brought in by the managers and higher-ups and their recognition of how corporate entrepreneurship could be used along with the tools that the fourth industrial revolution brought.

SOLUTIONS AND RECOMMENDATIONS

To tackle the challenges still faced by many businesses and organizations around the world. There is a need to understand and make use of the fourth industrial revolution in combination with proper corporate entrepreneurship. The tools that the fourth industrial revolution offers are invaluable if used correctly by managers and business leaders. It was seen from the above discussions where many solutions were analyzed and discussed, that many businesses were able to utilize those tools efficiently and think ahead and turn the problems into solutions. But that is only the beginning. The fourth industrial revolution is very much still in the early stages and many countries around the world are still trying to adapt to it. Governments should ensure that they introduce the fourth industrial revolution into their countries and encourage businesses to adapt to it as that is the future if inequality is to be demolished. By offering support for local schools, universities, and businesses to educate and train the future generation to be able to make use of the industrial revolution. They will be better equipped for the future, and individuals from any background can start utilizing those tools to better the quality of life for everyone around them. Businesses, and organizations around the world (and especially in developing countries) should ensure they hire qualified individuals. These employees should have the correct set of skills to train and educate future generations to better utilize what the industrial revolution offers. This will result in better more flourishing economies with reduced inequality and a better quality of life for everyone.

FUTURE RESEARCH DIRECTIONS

This research provided an idea of how businesses successfully used corporate entrepreneurship in the fourth industrial revolution to gain a market and economical advantage. Further research could be done on the inequality increasing gap between the 4IR users, businesses, and organizations. Also, it did not make use of the 4IR features and ended up losing money and shutting down the online and/or offline businesses. This can further show that the lack of innovation could not only be detrimental to the companies themselves, but also to the market and economy in which they operate in.

CONCLUSION

Extensive research was conducted by making use of journals and books. The methodology used to achieve this study was through desktop study which was mainly done by looking at secondary data from questionnaires and surveys conducted by researchers worldwide. Other research papers were also studied, analyzed, and reviewed. This study review shows that corporate entrepreneurship in the fourth industrial revolution increased significantly. Especially when the covid-19 pandemic introduced numerous challenges to businesses of all scales and from all industries. The covid-19 pandemic accelerated the implementation of corporate entrepreneurship and the use of the fourth industrial revolution. It was found that businesses that implemented corporate entrepreneurship by using the tools obtained from the fourth industrial revolution were able to survive and thrive by turning the challenges they faced into opportunities. This was proven by looking at many examples of businesses of different sizes and from different sectors in the African continent, Europe, and the United States. They profited from the use of corporate entrepreneurship and the tools from the fourth industrial revolution.

REFERENCES

Adams, R., Pienaar, G., Gastrow, M., Olorunju, N., Gaffley, M., & Ramkissoon, Y. (2021). *Human rights and the Fourth Industrial Revolution in South Africa*. HSRC Press.

Bashizi Bashige Murhula, P., & Nunlall, R. (2022). Covid-19 and the Ban of Alcohol Sales in South Africa: A Critical Overview. *Acta Criminological: African Journal of Criminology & Victimology, 34*(3).

Belitski, M., Guenther, C., Kritikos, A., & Thurik, R. (2021). Economic effects of the COVID-19 pandemic on entrepreneurship and small businesses. *Small Business Economics, 58*(2), 593–609. doi:10.100711187-021-00544-y

BioNTech. (2020). *A Phase 1/2/3 Study to Evaluate the Safety, Tolerability, Immunogenicity, and Efficacy of RNA Vaccine Candidates Against COVID-19 in Healthy Individuals*. Pfizer. Retrieved from https://cdn.pfizer.com/pfizercom/2020-11/C4591001_Clinical_Protocol_Nov2020.pdf

Bouchard, V., & Fayolle, A. (2018). *Corporate entrepreneurship*. Routledge.

Burns, P. (2020). *Corporate entrepreneurship and innovation*. Red Globe Press.

Cserháti, I. (2020). "Business is unusual" – Remote work after COVID-19. *Köz-Gazdaság, 2*. doi:10.14267/RETP2020.02.04

Gift Makgamatha, M., & Maureen Makgato-Khunou, P. (2021). Coronavirus (COVID-19) A Severe Push to the Fourth Industrial Revolution (4IR) Whether Ready or Not: African Realities. *CCSE, 12*, 62-74. Retrieved from https://static1.squarespace.com/static/5f2e7663885b2571f33c3d52/t/622e19dc9359524fc74b4f21/1647188448201/Conference+Proceeding+Final+Version_2022-03-14.pdf

Gray, R. (2017). Could the fourth industrial revolution combat inequality? *Horizon Magazine*. Retrieved 9 May 2022, from https://ec.europa.eu/research-and-innovation/en/horizon-magazine/could-fourth-industrial-revolution-combat-inequality

Guarda, D., & Hussin, R. (2019). *4IR AI Blockchain Fintech IoT - Reinventing a Nation*. EMIR Research.

Gwagwa, A., Kazim, E., Kachidza, P., Hilliard, A., Siminyu, K., Smith, M., & Shawe-Taylor, J. (2021). Road map for research on responsible artificial intelligence for development (AI4D) in African countries: The case study of agriculture. *Patterns, 2*(12), 100381. doi:10.1016/j.patter.2021.100381 PMID:34950903

Kafile, M. (2022). A framework of intrapreneurship development for corporate entrepreneurship: A case study of organisational development. *Educor Multidisciplinary Journal, 2*(1). Retrieved from https://journals.co.za/doi/abs/10.10520/EJC-13d336741d#

Kim, D., Trimi, S., Hong, S., & Lim, S. (2020). Effects of co-creation on organizational performance of small and medium manufacturers. *Journal of Business Research, 109*, 574–584. doi:10.1016/j.jbusres.2019.03.055

Layton-Matthews, S., & Landsberg, C. (2022). The Fourth Industrial Revolution (4IR) and its Effects on Public Service Delivery in South Africa. *Special Focus, 90*. Retrieved from https://journals.uj.ac.za/index.php/The_Thinker/article/download/1173/752

Lee, S., & Trimi, S. (2021). Convergence innovation in the digital age and in the COVID-19 pandemic crisis. *Journal of Business Research, 123*, 14–22. doi:10.1016/j.jbusres.2020.09.041 PMID:33012897

Lotz, H., & van der Merwe, S. (2018). An assessment of selected organizational-based factors on the perceived success of agribusinesses: A corporate entrepreneurship perspective. *Southern African Business Review, 17*(13). Retrieved May 10, 2022, from http://hdl.handle.net/10394/16625

Makamase, M. (2022). *The Fourth Industrial Revolution: Impact on unemployment and inequality in South Africa*. Retrieved 10 May 2022, from https://www.igd.org.za/infocus/12080-the-fourth-industrial-revolution-impact-on-unemployemnet-and-inequality-in-south-africa

Marwala, T. (2020). *Closing the Gap: The Fourth Industrial Revolution in Africa*. Pan MacMillan.

Mhlanga, D., & Moloi, T. (2020). COVID-19 and the Digital Transformation of Education: What Are We Learning on 4IR in South Africa? *Education Sciences, 10*(180), 180. Advance online publication. Retrieved May 12, 2022, from. doi:10.3390/educsci10070180

Morris, M., Kuratko, D., & Covin, J. (2019). *Corporate entrepreneurship and innovation*. South-Western Cengage Learning.

Ogunlela, O., & Tengeh, R. (2021). The fourth industrial revolution and the future of the entrepreneurial university in South Africa. *International Journal of Research in Business and Social Science, 10*(3), 91-100. doi:10.20525/ijrbs.v10i3.1103

Olaitan, O., Issah, M., & Wayi, N. (2021). A framework to test South Africa's readiness for the Fourth Industrial Revolution. *South African Journal of Information Management*, *23*(1). Advance online publication. doi:10.4102ajim.v23i1.1284

Onu, P., & Mbohwa, C. (2021). Industry 4.0 opportunities in manufacturing SMEs: Sustainability outlook. *Materials Today: Proceedings*, *44*, 1925–1930. doi:10.1016/j.matpr.2020.12.095

Ratten, V. (2021). *COVID-19 and entrepreneurship: Challenges and Opportunities for Small Business*. Routledge. doi:10.4324/9781003149248

Ravjee, B., & Mamabolo, M. (2019). The impact of corporate entrepreneurship on service innovation: A case of a South African banking institution. *The Southern African Journal of Entrepreneurship and Small Business Management*, *11*(1). Advance online publication. doi:10.4102ajesbm.v11i1.155

Sakhdari, K. (2016). Corporate Entrepreneurship: A Review and Future Research Agenda. *Technology Innovation Management Review*, *6*(8), 1–18. doi:10.22215/timreview/1007

Schwab, K. (2018). *The fourth industrial revolution*. Currency.

Sima, V., Georgiana Gheorghe, I., Subi'c, J., & Nancu, D. (2020). Influences of the Industry 4.0 Revolution on the Human Capital Development and Consumer Behavior: A Systematic Review. *Sustainability*, *12*(43), 4035. Advance online publication. doi:10.3390u12104035

Sobrosa Neto, R., Sobrosa Maia, J., de Silva Neiva, S., Scalia, M., & de Andrade Guerra, J. (2020). The fourth industrial revolution and the coronavirus: A new era catalyzed by a virus. *Research In Globalization*, *2*, 100024. Advance online publication. doi:10.1016/j.resglo.2020.100024

Soltanifar, M., Hughes, M., & Göcke, L. (2021). *Digital Entrepreneurship Impact on Business and Society*. Springer. doi:10.1007/978-3-030-53914-6

Telukdarie, A., Buhulaiga, E., Bag, S., Gupta, S., & Luo, Z. (2018). Industry 4.0 implementation for multinationals. *Process Safety and Environmental Protection*, *118*, 316–329. doi:10.1016/j.psep.2018.06.030

van Tonder, C., Schachtebeck, C., Nieuwenhuizen, C., & Bossink, B. (2021). Business Model Innovation Success in the Fourth Industrial Revolution. *Research Gate*, *21*. Advance online publication. doi:10.34190/EIE.21.038

Vizitiu, C., Agapie, A., Paiusan, R., Hadad, S., & Nastase, M. (2018). Adapting corporate entrepreneurship assessment instrument for Romania. *South African Journal of Business Management*, *49*(1). Advance online publication. doi:10.4102ajbm.v49i1.8

KEY TERMS AND DEFINITIONS

Artificial Intelligence: Simulating intelligence in machines.

Corporate Entrepreneurship: The process to develop newer businesses, services, and/or products for further growth.

COVID-19: A contagious virus caused by SARS-CoV-2.

Fourth Industrial Revolution: A way to describe the blurring of the boundaries between the digital and physical worlds.

Inequality: Unjust distribution of opportunity and/or resources between individuals.

Internet of Things: Products that transfer sensor, processing results, or other data with other devices and/or systems over the internet.

Pandemic: A global epidemic.

Chapter 6
Realizing the Economic Welfare of Farmers:
The Case of Digital Agriculture in East Java, Indonesia

Ermita Yusida
https://orcid.org/0000-0002-5274-5114
Universitas Negeri Malang, Indonesia

Vika Annisa Qurrata
https://orcid.org/0000-0003-4214-5956
Universitas Negeri Malang, Indonesia

Bunga Hidayati
https://orcid.org/0000-0003-2182-583X
Universitas Brawijaya, Indonesia

ABSTRACT

During this industrialization era, agriculture is still the key to the economic development of developing countries, such as Indonesia. This chapter aims to see how relevant the current agricultural model is. The method used is the literature review. With the development of digitalization, agriculture in Indonesia, which still uses little technology, must be encouraged to be more technologically literate. In the future, the government must pursue agricultural digitalization to increase the level of farmer welfare so that agriculture can become a driving sector for industrialization and economic growth.

DOI: 10.4018/978-1-6684-5289-9.ch006

INTRODUCTION

Indonesia is one of the countries where the majority of the people work as farmers. Therefore it is known as an agricultural country. Economic growth supported by the agricultural sector requires the government to pay special attention to this sector. However, when viewed together, farmers have always been marginalized until now. Its role, which is quite significant in supporting the economy and being the key in meeting food needs, does not seem to promise a decent life for farmers. Not because no one pays attention, but because the farmer's problem is a double squeeze phenomenon. Farmers have problems both externally and internally, especially in this era of digitalization, where farmers must be easier and faster to adopt and diffuse technology in agriculture. Therefore, it is crucial to reform traditional agriculture into modern agriculture by including digitalization in every up and downstream agricultural activity.

THE SCOPE OF DIGITALIZATION IN AGRICULTURAL SECTOR

Agricultural digitalization is a change and development of methods in agriculture, starting from the early planting period, processing, marketing to post-harvest. The development of traditional agricultural systems towards digitalization in agriculture is a possible solution to overcome the problems farmers face, both internally and externally. Therefore, the Ministry of Agriculture launched the Agriculture 4.0 program, precision agriculture combined with digital information technology, namely cloud computing, mobile internet, and big data (Ministry of Agriculture, 2019).

Cloud computing is a technology that utilizes the internet as central processing of applications and data, where users who have access rights can participate in managing them. One cloud computing implementation is digitizing agricultural training, for example, the integration of training reporting information systems, one-stop access to agricultural activity, and digital administration governance (Caya, 2020). Technology and internet-based applications, which are easier for farmers, have been widely developed by the Agricultural Research and Development Agency (Balitbang). Thus, farmers can take part in online training organized by the ministry of agriculture and other institutions to absorb information that has been integrated into one page using cloud computing.

In the agricultural sector, big data lead a significant role, like storing various data, including mapping agricultural land. The land mapping was accompanied by data collection on commodities and agricultural products (Wibowo & Dairoh, 2018). Apart from being owned by the Central Bureau of Statistics, this big agricultural data has also been developed by local governments, such as the Brebes Regency, which has set a system through the System Development Life Cycle method. The developed SDLC can facilitate and accelerate the flow of agricultural information so that the government can carry out the policymaking quickly and precisely.

According to Abiwodo (2021), the implementation of agricultural digitization is defined as smart farming, precision farming, precision agriculture, and smart agriculture. Precision agriculture is defined as a way for farmers to determine the proper techniques and inputs, where farmers can process to harvest with precision according to the information they get through the help of digital devices. For example, farmers can calculate the correct spacing. Then the farmers can obtain the farmers the need for seeds and fertilizers, even the quantity of crop yields correctly. Precision farming must be supported by GIS, GPS, pest sensors, plant sensors, soil sensors, and aerial photography to measure variables on agricultural land (Manalu, 2013). Therefore, precision agriculture can encourage sustainable agriculture.

The information obtained in digitization and various tools and machines resulting from technological developments can also benefit farmers. For example, they use advanced machinery such as planting robots, granular fertilizer drones, autonomous tractors, and integrated harvesting machines with tillage. In addition, other modern tools and machines integrated into digital systems can increase efficiency in resource use.

Setiana, Nuskhi, & Hidayat (2021) stated that the scope of agriculture in the era of industrial revolution 4.0 includes digital marketplaces, off-farming, and agriculture. Off farming is income in agriculture that comes from agricultural product processing activities such as sugar craftsmen, Tempe makers, soy milk processors, farm laborers, and so on (Edy, 2009). While on farming is the income obtained by the community by carrying out agricultural activities. The farmers can carry out these activities in rice fields or dry land. For example, farming corn, rice, green beans, and agriculture on dry land requires smart farming technology to increase sustainable production (Ekawati, 2019).

THE ROLE OF DIGITALIZATION IN AGRICULTURAL SECTOR

The development of traditional agricultural systems into digitalization systems is a solution to solve various problems experienced by farmers. Food security is closely related to the digitalization system in agriculture. At the International Conference of Nutrition (FAO, 1992), it is stated that food security is the availability of food that meets the needs of everyone, both in quantity and quality, with the aim that everyone can live a healthy, active and productive life. It is supported by the statement of Hakim (2014), which states that everyone has physical and economic access to sufficient food for a healthy and productive life. The four pillars of food security are food utilization, food physical and economic access to food, food availability, and stability of supply and access (Shinta, 2014). Food security, especially in villages, can be realized through independent agriculture by applying food from the people, people, and people (Utomo et al., n.d.). Thus, agricultural digitization that is used to make it easier for farmers to find information and market products can also be used by consumers to access various types of information about quality agricultural products.

The government must optimize the rapid development of technology to support the fulfillment of farmers' needs with the availability of facilities needed by farmers quickly and accurately. In general, digital agriculture facilitates farmer health insurance to oversee the entire production process of agricultural products. The East Java Regional Government in the Government's 2021 Work Plan proclaimed to increase competitiveness and food security through the modernization of agrarian infrastructure (East Java Bappeda, 2021).

Agricultural technology is vital for preserving agriculture, accelerating the transformation of agricultural science and technology, and supporting the achievement of agricultural modernization (Yin et al., 2018). Li, Zhang, & Cui (2018) mention that the extension of agricultural technology involves several elements, namely solving technical problems of online farmers, technical information, and providing agricultural technology that supports innovations in agriculture through smartphone applications. Diagne & Cabral (2017) also mentions that in some cases, innovation in agricultural technology plays an essential role in developing sustainable agricultural systems.

In the more modern digitalization of agriculture, agricultural technology systems are equipped with sensors that are useful for collecting and receiving data through intelligent machines (Poppe et al., 2015). Increasingly sophisticated agricultural digitization accompanied by various sensors will encourage agriculture to apply the smart farming concept (Sonka, 2015). Smart farming is an innovation in agriculture that utilizes artificial intelligence in the production process of agricultural products to ease the performance of farmers. In addition to facilitating the implementation of farmers, smart farming can also provide the correct dose of fertilizer and watering time so that agricultural productivity will also increase.

For farmers, digitalization in agriculture can increase knowledge and information about calculating fertilizers, seeds, or agricultural inputs more efficiently while also improving accuracy in making decisions regarding weather information, plant care, and market conditions (Amalia, 2019). The middlemen who often take greater profits from these farmers can also be minimized by digitizing them. Farmers can directly market or offer their crops in various available applications so that farmers and consumers can determine for themselves according to their wishes.

THE RELATIONSHIP OF DIGITALIZATION ON AGRICULTURAL SECTOR AND ECONOMIC WELFARE

1. Digitalization carried out in the agricultural sector positively impacts a region's economy. The data from Botta et al. (2020), released in the 2020 McKinsey Global Payments Report, estimates that the use of modern technology in the agricultural sector can increase economic output by up to US$ 6.6 billion per year. Furthermore, with the presence of various media, applications, and startups developing in the agricultural sector, this is the leading way for farmers to get more profits so that the welfare becomes more evenly distributed.

The need for agricultural products that continue to grow accompanied by technological developments that cannot be dammed is a real collaboration to improve the welfare of the community, especially farmers. Conventional farming systems that have long been adhered to cannot be quickly transformed into modern agriculture. However, internal and external problems require farmers to slowly move towards digitalization to maintain the presence of agricultural products. Unfortunately, this change towards digitalization is not immediately accepted by all levels of society, especially farmers.

Several factors affect the acceptance of technology among farmers, including human resources and land conditions in Indonesia. In terms of human resources, the majority of people who work as farmers are over 40 years of age and have a low level of education. Due to the conditions, the causing a lack of knowledge and difficulties in receiving and using technological updates, especially digitalization in the agricultural sector.

Furthermore, the unstable condition of agricultural land in Indonesia also makes it difficult for digitization to develop. There are still many vacant lands that are not optimized by the owner and some strategic lands that are expensive to be used as residential land. This limited agricultural land makes the farmers lack land to grow crops. As a result, local or domestic agricultural products become shortages and eventually lead to price increases, returning to the community.

With various obstacles and factors that occur in conventional farming systems, agricultural digitalization is here to solve these problems. The yearly survey in 2020 showed that nearly a quarter of youth or the millennial generation worked in the agricultural sector. The circumstances was increased from the previous period. It is in line with the reality that 85.62% of whom are internet users and have the opportunity to become early adopters of digital technology in agriculture. Thus, the obstacles regarding people who work as farmers who are in the age range of 40 years and over are answered, with the help of the younger generation who come from children, relatives, neighbors, or communities whose aim is to help and introduce various digital products in the agricultural sector to others. As a result, it is easier

Figure 1. The linkages between farmers, food security and welfare

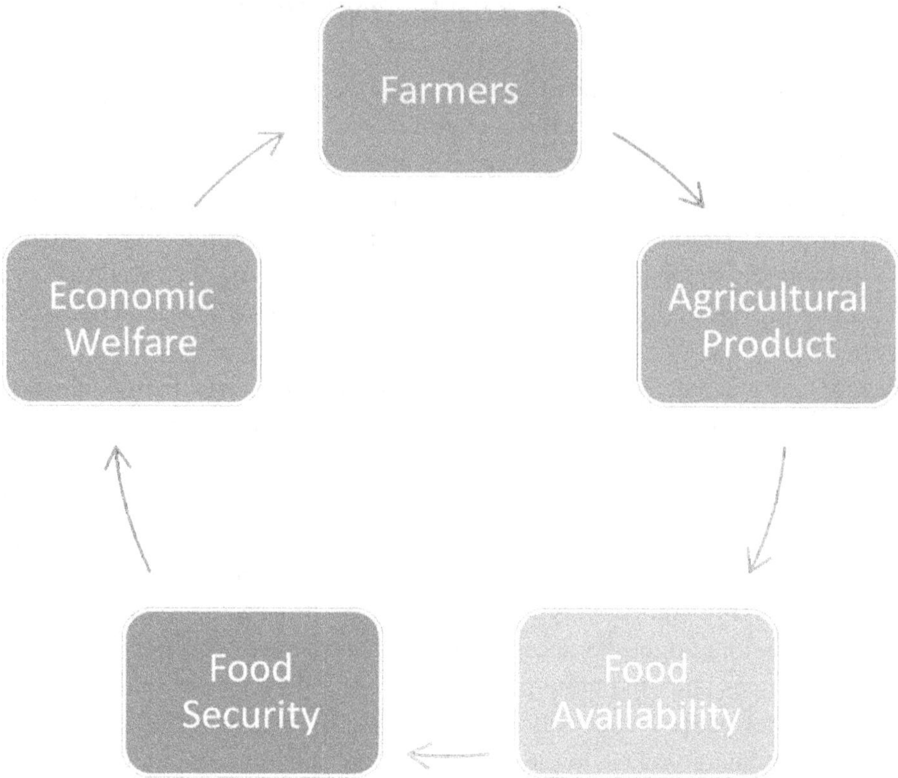

to find seeds, fertilizers, and market agricultural products using the technology. As a result, high-quality agricultural products and profits are maximized.

The ease of obtaining food sources and the abundance of food sources will increase food security. Food security is closely related to the digitalization system in agriculture. At the International Conference of Nutrition in 1992, it was stated that food security is the availability of food that meets the needs of everyone, both in quantity and quality, with the aim that everyone can live a healthy, active and productive life (FAO, 1992). Therefore, a country's high and intense level of food security will impact the welfare of its people. The linkage and causal process as shown in the chart below:

Based on Figure 1 above, we can see that farmers are upstream of community welfare, where agricultural products guarantee food availability. Availability of sufficient food and meeting all community needs is one indicator of food security. When people have strong food security, they will achieve and basic needs.

On the other hand, Santo (2021) mentions that agricultural digitalization will lead farmers into smart farming. Smart farming will improve farmer welfare through more efficient operating costs and higher productivity. Through technology-based intelligent agriculture, land area measurements cost calculations, and planting times can be accurately measured.

Digitization of agriculture through using various modern equipment that increases the efficiency of time and labor in cultivating agricultural land can reduce operational costs. Selvia, Hos, & Moita (2019) found that agricultural modernization can speed up land processing time and increase crop yields. As a result, the production costs can decrease, and crop yields rise, then the profits obtained by farmers will also be greater so that the income of farming families increases. This increase in revenue is one indicator of improving farmer welfare.

REALIZING ECONOMIC WELFARE OF FARMERS USING DIGITALIZATION IN AGRICULTURAL SECTOR MODEL

The following are several agricultural digitization models that farmers, namely, can apply:

1. Soil Fertilization Technology

Based on (Yusida, 2021), only 14% of farmers in East Java chose to use soil fertilization technology, while 51% chose not to use the technology. There are four soil fertilizers that farmers can choose from location-specific fertilizers, using new superior varieties, balancing the use of organic and inorganic fertilizers, and using soil fertility tests. Of the four technologies, 9% of farmers use technology, 29% choose new superior varieties, and the rest use other digital technologies.

2. Water-Saving Irrigation

Water-saving irrigation technology uses water for irrigation with a lower amount than usual. This technology is applied upstream to downstream, including water sources and irrigation channels. Problems arise when irrigation water passes through various agricultural areas, requiring water to irrigate crops. As a result, there is a water inequality for irrigation from upstream to downstream. In addition, waterways as infrastructure also require maintenance to prevent damage that hinders the water distribution process. If irrigation canals are damaged, then the national food security will also be threatened. More broadly, agricultural diversification will be realized

Figure 2. The Agricultural Digitalization Model

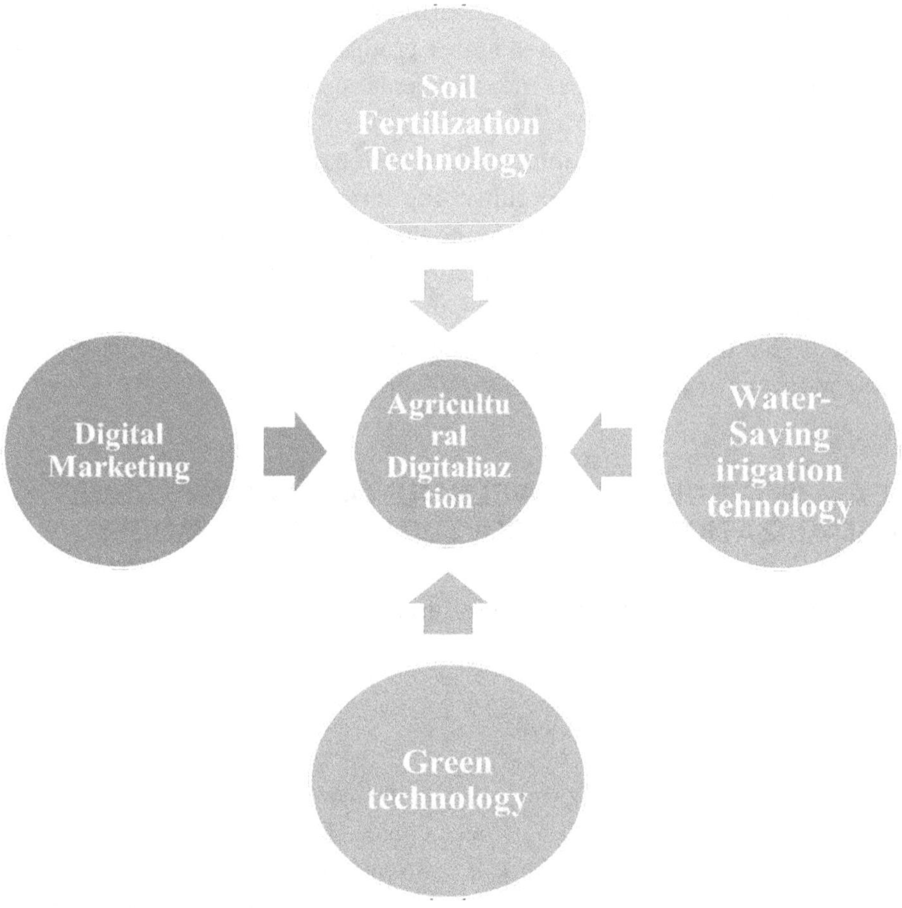

when irrigation channels are smooth so that social capital in irrigation maintenance is more maintained (Purwantini & Suhaeti, 2017).

Thus, digitalization in irrigation is essential for determining the level of plant water needs, water distribution, and monitoring irrigation channels. Determination of plant water needs can be known through smart farming technology with sensors specifically designed to measure soil moisture suitable for plants. When plants get the water content according to their needs, they can thrive and minimize water wastage.

Furthermore, when the water content requirements for each plant on the farmer's land have been met, the distribution of irrigation water can be arranged, for example, such as making an irrigation schedule. Thus, water will be distributed evenly, and conflicts in water use can be avoided.

Finally, it is necessary to form a team of farmers who specifically supervise irrigation infrastructure. These farmers routinely check the condition of the irrigation canals, whether they are clogged with garbage or a leak that results in wastage of irrigation water. Finally, water can continue to irrigate crops while saving on its use. If these three things can be integrated into agricultural digitization, which can be controlled via a smartphone application, it will make it easier for farmers and save water use.

(Yusida, 2021) found that farmers still do not take advantage of this digital technology. Most farmers (65%) chose not to use water-saving irrigation technology, while 19.7% often and only used this technology a few times. Farmers usually use irrigation technology in vertical mulch, wells, intermittent irrigation, reservoirs, and drainage.

3. Green Technology

The use of fertilizers aims to increase crop productivity. Farmers usually use two fertilizers, namely organic fertilizers and inorganic fertilizers. Digitization of fertilizers in agriculture is aimed at controlling the level of soil fertility. Currently, green technology is being applied intensively, which is based on increasing the combination of new and renewable energies. Green technology is also in harmony with environmentally friendly sustainable agriculture. Therefore, implementing green technology will increase agricultural productivity while preserving the environment.

This green farming technology has been developed and has given excellent results. Plant cultivation combines various components, such as technology, crop management, waste-free crops, and livestock, to automatic plant pest control. The integration of this agricultural system will increase crop productivity, reduce greenhouse gases from fuel emissions, and maintain soil fertility.

Research conducted (Yusida, 2021) shows that nearly half percent of farmers in East Java choose to use this green technology. Many farmers have implemented this green farming system without realizing it. Environmentally friendly agricultural actions that farmers usually carry out are the use of additional inorganic fertilizers to achieve optimal yields, maintain soil fertility and the sustainability of the rice field ecosystem, and control pests while still paying attention to the balance of the ecosystem.

4. Digital Marketing

Marketing of agricultural products often experiences inefficiency and causes new problems. Examples of emerging issues include:

- Weak infrastructure.
- Low information on commodity prices in the market.
- Insufficient knowledge of marketing techniques.
- High transaction costs.

Therefore, farmers need to know the marketing system of agricultural products, from input to output markets. Then, the farmers can use digital marketing of agricultural products to solve existing problems. Through digital marketing, selling agricultural products is more effective and efficient so that farmers still get a reasonable price. In East Java, nearly 70 percent of farmers still sell their agricultural products to middlemen (Yusida, 2021). Moreover, less than a quarter percentage of farmers have used digital marketing to market their crops. Sadly, many farmers have not used the marketplace to buy agricultural needs and equipment.

Based on these facts, digital marketing needs to be socialized, and its implementation intensified among farmers. Farmers need to be trained to do product packaging to be marketed online and process agricultural products so that they have a higher selling value. In addition, farmers also need to be taught how to sell on the marketplace, from registering to sending orders. Thus, digitalization of marketing can increase sales of agricultural products to increase their profits and increase their welfare.

The results of this study show that agricultural digitization is the use of digital technologies such as cloud computing, mobile internet, and big data in agriculture, from planting to post-harvest. Agricultural digitalization is very useful in increasing food security, efficiency and effectiveness of agricultural product production, and crop yields. As a result, farmers can sell their crops at reasonable prices, so farmers' welfare increases. However, the digitalization of agriculture in Indonesia has not been widely implemented by farmers due to the low level of education of farmers, the majority of farmers are over 40 years old, and the condition of agricultural land is unstable. Nevertheless, Indonesia has the potential that a quarter of young people work in the agricultural sector so that they can help introduce agricultural digitization products to others. Digitization of agriculture can be realized by several models, such as soil fertilization technology, water-saving irrigation, green technology, and digital marketing.

CONCLUSION AND RECOMENDATION

Based on the literature discussed above, it can be seen that there are still very few farmers in Indonesia who use technology and agricultural digitization. In fact, various studies and literature studies believe that the digitalization of agriculture can increase the effectiveness and efficiency of agricultural products. Therefore, increasing agricultural output will also improve the welfare of farmers. Therefore, farmers must be able to master and take advantage of technological advances, especially in agriculture. Farmers who are technology literate are called millennial farmers. With millennial farmers who can take advantage of existing technological developments in agricultural businesses, farmers in Indonesia will be helped to improve their welfare.

There are three main suggestions to support the digitalization of agriculture in Indonesia and increase the number of millennial farmers. The suggestions are as follows:

a. The government needs to socialize the innovations that have been produced, such as Agriculture 4.0 to farmers, especially young farmers, so that research can be accessed and utilized. The government also needs to provide counselling, training, and assistance related to digital agricultural technology.
b. The young generation who work in agriculture and young farmers are advised to actively follow the development of digital agricultural technology and disseminate it to other farmers.
c. Universities need to collaborate and collaborate with farmers and the agricultural industry to create innovations that are beneficial for accelerating agricultural digitization.

Thus, agricultural digitalization can be widely applied by Indonesian farmers so that the agricultural sector can strengthen food security and is a driver for the industrial sector, which leads to increasing Indonesia's economic growth.

REFERENCES

Abiwodo. (2021). Digitalisasi Pertanian dan Peran Bank Negara Indonesia dalam Ketahanan Pangan Paska Adaptasi Kebiasaan Baru. *Jurnal Kajian Lembaga Ketahanan Nasional Republik Indonesia, 8*(3), 227–243.

Amalia, N. (2019). 5G Siap Hadirkan Teknologi Canggih pada Ranah Pertanian. *whiteboard Journal*. https://www.whiteboardjournal.com/ideas/media/5g-siap-hadirkan-teknologi-canggih-pada-ranah-pertanian/

Bappeda Jawa Timur. (2021). *Rencana Kerja Pemerintah Daerah Provinsi Jawa Timur*. Author.

Botta, A., Bruno, P., Chaudhuri, R., Nadeau, M. C., Taya, G., & Trascasa, C. (2020). *The 2020 McKinsey Global Payments Report*. McKinsey Global.

BPS. (2020). *Statistik Pemuda Indonesia*. Badan Pusat Statistik (BPS). https://www.bps.go.id/publication/2020/12/21/4a39564b84a1c4e7a615f28b/statistik-pemuda-indonesia-2020.html

Caya, B. A. (2020). Strategi Digitalisasi Pelatihan Pertanian Berbasis Online di Era Revolusi Industri 4.0: Laporan Proyek Perubahan. In *Kementerian Pertanian Republik Indonesia*. PPMKP. http://repository.pertanian.go.id/handle/123456789/12648

Diagne, A., & Cabral, F. J. (2017). *Agricultural Transformation in Senegal: Impact of an Integrated Program*. Policy Analysis on Growth and Employment.

Edy. (2009). *Analisis Keberagaman Usaha Rumah Tangga Pertanian Lahan Kering di Kabupaten Banyumas*. Universitas Jenderal Soedirman.

Ekawati, I. (2019). Smart Farming: Teknologi PGPR untuk Keberlanjutan Pertanian Lahan Kering. *Seminar Nasional Optimalisasi Sumberdaya Lokal di Era Revolusi Industri*, *4*(0), 615–622.

FAO. (1992). *Final Report of the International Conference on Nutrition*. FAO.

Hakim, M. (2014). *Memperkuat Ketahanan Pangan Demi Masa Depan Indonesia 2015-2025*. CV Rumah Buku.

Kementerian Pertanian, R. I. (2019). *Kementerian Pertanian - Pertanian 4.0 Efisiensi Waktu dan Peningkatan Produktivitas*. https://www.pertanian.go.id/home/?show=news&act=view&id=3819

Li, J., Zhang, Y., & Cui, B. (2018). Internet +" is used to promote the upgrading of agricultural technology extension mode. *Agriculture Technology Extension*, *6*(1), 7–8.

Manalu, L. P. (2013). Aplikasi Kontrol Digital untuk Pemupukan Secara Variable Rate pada Sistem Pertanian Presisi. *Jurnal Sains dan Teknologi, 15*(3), 31–28.

Poppe, K., Wolfert, J., Verdouw, C., & Renwick, A. (2015). A European Perpective on The Economics of Big Data. *Farm Policy Journal*, *12*, 11–19.

Purwantini, T. B., & Suhaeti, R. N. (2017). Irigasi Kecil: Kinerja, Masalah, dan Solusinya. *Forum Penelitian Agro Ekonomi, 35*(2), 91–105.

Santo, S. Q. (2021). Digitalisasi Pertanian di Indonesia, Strategi Di Masa Pandemi dan New Normal. *Jurnal Teknologi dan Industri Pertanian Indonesia, 8*(10).

Selvia, S., Hos, J., & Moita, S. (2019). Dampak Modernisasi Pertanian terhadap Kondisi Sosial Ekonomi Masyarakat Petani Sawah (Studi di Desa Masagena Kecamatan Konda Kabupaten Konawe Selatan). *Neo Societal*, *4*(2), 767–776.

Setiana, L., Nuskhi, M., & Hidayat, S. (2021). Kompetensi Penyuluh Pertanian dalam Revolusi Industri 4.0 Menuju Pertanian Modern. *Prosiding Seminar Teknologi Agribisnis Peternakan (STAP) Fakultas Peternakan Universitas Jenderal Soedirman, 8*, 602–607. http://jnp.fapet.unsoed.ac.id/index.php/psv/article/view/1225

Shinta, N. (2014). *Pemetaan Ketahanan Pangan di Indonesia: Pendekatan TFP dan Indeks Ketahanan Pangan* (No. 4). Academic Press.

Sonka, S. (2015). Big Data; from hype to agricultural tool. *Farm Policy Journal, 12*, 1–9.

Utomo, S. H., Mukhlis, I., & Yusida, E. (n.d.). A Model for Predicting Food Security Status Among Indonesian Farmer's Households During Covid-19 Pandemic. *Pertanika. Journal of Tropical Agricultural Science*, 1–17.

Wibowo, D. S., & Dairoh, D. (2018). Sistem Digitalisasi Pemetaan Lahan Pertanian Di Kabupaten Brebes. *Sinkron : Jurnal dan Penelitian Teknik Informatika, 3*(1), 20–30. https://www.polgan.ac.id/jurnal/index.php/sinkron/article/view/157

Yin, R., Luo, X., Li, R., & Huang, Y. (2018). Under the background of informatization, why do farmers favor agricultural technicians to carry out agricultural technology extension in the field? *Nongye Xiandaihua Yanjiu, 39*(4), 576–583.

Yusida, E. (2021). The Digital Agriculture Model For Sustainable Food System: An Analysis of Agricultural Technology Adoption in Jawa Timur, Indonesia. *Journal of Sustainability Science and Management.*

KEY TERMS AND DEFINITIONS

Agriculture: The science or practice of farming, including cultivation of the soil for the growing of crops and the rearing of animals to provide food, wool, and other products.

Farmer Welfare: In Indonesia, economic welfare of any individual or a class of people, including that of the farmers, is catered to by governments through various schemes that offer direct support besides creating or facilitating generation of job opportunities. The implication is that both personal incomes and governmental support determine the intensity and extent of welfare that is available to the Indonesian including the farmers

Agricultural Digitalization: A change and development of methods in agriculture, starting from the early planting period, processing, marketing to post-harvest

Section 3

Inequality in Changing Times

Chapter 7
Gross Domestic Savings, Household Consumption, and Inequality in Africa:
A Panel Analysis

Shafiu Ibrahim Abdullahi
https://orcid.org/0000-0003-3471-4493
Bayero University, Kano, Nigeria

Ahmad Muhammad Tsauni
Bayero University, Kano, Nigeria

Mosab I. Tabash
Al Ain University, UAE

ABSTRACT

The chapter analyses gross domestic saving, household consumption, and inequality in African countries. The study covers the period from 1989 to 2019, a length of 31 years, for 24 Africa nations from all the regions of the continent. The main econometric methods of analysis employed for the work is panel cointegration analysis. The variables used for the study to explain both gross domestic savings and household consumption trajectories in Africa include income, inequality, financial development, and government final consumption expenditure. The results show that inequality has negative effects on gross domestic saving but positive effects on household consumption in countries across Africa.

DOI: 10.4018/978-1-6684-5289-9.ch007

INTRODUCTION

The importance of domestic savings and strong domestic consumption in the development of nations in modern era cannot be taken for granted. Over the years nations in Africa have suffer from lack of domestic savings; and international capital mobility into Africa is not significant to offset the lack of domestic savings. According to Keynesian theory, there is presumed equality of saving and investment. Thus, where nation's saving is lower than investment as is the case in Africa, foreign investment and debts sometimes fill the gap. This has been going on for decades since African countries experiences serious shortfalls due to falls in export revenues. Notable works such as Feldstein and Horioka (1980) has demonstrated that saving and investment rates are strongly correlated. Other works such as that of Baxter and Crucini (1993) and Irandoust (2019) pointed to the same conclusion. Liquidity problems and less than competitive insurance markets are some of the prominent features of financial markets in Sub-Saharan Africa (Aryeetey andUdry, 2000). The importance of saving to economic growth and development of nations has been emphasized by Solow growth model and by other scholars such as Hanson (1978). Saving reduces the demands for consumer goods, thus freeing resources for the production of capital goods. Modern governments use taxation to force people into saving in the situation where saving fall short of investment. The performance and subsequent crisis of 1997 in the East Asian economies put to rest the belief that developing countries are madly in need of capital from developed countries to achieve development. Instead of capital to move from developed to developing countries it was reverse of the case for these Asian economies as they become important sources of capital for developed economies. According to Flassbeck (2008), the fact that capital is moving "uphill", from poor to rich nations, contradicts conventional neoclassical economic theory. He noted that this might have contradicted a very long accepted economic theory, seeing developing countries that export surplus capital growing faster and having higher investment ratio than their peer developing countries who receive net capital inflows'.

According to Aryeetey and Udry (2000) some level of empirical evidences have indicated that the monetary value of formal sector financial assets in Africa is below the value of financial assets held by households, and financial assets in total are relatively small part of the portfolio of assets held by households. This contrast with what is found in developed countries where households hold substantial amount of their wealth in financial assets. Generally, demand in an economy composed up of demands for consumer goods and demands for capital goods. Both of them depend on factors such as level of income, inequality, prevailing interest rate, and government policies among others. Government is the most important spender in most economies around the world. Modern government use taxes to influence what is happening in the economy. But, government also uses its own expenditure to influence the economy. The greatest source of revenue for modern states is taxation which is also used to regulate consumption level in the economy. By changing its expenditure or the level of taxes its enforces, government in turn changes the demand for output of goods and services in the economy and changes aggregate saving, investment, level of inequality and the equilibrium interest rate (ManKiw, 2007). Scholars such as Lewis, (1954), Solow (1956), Kaldor(1957) and Pasinetti(1962) had shown how income distribution, saving and growth are related to one another. Later day's works such as that of Schmidt-Hebbel and Serven (2000) failed to find any continuous effect of income inequality on aggregate saving. The empirical relationship between saving, economic growth and consumption is not very straight forward as some simple economic theories have depicted it. Keynesian economics have emphasis the role of consumption through demand creation in realizing economic growth. Here aggregate demand is the same thing as aggregate planned expenditure and the real expenditure is equal to output. According to Solow (1956) growth model, economic growth relies on capital stock and capital stock depends on investment and investment depends on savings; it therefore follows that economic growth relies on savings. These chains of events were the explanation of the socalled East Asian economic miracles of the 1980s and 1990s. Empirical works like that of Carroll, Weil and Summers (1993) and the World bank study on East Asian success stories (1993) found that rapid economic growth cause saving rate to increase.

According to Nel (2018) inequality is simply the skewed distribution of valued and scarce resources, both within nations and across national borders. Crises such as the COVID-19 pandemic are believed to have caused increase in inequality around the world, especially in poor countries (Global Economic Prospects, 2022). Due to wide spread stay at home orders in order to curtail the spread of the COVID virus, millions of poor and middle class people have lost their jobs and other sources of income. Global crises such as the global financial crisis of 2008 have further manifested the tendency of aggregate demand to fall relative to aggregate supply (Martins, 2010). According to Ferreira & Ravallion, (2009) empirical works on inequality in Africa have focused on household consumption expenditure. Inequality can be noticed not only in monetary term but can be seen in other variables such as health, education, and housing distribution. Despite the obvious connection between inequality and poverty they are distinct concepts and it is mostly noted that inequality is an important cause of poverty; but, some time poverty itself can result in increase in inequality. This research work was undertaken within the general milieu of cross country studies and the underlying macroeconomic problems faced by African nations in the past decades. The study covers the period from 1989 to 2019, a length of 31 years for 24 Africa nations from all the regions of Africa. The econometric method of analysis employed for the work is cointegration analysis. Among the objectives of the work include discovering whether the predicted impact of inequality on savings and consumption is true for Africa. But the specific objectives of the paper are to find out what explains gross domestic saving and household consumption in Africa in recent decades. The variables used for the study to explain both savings and consumption trajectories include income, inequality, financial development and government final consumption expenditure. The paper delves into theoretical literature behind saving and consumption theory to choose the appropriate theoretical framework. The results of the work show that inequality has negative effects on saving but positive effect on consumption.

RELATED EMPIRICAL STUDIES

There are a number of studies on the main variables used for this work which are inequality, economic growth, financial development, consumption and savings in Africa. Some of these studies and other related research has been reviewed to serve as background to this work. Alvarez-Cuadrado and Vilalta (2018) provide evidence that when households are more concern about their own consumption compare with other households, individual saving decrease with reference income while total saving declines with income inequality. De Nardi and Fella (2017) found that transmission of inheritance assets and human capital, health expense risk and entrepreneurship are important determinants of savings and wealth disparity. A paper on international consumption patterns by Seale and Regmi (2006) found that poor countries are more affected by changes in income and cost prices than rich countries. Aryeetey and Udry (1999 and 2000) found high positive correlation between possession of financial assets and holdings of economic assets in a study on Household Asset Choice in Ghana and other African countries. Shawa (2016) use panel GMM to analyze saving function for 39 African nations. Results indicate a persistent saving rate. The finding shows that urbanization ratio, per capita income growth, youth dependency ratio, elder dependency ratio, increase in terms of trade, public saving rate, real interest rate, government consumption, credit to private sector, inflation and current account deficit have important effects on saving rate. Geda and Kebret (2006) found that saving is positively related to rate of investment, income level, growth, and short-run changes in terms of trade. But, negatively related with foreign aid, macroeconomic instability and age-dependency ratio.

Akadiri and Akadiri (2018) look at the relationship between economic growth and income inequality in Africa during the period 1991 to 2015. Using Panel fixed effect model, the result of the analysis shows that there is a long run positive relationship between growth and inequality. In a paper on historical income inequality in Africa focusing on country level inequality trend, Hillbom, Bolt, Haas and Tadei (2021) noted that inequality increase with increase in commercialization, colonial heritage influence relative inequality and that capital intensive commodities were linked with higher inequality. Dabla-Norris, Kochhar, Suphaphiphat, Ricka, Tsounta (2015) in a study on causes and consequences of income inequality around the world observes that income distribution in view of wide inequality matters for economic growth. The study further suggested that technological change and changes in labour markets have caused increase in inequality in both poor and rich countries. Another cause agent for increase in inequality is financial deepening which has positive relationship with inequality. Sembene (2015) studied relationship between poverty, inequality and economic growth in Sub Saharan Africa in view of Poverty Reduction Strategy Paper (PRSP) program of the World Bank. It findings show that there is sign of strong growth in the aftermath of the global crisis of 2008. But, growth benefits the rich more than the poor. But Shimeles and Nabassaga (2017) in a study on why inequality is high in Africa noted that between country inequality is negatively related with the ration of households that completed tertiary education. And that countries with high remittance flows have lower inequality than those with lower remittance inflows. They also observed that assets or goods market distortions played important role in driving inequality on the continent. The results show that close to 40% of asset inequality inside countries are due to inequality of opportunities. While political governance and ethnic fractionalization explained 25% of inequality in opportunities but level of development is uncorrelated with it. In addition, inequality of opportunity is strongly correlated with child and maternal mortality and other measures of disease burden. Onwuka (2022) has analyzed relationship between poverty, income inequality and economic growth in Nigeria using data from 1981 to 2019 and cointegration and error correction model for the analysis. The findings of the study indicated that income inequality has negative relationship with economic growth while poverty has positive relation with economic growth.

Koo and Song (2016) investigate how aggregate saving ratio is related to income inequality. They estimated a fixed-effect model build with a panel data of 48 countries for the period 1991 to 2010. The result shows that saving rate increases with increase in disparity. Particularly, the impact of income distribution on saving is higher in rich countries. Aguiar and Bils (2015) noted that consumption inequality followed income inequality much more closely than found through direct responses on expenditures. Krueger and Perri (2005) using data from the US Consumer Expenditure Survey, found that higher income disparity in the United States was followed by an equal rise in consumption inequality. Cingano (2014), using over 30 years data covering OECD countries, noted that income inequality had a negative impact on subsequent economic growth. Gui-Diby (2014) examines the effect of foreign direct investment on economic growth in Africa. He used data of 50 African countries during the period 1980 to 2009. Using the system generalized method of moment estimators; the study finds that FDI inflows impacted economic growth. Adams (2009) analyzes the effect of domestic investment (DI) and foreign direct investment (FDI) on economic growth in Africa south of the Sahara during the period 1990–2003. The results show that Domestic Investment is positively related with economic growth. The study also found that FDI, first, has a negative effect on Domestic Investment and later on a positive effect. The study also found a net crowding out effect in respect of FDI.

Using panel data of 19 African countries for the years 1982-2000, Ndambiri, Ritho, Ng'ang'a, Kubowon, Mairura, Nyangweso, Muiruri andCherotwo(2012) explores the determinants of economic growth in Sub-Saharan Africa. The findings show that capital formation, a strong export sector and human capital development boost economic growth. Hassan, Sanchezb and Yu (2011) provide evidence on how financial development helps economic growth in non rich countries along geographic regions. The study estimates the panel regressions and variance decompositions of GDP per capita to find out what measures of financial development are important. They found positive relationship between economic growth and financial development. The study also found that other real sector variables such as trade and government expenditure play an important role in explaining economic growth. They concluded that a strong financial system is important for economic growth in these countries. In Sub-Saharan Africa, Olagbaju and Akinlo (2018) observed that FDI did not out rightly lead to economic growth. But the financial system by way of banking sector boosts the impact of FDI on economic growth. Ndikumana (2000) analyzes the impacts of financial development on domestic investment in Africa. He studied 30 sub-Saharan African countries and employed a dynamic serial-correlation investment model as well as various indicators of financial development. Results show a positive correlation between domestic investment and other indicators of financial development. He found that strong financial development resulted in higher future levels of investment. The findings support the hypothesis that financial development stimulates economic growth by means of capital accumulation. Yasin (n.d.) investigates the effect of government expenditure on economic growth using data set from Africa. The paper takes government expenditure, foreign aid for development and trade-openness as inputs. He used fixed-effects and random-effects estimation techniques. The results indicated that government expenditure, trade-openness and private investment expenditure have positive impact on growth.

Theoretical Framework for the Research

Life Cycle Hypothesis has been the dominant theory frequently applied to provide a theoretical basis for studies concerning savings, consumption and intertemporal decision (Romer, 2005; Aryeetey and Udry, 2000; Adewuyi, Bankole and Arawomo, n.d.). Modifying asset allocation and intertemporal consumption models used by Aryeetey and Udry (2000) and in Romer (2005) household utility is of the form:

$$U_t = E_t \sum_{i=t}^{T} V_t(C_t) \tag{1}$$

Where,
U_t = household utility at time t
C_t = household consumption at time t
The intertemporal dimension of the model is captured by β:

$$V_t^{'}(C_t) = \beta V_{t+1}(C_{t+1}) \tag{2}$$

for any c_t and c_{t+1}.
The budget constraint is of the form:

$$\sum^{T} C_t \leq A_t + \sum^{T} Y_t \tag{3}$$

Where,
A_t = Endowment, including holding of financial assets
Y_t = labour incomes over lifetime-period T, including holding of production assets

Households hold two assets: financial asset (W_f) and production asset (W_p). Financial asset refer to assets invested in financial market (money market/capital market), while production assets refer to assets directly invested in physical production. Because of the informal nature of most African economies physical asset is inclusive of the household labour of the participating households. Because of the dominance of informal sector in Africa, the bulk of portfolios holds by household are used directly in household production (Aryeetey and Udry (2000). For these assets, the return is dependent on the outcome of the household production process. But, for the other assets not used in household production, the return is a market return which depends on factors not specific to the household.

Household allocate its resources between consumption (C_t) and assets holding (W_{it}):

$$C_t + W_{ft} + W_{pt} = A_t + Y_t \tag{4}$$

Where
W_{ft} = financial assets
W_{pt} = production assets
Saving which is a form of asset holding is arrived simply by:

$$S_t = Y_t - C_t \tag{5}$$

In both the Classical and Keynesian models saving is equal to investment:

$$S_t = I_t \tag{6}$$

Saving equation is as follows:

$$S_t = \left(Y_t - \frac{1}{T}\sum^{T} Y_i \right) - \frac{1}{T} A_t \tag{7}$$

The equation indicates that savings is strong when current income is high. Saving is usually regarded as future consumption; hence, the opportunity cost of postponing current consumption (saving) for a high level of future period consumption is the interest rate available at the period. Equation 8 shows that saving depends on current income relative to its average, wealth level and interest rate.

$$S_t = \left\{ (Y_t / 1 + r) - \frac{1}{T}\sum^{T} (Y_t / 1 + r) \right\} - \frac{1}{T} A_t \tag{9}$$

The life cycle hypothesis predicts that an increase in the rate of growth of income leads to an increase in saving.

Data and Sources

Study of this nature normally involves a lot of variables which make the work a bit complex and data consuming. Add to that is the fact that the work is a macro panel study that involves many countries and large time series data. Among the variables used for the study, savings, as an endogenous variable, is influenced by the level of financial development; hence, financial development is one of variables of interest for this work. It among other things measures the ability of formal financial institutions to attract deposits. It also shows the level of financial sophistication of an economy. Income is a traditional variable in measuring saving and consumption. Government expenditure is also an important variable that explains savings and consumption especially in developing economies such as those in Africa. Inequality is another widely used variable in study involving saving and consumption. Studies such as that of Koo and Song (2016), De Nardi and Fella (2017) and Aguiar and Bils (2015) have tried to gauge the influence of inequality on saving and consumption.

Dependency ratio of population, as variable of interest, is one of the determinant (exogenous) factors under traditional life cycle hypothesis. This is because it is hypothesis that the young and the old have a low saving culture; while working age group have the highest saving rates. The dependency ratio is proxy by Dependency Ratio, as percentage of Working Age Population. In the case of consumption, financial development measures the level of access household may have to credit facilities provided by banks for the purpose of consumption. This is possible through the various bank's facilities that banks make available through consumer credits for the banking public. Also, inequality variable is important in studying savings and consumption; because economic theory noted that the poor have higher marginal propensity to consume (MPC), while the rich has lower MPC. At the same time the poor is theorized to save less than the rich, hence inequality has role to play in determining both saving and investment levels. In this work, inequality is proxy by Gini coefficient. The data used for savings is gross domestic savings as percentage of GDP, while the consumption data is proxy by household consumption data. The data was collected on 24 African countries which include Nigeria, Cameroon, Chad, Cote d'Ivoire, Djibouti, Algeria, Burkina Faso, Egypt, Benin, Mauritania, Gabon, Gambia, Guinea, Guinea-Bisaau, Mali, Morocco, Mozambique, Niger, Senegal, Sierra-Leone, Sudan, Togo, Tunisia and Uganda. Countries were chosen from all the regions of Africa i.e. N. Africa, W. Africa, C. Africa, E. Africa and S. Africa, in order to give the study geographical and economic spread. Data was generated from World Bank's World Development indicators, various countries statistical agencies and African Development Bank data base. The data ranges from 1989 to 2019.

EMPIRICAL MODELS

The paper tests the factors that determine consumption across Africa, taking into consideration theoretical and empirical precedents. For the saving model the paper tests factors that determine saving.

Model 1:

$$consm_{it} = \beta_0 + \beta_1 y_{it} + \beta_2 ineq_{it} + \beta_3 fd_{it} + \beta_4 ge_{it} + \mu_{it} \quad (11)$$

Where,

$consm_{it}$ = consumption
y_{it} = income
$ineq_{it}$ = Inequality level
fd_{it} = Financial Development
ge_{it}= Government Expenditure
μ_{it} = error term
Model 2:
$savng_{it} = \beta_0 + \beta_1 y_{it} + \beta_2 ineq_{it} + \beta_3 fd_{it} + \beta_4 dr_{it} + \beta_5 ge_{it} + \mu_{it}$ (12)
Where,
$savng_t$ = saving
y_t= income
$ineq_t$ = Inequality level
fd_t = Financial Development
dr_t = Dependency Ratio
ge_{it}= Government Expenditure
μ = error term

Method of Analysis

Panel cointegration tests

The main econometric method for the data analysis is panel cointegration model. Because the study is Africa-wide analysis of the behaviour of saving, consumption and growth, the appropriate estimation techniques for the analysis is panel data. In recent years, the emphasis of panel data econometrics has moved towards asymptotics of macro panels. Panel data econometrics have some leverage over a cross sectional or time series data econometrics. The use of panel data enables the exploitation of the time series nature of the data. The panel analysis includes better information than pure cross-country model with positive implications on accuracy of coefficients. In pure cross-country regression, any neglected country-specific effect belongs to the error term, which may bias the estimation of the coefficient. The potential endogeneity of all explanatory variables is controlled by the panel estimator. Through combining time series of cross section variables, panel econometrics provide better variability, less colinearity between variables, better degrees of freedom and more efficiency. (Baltagi, 2005; Gujarati, 2005: Wansbeek, 2001; Hsiao, 2003). The long run effects and the speed of adjustment to the long run are the parameters of interest in testing a panel cointegration model. Pedroni (2000, 2004) put forward different tests for cointegration in panel data models that permit high degree of heterogeneity. Pedroni tests make it possible for multiple regressors, cointegration vector to change

Table 1. individual variables statistics. Source: author's analysis using Eviews

	CONSM	SAVNG	INC	INEQ	FD	DR	GE
Mean	2.06E+10	7.04E+09	3.12E+10	40.47621	0.127944	86.63179	3.60E+09
Median	5.68E+09	1.15E+09	8.30E+09	40.30000	0.110000	89.23000	1.02E+09
Max	4.15E+11	1.49E+11	5.68E+11	54.10000	0.450000	111.9400	4.25E+10
Min	2.91E+08	-1.13E+09	3.63E+08	27.60000	0.000000	44.44000	35142213
Std. Dev.	4.87E+10	1.74E+10	6.86E+10	5.518364	0.066948	15.16266	7.06E+09
Skewness	4.922483	4.193916	4.336356	0.138324	1.801819	-0.996843	3.310661
Kurtosis	30.37500	22.61978	24.85274	2.968533	6.802769	3.457659	14.25442
Jarque-Bera	26235.73	14114.04	17135.50	2.403238	850.8649	129.7113	5285.619
Prob.	0.000000	0.000000	0.000000	0.300707	0.000000	0.000000	0.000000
Sum	1.53E+13	5.24E+12	2.32E+13	30114.30	95.19000	64454.05	2.68E+12
Sum Sq. Dev.	1.77E+24	2.26E+23	3.50E+24	22626.09	3.330154	170820.2	3.71E+22
Obs.	744	744	744	744	744	744	744

across different parts of the panel and for heterogeneity in the errors across cross sectional units.

Panel Unit Root Tests

Due to unit root problems, the variables in the model were tested for unit roots using the Levin-Lin-Chu (LLC) and Im, Pesaran and Shin (2003) methods. Im, Pesaran and Shin (2003) is advancement of the Levin, Lin and Chu (2002) test. Spurious regression and inconsistent results may be gotten if a level form regression is run when the variables in the model are spurious. Inferences using such data tend to be meaningless. Other unit root tests included are ADF-Fisher Chi-square and PP-Fisher Chi-square tests.

Discussion of results

Descriptive Statistics

The table of statistics shows the mean, median and standard deviation of the data used to represent the variables of the study. The overall number of observations is 744. Consumption has the highest Kurtosis and Jarque-Bera, while inequality has the lowest.

The correlation table shows there is strong correlation between income and both household consumption and gross domestic saving, but the relation is far stronger

Table 2. Correlation analysis. Source: author's analysis using Eviews

Sample: 1989-2019
Included observations: 744

Correlation Probability	CONSM	SAVNG	INC	INEQ	FD	DR	GE
CONSM	1.000000 -----						
SAVNG	0.727323 0.0000	1.000000 -----					
INC	0.976266 0.0000	0.854693 0.0000	1.000000 -----				
INEQ	-0.287864 0.0000	-0.276051 0.0000	-0.315930 0.0000	1.000000 -----			
FD	0.536817 0.0000	0.399507 0.0000	0.544834 0.0000	-0.233436 0.0000	1.000000 -----		
DR	-0.274252 0.0000	-0.363931 0.0000	-0.341632 0.0000	0.319664 0.0000	-0.615990 0.0000	1.000000 -----	
GE	0.804117 0.0000	0.830087 0.0000	0.884041 0.0000	-0.400459 0.0000	0.606324 0.0000	-0.526556 0.0000	1.000000 -----

with household consumption. Inequality is negatively related with all the variables except dependency ratio. Consumption and saving have near similar relationship with all the variables.

Results from Panel Stationarity Tests

Table 3 provides the results of various unit root tests conducted on variables in the study. It confirms that the indices are not stationary at level, hence the need for cointegration analysis.

Results of the Main Econometric Tests

This section provides the result of the various econometric tests.

Table 3. Unit root tests. Source: author's calculation using Eview; Note: panel unit root analysis was conducted at level

	Consumption		Saving		Income		Inequality		Financial development		Government expenditure		Dependency ratio	
	Statistic	*Probability*	*Statistic*	*Probability*	*Statistic*	*Probability*	*Statistic*	*Probability*	*Statistic*	*Probability*	*Statistic*	*Probability*	*statistic*	*Probability*
Im, Pesaran and Shin W-stat	9.91096	1.0000	4.42160	1.0000	9.43708	1.0000	0.97759	0.8408	-1.54308	0.0614	8.69412	1.0000	0.98483	0.8376
Levin, Lin & Chu	6.74775	1.0000	4.04809	1.0000	6.31104	1.0000	-0.67995	0.2483	-1.0228	0.1533	5.17200	1.0000	-7.29901	0.0000
ADF - Fisher Chi-square	5.47770	1.0000	30.9894	0.9731	5.76607	1.0000	32.3594	0.9593	64.3962	0.0570	7.79084	1.0000	87.6555	0.0004
PP-Fisher Chi-square	4.62761	1.0000	44.1195	0.6326	5.84737	1.0000	34.5053	0.9283	96.6112	0.0000	8.09089	1.0000	29.9101	0.9811

Model 1:

The results of Pedroni cointegration tests show the present of long run relationship between the variables in the study, see table 4. The result from the Panel Dynamic Least Squares (DOLS) analysis shows that income and inequality are positively related with consumption, while government final consumption expenditure is negatively related with consumption. Financial development is positively related with consumption but is not statistically important; see table 5. The result from

Table 4. Residual Cointegration Test. Source: Author's calculation using Eview

Individual intercept/No deterministic trend

Alternative hypothesis: common AR coefs. (within-dimension)

	Statistic	Prob.	Weighted Statistic	Prob.
Panel v-Statistic	3.558749	0.0002	-0.614635	0.7306
Panel rho-Statistic	-5.002701	0.0000	-0.125367	0.4501
Panel PP-Statistic	-10.62286	0.0000	-4.473967	0.0000
Panel ADF-Statistic	-1.475196	0.0701	-2.478734	0.0066

Alternative hypothesis: individual AR coefs. (between-dimension)

	Statistic	Prob.
Group rho-Statistic	1.377649	0.9158
Group PP-Statistic	-5.302588	0.0000
Group ADF-Statistic	-1.359467	0.0870

Individual intercept and individual trend/Deterministic intercept and trend

Alternative hypothesis: common AR coefs. (within-dimension)

	Statistic	Prob.	Weighted Statistic	Prob.
Panel v-Statistic	0.675816	0.2496	-2.495659	0.9937
Panel rho-Statistic	-3.505644	0.0002	0.973925	0.8350
Panel PP-Statistic	-9.856622	0.0000	-6.590801	0.0000
Panel ADF-Statistic	0.349967	0.6368	-3.812446	0.0001

Alternative hypothesis: individual AR coefs. (between-dimension)

	Statistic	Prob.
Group rho-Statistic	2.474834	0.9933
Group PP-Statistic	-6.000670	0.0000
Group ADF-Statistic	-1.535821	0.0623

No intercept or trend /No deterministic intercept or trend

panel fully modified least squares (FMOLS) show similar signs as in the case of DOLS model but with all the signs statistically significant. The positive relationship between inequality and consumption in this work is in conformity with the findings of Aguiar and Bils (2015), Krueger and Perri (2005).

Table 5. Cointegration analyses. Source: author's calculation using Eview; Note: value in parenthesis is p-value

Variables	Panel Fully Modified Least Squares (1)	Panel Dynamic Least Squares (2)
INC	0.977105 (0.0000)	0.979889 (0.0000)
INEQ	1.33E+08 (0.0000)	1.88E+08 (0.0368)
FD	1.28E+10 (0.0000)	1.35E+10 (0.3062)
GE	-2.308420 (0.0000)	-2.578851 (0.0000)
Observations	720	672
R^2	0.986854	0.995716

Model 2:

The result of panel fully modified least square analysis shows that income and government final consumption expenditure have positive relationship with saving; while inequality, financial development and dependency ratio have negative relationship with saving. The negative correlation between inequality and dependency ratio on the one hand and saving on the other hand was expected a priori, the same thing apply to positive relationship in case of income and government expenditure. The negative correlation between inequality and saving found in this study is in line with the findings of Cingano (2014) and Onwuka (2022) and it does not contradict the findings of Schmidt-Hebbel and Servén (2000). The result of panel dynamic least square analysis shows similar result, but with financial development and government final consumption expenditure not significant. Results of cointegration analysis using Pedroni show cointegration among the variables in the study; see table 6 and 7.

Implications

The positive relationship found between inequality and household consumption is a pointer to the positive/boosting effect of inequality on consumption across Africa. Higher inequality, which point to the ravage of poverty in one hand and wider gap between rich and poor on the other, across Africa means more inequality causes more household consumption across most of Africa. This is not surprising looking at the level of poverty in Africa and when one compares the aggregate consumption figures from Africa with those from other continents of the world. According to

Table 6. Cointegration analyses. Source: author's calculation using Eview; Note: values in parenthesis is p-value

Variables	Panel Fully Modified Least Squares (1)	Panel Dynamic Least Squares(2)
Income	0.051906 (0.0000)	0.147586 (0.0000)
INEQ	-1.13E+08 (0.0000)	-24590621(0.0118)
FD	-1.95E+10 (0.0000)	-3.31E+09 (0.1386)
DR	-1.04E+08 (0.0000)	-33971723 (0.0001)
GE	1.237470 (0.0000	0.059630 (0.5495)
Observation	720	672
R^2	0.899886	0.986961

the theoretical literature on consumption, the poor has higher marginal propensity to consume than the rich. Despite that, in order for African nations to increase household consumption they must fight poverty and reduce inequality. African nations shall take very seriously their efforts towards reducing inequality. The negative relationship between saving and both inequality and dependency ration mean that higher inequality (which, especially in Africa, goes hand in hand with poverty) reduces the level of saving. This can be further rationalized looking at the fact that inequality induced poverty reduce the saving and purchasing ability of households across Africa compare with richer continents. But on the other hand, the negative relationship between saving and dependency ratio means that higher dependency ratio exact negative effect on saving. This shall be expected, because as the number of dependents in a household increase in relation to the number of active household members the surplus income allocated to saving will be reduced or in many cases eliminated with some household going into debit by taking loan. The relationship between saving and income, financial development and government final consumption expenditure are positive; while inequality and dependency ratio are negatively related with saving.

These have important implications for policy makers across Africa. It means that policy makers have to set their priorities right. Policies that boost consumption and saving level shall be given priority for the sake of achieving economic growth and higher income level. Reduction in all types of inequality shall be the priority of African governments. The impact of inequality manifest in the quality and affordability of health services, education and housing. The implication of the negative effect

Table 7. Pedroni Residual Cointegration result. Source: author's analysis using Eviews

Individual intercept/No deterministic trend

Alternative hypothesis: common AR coefs. (within-dimension)

	Statistic	Prob.	Weighted Statistic	Prob.
Panel v-Statistic	2.093241	0.0182	-1.772695	0.9619
Panel rho-Statistic	-1.132131	0.1288	0.776807	0.7814
Panel PP-Statistic	-10.36740	0.0000	-5.842102	0.0000
Panel ADF-Statistic	-0.656688	0.2557	-1.810015	0.0351

Alternative hypothesis: individual AR coefs. (between-dimension)

	Statistic	Prob.
Group rho-Statistic	2.615025	0.9955
Group PP-Statistic	-6.542872	0.0000
Group ADF-Stat.	-1.559655	0.0594

Individual intercept and individual trend/Deterministic intercept and trend

Alternative hypothesis: common AR coefs. (within-dimension)

	Statistic	Prob.	Weighted Statistic	Prob.
Panel v-Statistic	1.929418	0.0268	-3.175776	0.9993
Panel rho-Statistic	-0.007695	0.4969	1.684648	0.9540
Panel PP-Statistic	-12.56425	0.0000	-9.732962	0.0000
Panel ADF-Statistic	-2.054508	0.0200	-4.239115	0.0000

Alternative hypothesis: individual AR coefs. (between-dimension)

	Statistic	Prob.
Group rho-Statistic	3.590381	0.9998
Group PP-Statistic	-11.08356	0.0000
Group ADF-Statistic	-4.686063	0.0000

No intercept /No deterministic intercept

Alternative hypothesis: common AR coefs. (within-dimension)

	Statistic	Prob.	Weighted Statistic	Prob.

of government expenditure on consumption means that government expenditure is not consumption enhancing. This may be as a result of government expenditure concentration on capital expenditure and leakages through corruption and inefficiency. The positive relationship between government expenditure and saving confirms the focus of government expenditure on capital projects instead of recurrent projects. In view of the COVID-19 crisis and the possible increase in poverty and inequality as a result, African nations shall increase the amount of their recurrent expenditure in order to help alleviate poverty and inequality. Government shall provide more income generation means for the poor and the middle class through adopting policies that redistribute income and various types of empowerment programs. At this time of COVID-19 crisis, government income transfer policies such as food subsidy, income transfer through government direct assistances to the poor and other form of subsidy shall be encouraged.

SUMMARY AND CONCLUSION

This study was conducted to find out how inequality, consumption and saving fair in relation to one another and other variables in 24 countries across the length of Africa. Studies of this nature are complex and demanding, but they are equality relevant to the understanding of African economies. The study findings collaborate some of the past findings about African economies. For example, a number of previous studies have found the level of inequality in Africa to be high. The levels of saving and household consumption across Africa have been equally affected by the economic fortune of the continent. Both theoretical and empirical literatures are filled with works on importance of saving and consumption. Policy makers in Africa must take cognizance of the fact that for the continent to achieve sustain economic growth, major macroeconomic variables such as consumption and saving must be set right. Policies that boost consumption such as higher government expenditure, reduction in inequality and increase in economic opportunities for citizens that also reduce dependency ratio shall be encouraged. Equally important are policies that increase saving such as financial development which have a positive effect on saving. Because of the devastating effects of global crises such as COVID-19 and the global financial crisis of 2008, African economies shall prepare themselves for future crises by building their economies to be resilience and absorbed shocks whenever they come. Solid economic growth and development is a must for reducing the impact of any future crisis on African economies. Nations in this part of the world shall support programs that further develop their agricultural sectors, as the largest employer of labour on the continent and to avoid further problem of food insecurity. The lack of huge foreign reserves and financial war chest have been an important barrier that held back any serious respond to crises of COVID-19 magnitude on the continent. This work contributed to the literature on inequality by emphasizing it links with consumption and saving. It emphasis the importance of household consumption and saving and show how they are in turn influenced by other factors such as government expenditure, financial development and dependency ratio.

REFERENCES

Adams, S. (2009). Foreign Direct investment, domestic investment, and economic growth in Sub-Saharan Africa. *Journal of Policy Modeling*, *31*(6), 939–949. doi:10.1016/j.jpolmod.2009.03.003

Adewuyi, A. O., Bankole, A. S., & Arawomo, D. F. (n.d.). what determines saving in the Economic Community of West African State (ECOWAS)? *Journal of Monetary and Economic Integration*, *10*(2), 71–100.

Aguiar, M., & Bils, M. (2015). Has Consumption Inequality Mirrored Income Inequality? *The American Economic Review*, *105*(9), 2725–2756. doi:10.1257/aer.20120599

Akadiri, S. S., & Akadiri, A. C. (2018). Growth and Inequality in Africa: Reconsideration. *Academic Journal of Economic Studies*, *4*(3), 76–86.

Alvarez-Cuadrado, F., & Vilalta, M. E. (2018). Income inequality and saving. *Oxford Bulletin of Economics and Statistics*, *80*(6), 1029–1061. doi:10.1111/obes.12236

Aryeetey & Udry.(1999). *Rural Household Asset Choice in Ghana*. ISSER and Yale.

Aryeetey, E., & Udry, C. (2000). *Saving in Sub-Saharan Africa*. Center for International Development, Working Paper no. 38.

Baltagi, B. H. (2005). *Econometric Analysis of Panel Data* (3rd ed.). John Wiley & Sons Ltd.

Baxter, M., & Crucini, M. J. (1993). Explaining Saving—Investment Correlations. *The American Economic Review*, *83*(3), 416–436.

Carroll, C., Weil, D., & Summers, L. H. (1993). *Savings and Growth: A reinterpretation*. Paper Presented at the Carnegie-Rochester Public Policy Conference, Bradley Policy Research Centre. 10.3386/w4470

Cingano, F. (2014). *Trends in Income Inequality and its Impact on Economic Growth*. OECD Social, Employment and Migration Working Papers, No. 163. OECD Publishing. doi:10.1787/1815199X

Dabla-Norris, E., Kochhar, K., Suphaphiphat, N., Ricka, F., & Tsounta, E. (2015). *Causes and Consequences of Income Inequality: A Global Perspective*. International Monetary Fund Discussion Note, SDN/15/13.

De Nardi, M., & Fella, G. (2017). Saving and wealth inequality. *Review of Economic Dynamics*. doi:10.1016/j.red.2017.06.002

Feldstein, M., & Horioka, C. (1980). Domestic Saving and International Capital Flow. *Economic Journal (London)*, *90*(358), 314–329. doi:10.2307/2231790

Ferreira, F., & Ravallion, M. (2009). Poverty and Inequality: The Global Context. In *The Oxford Handbook of Economic Inequality* (pp. 599–636). Oxford University Press.

Flassbeck, H. (2008). *Savings, investment and growth: theory and reality*. G-24 Policy Brief No. 35.

Geda, A., & Kebret, H. (2006). Aggregate Saving Behavior in Africa: A Review of the Theory and the ExistingEvidence with a New Empirical Results. *Ethiopian Journal of Economics*, *12*(1), 13–42.

Global Economic Prospects. (2022). *Impact of COVID-19 on Global income inequality*. Author.

Gui-Diby, S. L. (2014). Impact of foreign direct investments on economic growth in Africa: Evidence from three decades of panel data analyses. *Research in Economics*, *68*(3), 248–256. doi:10.1016/j.rie.2014.04.003

Gujarati, D. N. (2004). Basic Econometrics (4th ed.). The McGraw−Hill.

Hanson, J. L. (1978). *Monetary theory and practice*. Macdonald and Evans.

Hassana, M. K., Sanchezb, B., & Yu, J. (2011). Financial development and economic growth: New evidence from panel data. *The Quarterly Review of Economics and Finance*, *51*(1), 88–104. doi:10.1016/j.qref.2010.09.001

Hillbom, E., Bolt, J., Haas, M., & Tadei, F. (2021). *Measuring historical inequality in Africa: What can we learn from social tables?* African Economic History Working Paper Series No. 63/2021.

Hsiao, C. (2003). Analysis of Panel Data (2nd ed.). Econometric Society Monograph No. 34. Cambridge University Press. doi:10.1017/CBO9780511754203

Im, K. S., Pesaran, M. H., & Shin, Y. (2003). Testing for Unit Roots in Heterogeneous Panels. *Journal of Econometrics*, *115*(1), 53–74. doi:10.1016/S0304-4076(03)00092-7

Irandoust, M. (2019). Saving and investment causality: Implications for financial integration in transition countries of Eastern Europe. *International Economics and Economic Policy*, *16*(2), 397–416. doi:10.100710368-017-0390-6

Kaldor, N. (1957). A model of economic growth. *Economic Journal (London)*, 57.

Koo, J., & Song, Y. (2016). The relationship between income inequality and aggregate saving: An empirical analysis using cross-country panel data. *Applied Economics*, *48*(10), 892–901. doi:10.1080/00036846.2015.1090548

Krueger, D., & Perri, F. (2005). *Does Income Inequality Lead to Consumption Equality? Evidence and Theory*. Federal Reserve Bank of Minneapolis Research Department Staff Report 363.

Levin, A., Lin, C., & Chu, C. J. (2002). Unit Root Test in Panel Data: Asymptotic and Finite Sample Properties. *Journal of Econometrics*, *108*(1), 1–24. doi:10.1016/S0304-4076(01)00098-7

Lewis, W. A. (1954). Economic development with unlimited supplies of labor. *Manchester School*, *22*(2), 139–191. doi:10.1111/j.1467-9957.1954.tb00021.x

Mankiw, N. G. (2007). *Macroeconomics*. Worth publishers.

Martins, N. (2010). Globalisation, Inequality and the Economic Crisis. *New Political Economy*.

Ndambiri, Ritho, Ng'ang'a, Kubowon, & Mairura, Nyangweso, Muiruri, & Cherotwo. (2012). Determinants of Economic growth in sub-Saharan Africa: A Panel Data Approach. *International Journal of Economics and Management Sciences*, *2*(2), 18–24.

Ndikumana, L. (2000). Financial Determinants of Domestic Investment in Sub-Saharan Africa: Evidence from Panel Data. *World Development*, *28*(2), 381–400. doi:10.1016/S0305-750X(99)00129-1

Nel, P. (2018). Inequality in Africa. In T. Binns, K. Lynch, & E. Nel (Eds.), *Routledge Handbook of African Development*. Routledge.

Olagbaju, I. O., & Akinlo, A. E. (2018). FDI And Economic Growth Relationship In Sub-Saharan Africa: Is The Domestic Financial System A Significant Intermediator? *Archives of Business Research*, *6*(5), 90–112. doi:10.14738/abr.65.4540

Onwuka, C. E. (2022). Poverty, Income Inequality and Economic Growth in Nigeria (1981-2019). *J Eco Res & Rev*, *2*(2), 92–100.

Pasinetti, L. (1962). Rate of profit and income distribution in relation to the rate of economic Growth. *The Review of Economic Studies*, *29*(4), 267–279. doi:10.2307/2296303

Pedroni, P. (2000). Fully Modified OLS For Heterogeneous Cointegrated Panels, Nonstationary Panels, Panel Cointegration, and Dynamic Panels. *Advances in Econometrics*, *15*, 93–130. doi:10.1016/S0731-9053(00)15004-2

Pesaran, M. H., & Smith, R. (1995). Estimating long-run relationships from dynamic heterogeneous Panels. *Journal of Economics*, *68*(1), 79–113. doi:10.1016/0304-4076(94)01644-F

Raut, L. K., & Virmani, A. (1989). Determinants of Consumption and Savings Behavior in Developing Countries. *The World Bank Economic Review*, *3*(3), 379–393. doi:10.1093/wber/3.3.379

Romer, D. (2005). *Advanced Macroeconomic* (3rd ed.). University of California.

Schmidt-Hebbel, K., & Serven, L. (2000). Does income inequality raise aggregate saving? *Journal of Development Economics*, *61*(2), 417–446. doi:10.1016/S0304-3878(00)00063-8

Seale, J. L., & Regmi, A. (2006). Modeling international consumption patterns. *Review of Income and Wealth Series*, *52*(4), 603–624. doi:10.1111/j.1475-4991.2006.00204.x

Sembene, D. (2015). *Poverty, Growth, and Inequality in Sub-Saharan Africa: Did the Walk Match the Talk under the PRSP Approach?* IMF Working Paper, WP/15/122.

Shawa, K. C. (2016). Drivers of private saving in sub-Saharan Africancountries. *Journal of Economic Development*, *41*(2), 77–110. doi:10.35866/caujed.2016.41.2.004

Shimeles, A., & Nabassaga, T. (2017). *Why is inequality high in Africa?* Working Paper Series N° 246. African Development Bank.

Wansbeek, T.J. (2001). GMM Estimation in Panel Data Models with Measurement error. *Journal of Econoimetrics*, 104.

World Bank. (1993). *The East Asian miracle: Economic growth and public policy.* Oxford University Press.

Yasin, M. (n.d.). *Public spending and economic growth: empirical investigation of Sub-Sahara Africa. Southwestern Economic Review.*

KEY TERMS AND DEFINITION

Africa: Africa comprises all the countries in the African continent.

Consumption: Consumption is the act of using resources to satisfy current needs and wants whether by individual or group. Consumption in economics is frequently associated with the use of goods and services by households. Consumption is distinct from consumption expenditure, which is the purchase of goods.

Financial Development: Financial development is the development of financial institutions, financial markets, and financial instruments. It involves funding of entrepreneurial activity and innovations.

Government Expenditure: Government expenditure means money spent by public sector on acquisition of goods and provision of services. It includes all government consumption, investment, and transfer payments.

Inequality: Inequality in economics means unequal (unjust) distribution of resources and opportunities among members of a given society.

Panel Data: Panel data is a type of data that contains observations about different cross sections across time.

Poverty: Poverty is the inability of individual or household to meet basic needs including food, clothing, and shelter. Absolute poverty measures poverty as those earning less than $1.90 a day.

Saving: Saving is the opposite of consumption; it is the amount of money kept for future consumption. Hence, saving is income not spent.

Chapter 8
Cross-Country Analysis of Competitiveness in GDP per Capita, Health, Social Support, Freedom

Evin Tom Xavier
Amity University, India

Shilpi Sharma
Amity University, India

Aayush Agarwal
Amity University, India

ABSTRACT

Happiness supports growth, this chapter aims to further explain how developed countries achieve peace and prosperity by keeping their population happy. The aim of this chapter is to analyze the interdependence between the various factors that affect the happiness of a population measured on happiness scale. This analysis is done by using the World Happiness Report 2020. This report includes the data from 154 countries from different regions of the world taking into account the country's GDP per capita, freedom to make life choices, social support, health life expectancy, among other factors. The research results are based on descriptive and inferential statistics methods. The target of this chapter is to explain the possible reasons behind the success or the failure of the country to provide for its population. This chapter investigates the positive relation between factors like GDP per capita, freedom, health life expectancy, and social support to the happiness of the population.

DOI: 10.4018/978-1-6684-5289-9.ch008

INTRODUCTION

Happiness is a hard thing to measure, it cannot be quantified but there are always some parameters that affect the happiness of a population. People tend to migrate for relatively peaceful and prosperous life even at the cost of cultural alienation. Sustainable happiness comes with a lot of benefits:

- Better social relationship- better family connections and less chance of divorce (Tofallis, 2020).
- Generosity- more likely to help, volunteer or donate to social wellbeing.
- Better mental health- better focus on mental health and ability to bounce back after something bad happens. (Tofallis, 2020)
- Better health and better life expectancy- happier population experience not only a longer life but also a better health experience. (Esmail & Shili, 2018)

Alternative concept of Gross National Happiness (GNH) was first coined in 1970s (Tideman, 2011, pp. 133-153) by the king of king of Bhutan in response to western developed countries who regarded Bhutan as a poor country with respect to Gross Domestic Product (GDP). Moving forward to 21st century to highlight the Importance of happiness the world celebrates international happiness day on 20th March to highlight its importance in everyone's life. The United Nation (UN) has now taken a step further by publishing world happiness report every year starting from April 2012. Now more and more countries are investing to better understand the people by conducting various reports and studies regarding the society's suffering versus flourishing.

The data is based on global survey where residents of each country rated their happiness ranging from 0 to 10 with 0 being the lowest and 10 being the highest. This report also includes other factors like GDP per capita, social support, freedom to make life choices, health life expectancy, generosity and perception of corruption. No single factor can completely overweigh other for example, it is always observed that a growing GDP per capita always reflect to a happier population this is only true to an extent, it has been observed that a GDP per capita exceeding $40,000 in southeast European countries has no positive correlation with the happiness of the population (Pupavac et al., 2020). The paper first divides the world into different regions and then analysis the factors of growth in each region, it then studies each region carefully trying to explain extremities observed.

LITERATURE REVIEW

Happiness is a very hard topic to summarize it can be a good standard of living for some, it could be a positive approach or it could just be things that people find amusing, so it is hard to examine which factors contribute to its development. The UN World happiness report tries to assess the happiness of the population using 6 different factors. The report includes analysis by experts in economics, neuroscience and statistics, and shows how measurements of well-being can be used to evaluate a country's progress. The report can be used to find collaborative solutions to problems for citizens of the country. National government around the world can contribute to reduce the misery faced by its population be designing policies to tackle mental health problems, declining social support systems. It is very important for a country to have a strong social fabric; this leads to people working together to solve problems. For example, during the financial crisis both Iceland and Ireland suffered decimation of banking systems, this however was not reflected on overall happiness of the population due to strong social support that is having someone to count on, while Greece happiness rank crumbled during the recession also because it had lost social support. It is a very common mistake made by the political leaders which very conveniently link the happiness score to the GDP growth, this argument holds only for a short duration, consider comparing the income levels of USA and UK (Oswald, 2006). The US boasts 6 times more income level than UK and yet the suicide rate ratio in both of these countries are still similar. This leads to speculations that there are non-economic factors that come into play, further studies indicate how the government's ambition to increase the GDP and at the same time elevate the happiness of the population fails in the long term (Roka, 2020). Increase in economic growth creates more opportunity but it also gives more false aspirations to people and on further failing to keep up to the dreams it in turn creates more dissatisfaction among the population. This is evident in advanced economies, while happiness did help to elevate the happiness of the population but when income inequality was added as a factor, countries with higher income-inequality (UK, USA) as compared to countries with low income-inequality (Denmark, Sweden) performed poorly. Another study which focuses more on cultural aspect and focuses on "good life" over "good's life" explains how the pursuit for money, fame and image only suffices to a low quality of life, it focuses for personal growth to achieve happiness and enhanced wellbeing (Kasser, 2004). Health and happiness can be linearly related, this explains how healthy people tend to live longer and that how public health can be further improved by introducing policies that aim to increase the happiness of the population (Veenhoven, 2008). Happiness and success can also be related to the genes, families and the psychological effects of socio-economic position and social support (Schnittker, 2008), but this has its own limitations. The major being measuring of parameters is based on self-report, this may lead to interpretive ambiguity. China presents an interesting example on how happiness cannot only be related to economic factor, even though China experienced a rapid growth since 1990, the happiness has ever since plummeted (Brockmann et al., 2009). From happiness perspective, freedom has not been reached even in countries experiencing high levels of freedom. People crave for more freedom even in developed countries with high happiness index, (Rahman & Veenhoven, 2017) concluded how happiness and freedom have been observed to be predominantly positive. Another positive relation was found between happiness and social support during research conducted among elderly in Iran, the study found that higher social support increased happiness among elders (Moeini et al., 2018).

METHODOLOGY

Firstly, the countries are ranked based on happiness score as provided from UN world happiness report 2020 then, factors that affect happiness of a population is compared between the happiest countries and the most unhappiest countries as per the UN world happiness report. GDP per capita, life expectancy, social support and freedom to make life choices are the key factors using to assess the happiness of a population. The factors are then graphically compared to the happiness score to determine the relationship between them, if the relationship is linear it implies that with the increase in magnitude of factor 'A' the happiness of the population reacts positively, if the relationship is scatter it would suggest a weak or no relationship between the two. One disadvantage of linear relationship is that it assumes that with unit increase in factor 'A' it will bring unit improvement in happiness score, this isn't true, for example with increase in GDP per capita one might think this will bring positive growth in happiness index this holds only for a certain point. With increase in GDP per capita new problems may arrive like income inequality. Income inequality basically refers to distribution of wealth, it compares how a fraction of rich population possess wealth as compared to magnitude of wealth of poor population. High income inequality gives a false impression of a country's economic growth. After assessing the factors we then divide the world into various regions and then compare how each region scores in the subject of logged GDP per capita, Health life expectancy, social support and freedom to make life choices and then compare the happiness score of the region to the world average, each region is further analysed to find the possible reasons how one country succeeds or fails in the happiness score of its population.

RESULTS

Table 1. Top 10 most happiest countries in the world (2020). Source: UN world happiness report 2020.

RANK	COUNTRY	SCORE
1.	FINLAND	7.8087
2.	DENMARK	7.6456
3.	SWITZERAND	7.5599
4.	ICELAND	7.5045
5.	NORWAY	7.4880
6.	NETHERLANDS	7.4489
7.	SWEEDEN	7.3535
8.	NEW ZEALAND	7.2996
9.	AUSTRIA	7.2942
10.	LUXEMBOURG	7.2375

A whopping 9 countries belong to western Europe region and only one country is located with oceanic regions.

Table 2. Top 10 most unhappiest countries in the world (2020). Source: UN world happiness report 2020.

RANK	COUNTRY	SCORE
1.	AFGANISTAN	2.5669
2.	SOUTH SUDAN	2.8166
3.	ZIMBABWE	3.2992
4.	RAWANDA	3.3123
5.	CENTRAL AFRICAN REPUBLIC	3.4759
6.	TANZANIA	3.4762
7.	BOTSWANA	3.4789
8.	YEMEN	3.5274
9.	MALAWI	3.5380
10.	INDIA	3.5733

Figure 1. Happiness score (y) versus log (GDP per capita) on x-axis.

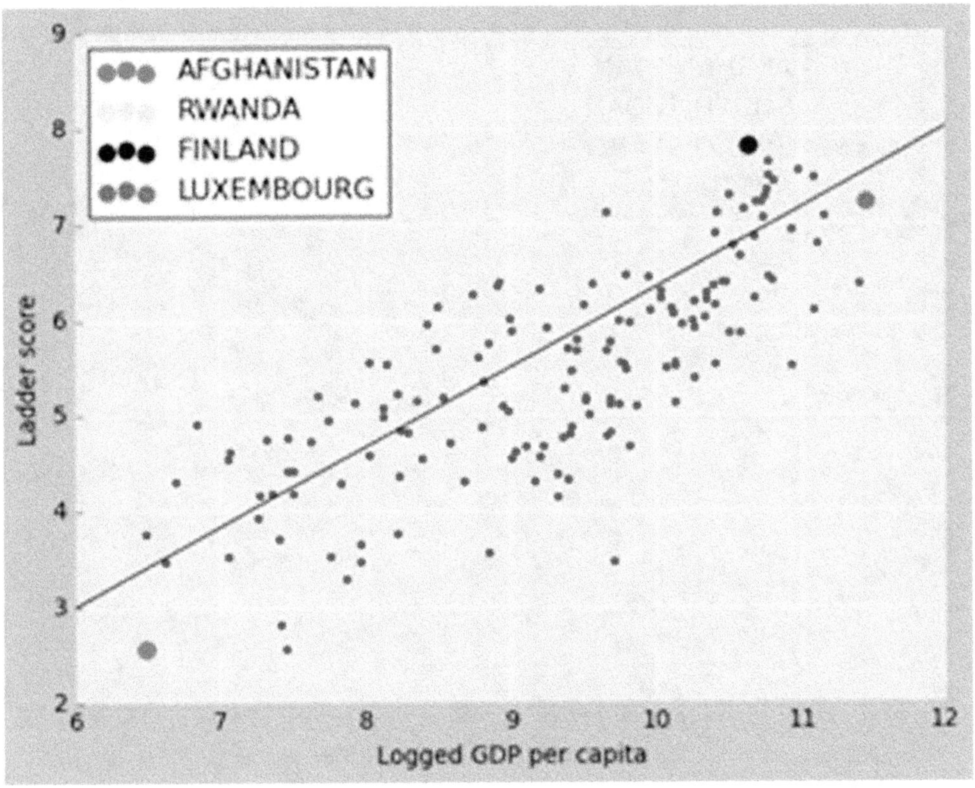

Seven of the above countries belong to Sub-Saharan Africa while 2 of the countries belong to south Asia and only one from middle east and north Africa region.

The following factors tries to explain behind the achievement or the failure of the countries mentioned:

- GDP per capita

Up to a certain point economist have always considered the growing GDP per capita influences the happiness score of the population linearly.

The above figure presents the scatter plot of happiness score of different countries, the main objective is to further emphasis the importance of a growing GDP per capita to the happiness of the population. The graph clearly shows the linear relationship between high GDP per capita of a nation to its happiness of the population. Countries like Rwanda and Afghanistan who perform poorly in happiness score also reflect a poor logged GDP per capita when compared to countries like Finland and Luxembourg.

Figure 2. Happiness score (y) versus health life expectancy on x-axis.

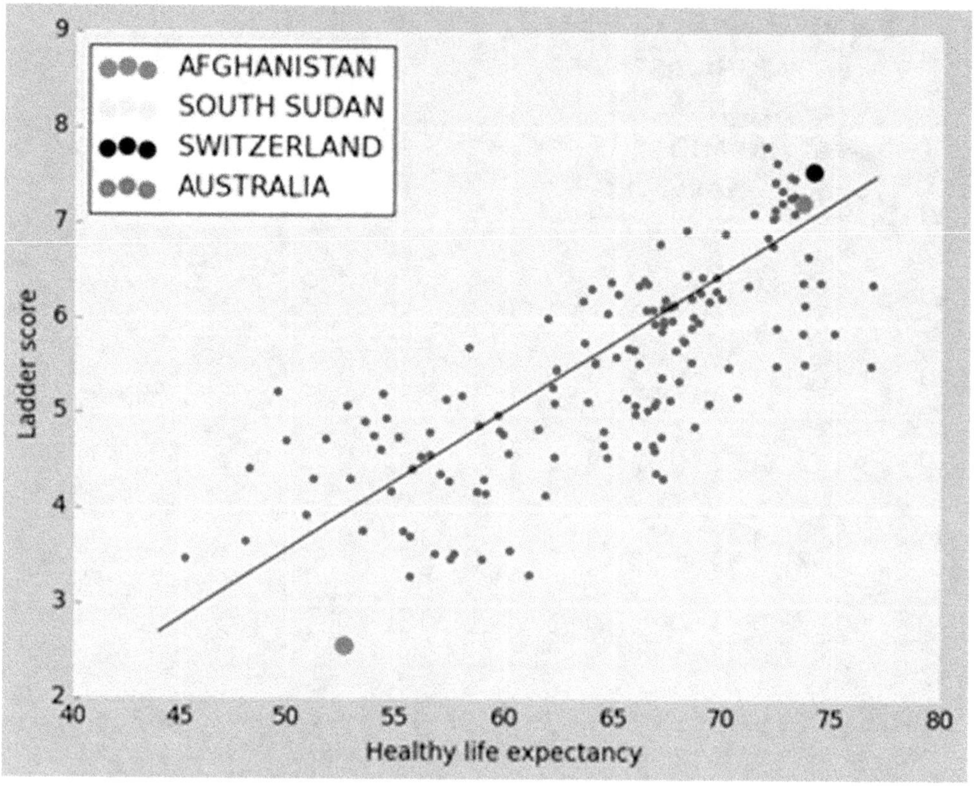

- Health life expectancy

As expected, the health of the population directly affects the happiness. The above graph shows a linear relationship between the health of the nation to the happiness experienced by the nation, countries like South Sudan and Afghanistan have poor life expectancy of 51 and 52.59 years respectively have low happiness score when compared to countries like Australia and Switzerland who with their high happiness score tend to keep a healthier population.

- Social support

Social support refers to individual's relationship with their friends, their family basically anyone who they find their refuge in case of adverse life events. The above graph shows the relationship between social support and happiness of a population. Countries like Burundi and Central African Republic which have high social unrest perform poorly in this scale.

Figure 3. Happiness score (y) versus social support on x-axis.

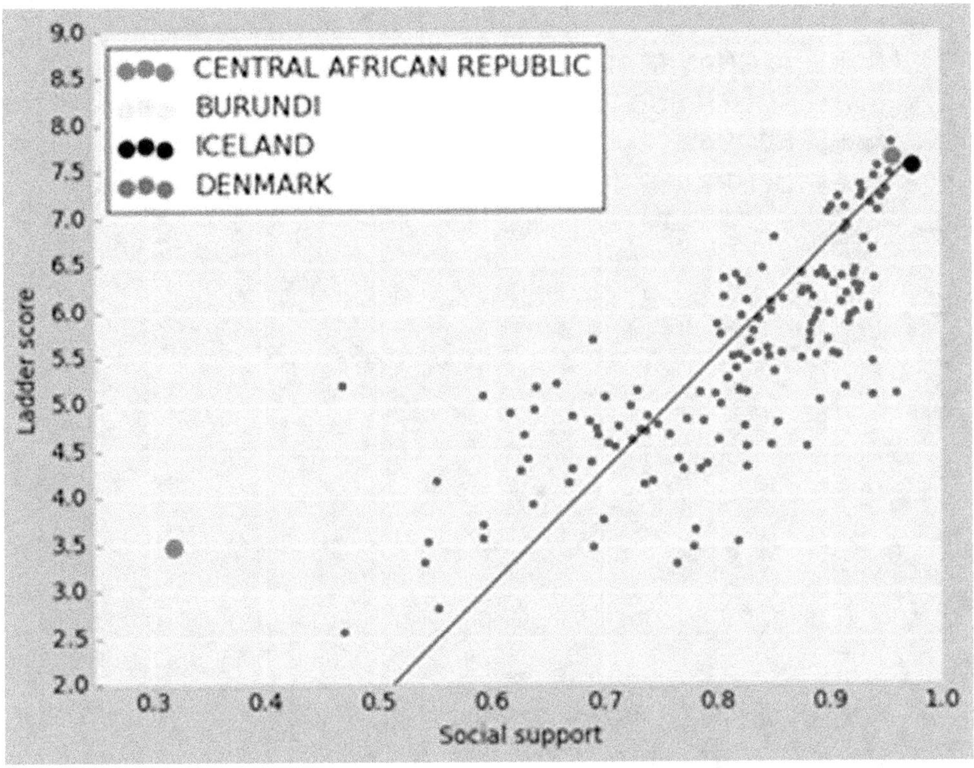

- Freedom to make life choices

The relationship between happiness of a population and relative freedom of life choices isn't linear but the countries that experience more freedom tend to perform good in happiness scale.

Analysis based on different region:

1. Western Europe

Western European countries have among the highest happiness index among different regions, a survey in 2020 indicated it is because of relatively good stability and high level of trust in the government.

World happiness index (mean): 5.47

Western Europe happiness index (mean): 6.89

The above table confirms how Western European countries have dominated in all the factors which is reflected in its happiness score, hence this region not only

Figure 4. Happiness score (y) versus Freedom to make life choices on x-axis.

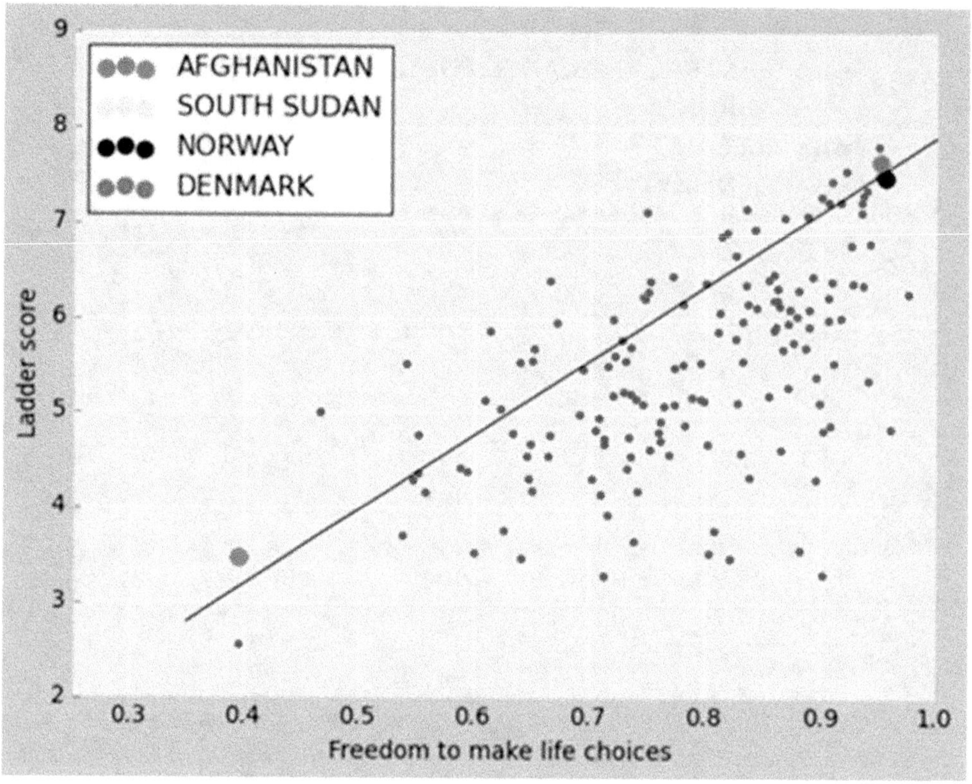

belongs to one of the happiest region but also one of the progressive regions in the world.

Most successful country based on happiness (region-wise): Finland

It is the fourth time running Finland has ranked 1st in UN World Happiness report 2020.

Table 3. Comparing factors that affect happiness (Western Europe).

	Logged GDP per capita	Health life expectancy (years)	Social support	Freedom to make life choices
World	9.29	72.63	0.80	0.78
Western Europe	10.68	81.50	0.91	0.85

Table 4. Comparing factors that affect happiness (Central and Eastern Europe).

	Logged GDP per capita	Health life expectancy (years)	Social support	Freedom to make life choices
World	9.29	72.63	0.80	0.78
Central and Eastern Europe	9.80	74.29	0.85	0.75

- Finland is blessed when it comes to natural beauty. The country possesses beautiful landscape, pristine forests, clear lakes with incredibly less pollution levels.
- Low crime rate is another reason why people feel safe, secure and live a happier life
- Finland's focus on healthcare is also a major contributing factor, the citizens are offered universal healthcare this has helped to promote healthy lifestyle while maintaining a very reasonable cost.

Most unsuccessful country based on happiness (region-wise): Greece

The country ranks 77 in 2020 which is a major improvement considering the fact that it stood at 102nd rank in year 2015.

- Ever since the debt crisis the country economy has been the same, unemployment among youths (15-24) is at astonishing 40.4%, this is much more when compared to EU youth unemployment rate at 14.3%.
- The debt problem has forced the country to spend low in public healthcare expenditure currently it stands at 5% of GDP which when compared to EU average of 7.2% makes it among the underperformers.

2. Central and Eastern Europe

Many countries in this region even with a relative developed economy experience less happiness due to slow growth in economy, poor government performance and problems dating back to pro-socialist governance. Even after the fall of socialism countries in this region still face sluggish growth due to ideological, political and economic problems.

World happiness index (mean): 5.47

Central and Eastern Europe happiness index (mean): 5.65

The above table shows how an average score in all the four factors result in an average happiness score when compared to the mean world happiness.

Most successful country based on happiness (region-wise): Czech Republic

Table 5. Comparing factors that affect happiness (Latin America and Caribbean).

	Logged GDP per capita	Health life expectancy (years)	Social support	Freedom to make life choices
World	9.29	72.63	0.80	0.78
Latin America and Caribbean	9.30	75.24	0.85	0.83

Czech Republic ranks at 19th place in UN World Happiness report 2020, the happiness index has been steadily improving in recent years.

- The unemployment rate in Czech Republic stood at 2.01% which is comparatively among the lowest in Europe, the various incentives offered by the government have made Czech Republic an attractive location for global companies.
- Czech Republic has one of the best healthcare system in central and eastern Europe, the number of doctors per citizens is among the highest in EU countries. It is important to note that free medical care is provided not only to Czech citizens but also to foreigners working for a local company through compulsory contributions made to health insurance company approved by government.

Most unsuccessful country based on happiness (region-wise): Ukraine

Ukraine ranks 123rd in UN World Happiness report 2020, climbing by 11 positions as compared to last year.

- Ukraine has among the highest crude death rates in the world, the healthcare system has been unreformed since the soviet era left it in poor and under-financed condition, widespread abuse of alcohol and drug is another major reason why the country has performed poorly in health-care index.
- From being the 2nd largest economy in Soviet era, the country now ranks 2nd in the list of Europe's poorest countries with a GDP per capita of just $3245.

3. Latin America and Caribbean

This region extends from Bahamas and Mexico to Argentina and Chile covering a number of developing countries. This region performs significantly lower when compared to its North American neighbour because of a lot of reasons including poor governance, drug trafficking, poor economic performance and high crime rates.

World happiness index (mean): 5.47

Latin America and Caribbean happiness index (mean): 5.98

Since the 1980s and 1990s drug trafficking has led to sharp increase in crime rates all over Latin America, this resulted in affecting the happiness of the population directly hence Latin America and Caribbean countries just manage an above average happiness score.

Most successful country based on happiness (region-wise): Costa Rica

The country ranks 15th in UN World Happiness report 2020.

- Costa Rican people have among the highest social support. Family life is given a major priority, it is common for people to live with their parents even in their late 30s or even 40s.
- Costa Rican's follow a very sound and healthy diet, rice and beans are among the major staple and the diet also includes meat and vegetables so in average people tend to consume more nutrients this has helped the nation to maintain a very high health life expectancy, higher than that of United States at 80.38 years.

Most unsuccessful country based on happiness (region-wise): Haiti

Haiti ranks 142nd in UN World Happiness report 2020, the country has been consistently performing poorly over the past several years.

- More than two-fifths of the country's population depend on agriculture sector which is vulnerable to frequent natural disasters, Haiti's economy has faced some major shocks over the years, a 1.7% contraction in 2019 followed by an estimated 3.8% contraction due to COVID-19, this has resulted in 14.50% unemployment rate in 2020.
- Due to the economic limitation the country is forced to spend a very limited amount in health-care infrastructure, this had led to a very poor health life expectancy of just 63.5 years.

4. North America

Only 2 countries are included in this region the United States and Canada. Both of these countries perform among the highest when it comes to satisfying its population, also these countries possess high scores in all four factors that affect the happiness of the population.

World happiness index (mean): 5.47

North America happiness index (mean): 7.08

Major focus on healthcare and educational institutions has enabled this region to progress and maintain a high happiness score.

Both countries USA and Canada perform exceptionally well in happiness score.

Canada ranks 11th in UN World Happiness report 2020.

Table 6. Comparing factors that affect happiness (North America).

	Logged GDP per capita	Health life expectancy (years)	Social support	Freedom to make life choices
World	9.29	72.63	0.80	0.78
North America	10.80	80.44	0.92	0.88

- Canada's economy is highly developed and is one of the largest economies in the world. The job market is also very vibrant making it easy for the people to find employment.
- When it comes to health-care infrastructure Canada invests heavily on it, it ranks 11th among health-care systems in OECD. The funds for universal health-care system is paid through taxes, even if a citizen or a permanent resident does not have a government health care he/she can still avail most health-care services for free.

The United States happiness index has been on a bumpy road for a few years, it ranked 11th back in 2012 followed by 17th rank a year later but after climbing a few spots it dropped to 18th in 2020.

- Even though the United States has the largest GDP in the world, its economic achievement does not tell the complete picture. Income inequality is a growing concern, the country ranks highest in income inequality among G7 nations.
- The health-care system in US is also very costly, there is no universal health-care system so the US government do not provide any health benefits to its citizens or tourists.

5. East Asia and Pacific

This region consists majorly of developing countries, characteristics include large population and rich diversity.

World happiness index (mean): 5.47

East Asia and Pacific happiness index (mean): 6.09

The Happiness of this region is deceptive this is because a majority of countries located in oceanic regions were not included in UN World Happiness report, only developed countries in oceanic region like Australia and New Zealand were included.

Most successful country based on happiness (region-wise): New Zealand

New Zealand ranks 8th in UN World Happiness report 2020, this is the only non-European in the top 10 performers.

Table 7. Comparing factors that affect happiness (East Asia and Pacific).

	Logged GDP per capita	Health life expectancy (years)	Social support	Freedom to make life choices
World	9.29	72.63	0.80	0.78
East Asia and Pacific	10.38	70.85	0.87	0.80

- The economy is highly developed and free market economy, the strengthening of the currency in recent years against the US dollar has had a major impact and with unemployment rate at just 4.5% New Zealand performs good in economic factor.
- The government also runs the universal health-care system, this has allowed most of the health care services in the country to be free. The healthcare is funded through taxes and has helped the country to maintain a high health life expectancy.

Most unsuccessful country based on happiness (region-wise): China
China ranks 94th in UN World Happiness report 2020.

- Even though China boasts the second largest GDP in the world the country still faces problems regarding its economic activity. The GDP per capita according to world bank is $10,500 making it in 76th rank in the list of largest GDP per capita, the massive infrastructure projects have also accumulated a large debt thus slowing its economic growth.
- Due to high difference in health-care standards between rural areas and cities, the country ranks 144th in World Health Organization report. The country spends 5.5% of its GDP on health but still manages a relatively low number of doctors per population (1.6 per 1000 population).

6. South-east Asia

This region contains mostly of under-developed and developing countries, it is also famous for affordable tourist destination.

World happiness index (mean): 5.47

South-east Asia happiness index (mean): 5.38

This region further contains a host of developing countries which perform fairly in world happiness report.

Most successful country based on happiness (region-wise): Singapore

Singapore ranks 31st in UN World Happiness report and is ranked the happiest country in Asia.

Table 8. Comparing factors that affect happiness (South-east Asia).

	Logged GDP per capita	Health life expectancy (years)	Social support	Freedom to make life choices
World	9.29	72.63	0.80	0.78
Southeast Asia	9.36	73.10	0.82	0.91

- One major reason why Singapore is highly ranked in Asia is due to the government's performance in job creation and its effective measures in proving basic necessities like housing. The poverty is very low and the country's unemployment rate is among the lowest in the world.
- Singapore's health care has consistently ranked among the best in the world, health care in government hospitals is either highly subsidized or sometimes even made free for its citizens thus helping the country to achieve high health life expectancy.

Most unsuccessful country based on happiness (region-wise): Myanmar

Myanmar ranks 133rd in UN World Happiness report, the country has continuously performed poor since the report was first launched in 2013.

- The country has failed to have a stable democratic government ever since it gained independence from Britain in 1948, the widespread persecution of Rohingyas has affected its international relations, the US, UK and European union have all responded with economic sanctions thereby hurting its economy.
- The country fails to provide freedom of speech and expression by law in fact the country follows colonial era laws to arrest and prosecute anyone who exercises their right to form association or peaceful assembly.

7. South Asia

This region even though with a good economic potential performs poorly when compared to happiness index, challenges include over population, unemployment, failing government and mass poverty.

World happiness index (mean): 5.47

South Asia happiness index (mean): 4.47

Poor focus on health care infrastructure and educational institutions coupled with poor technological background and growing territorial disputes has pushed this region among the worst performers in UN World Happiness report.

Table 9. Comparing factors that affect happiness (South-east Asia).

	Logged GDP per capita	Health life expectancy (years)	Social support	Freedom to make life choices
World	9.29	72.63	0.80	0.78
South Asia	8.55	69.64	0.70	0.77

Since this region accounts for one of the most unhappiest regions in the world it is hard to call a country successful in terms of happiness, the ranking ranges from 66th for Pakistan to the lowest 153rd for Afghanistan.

- Due to rapid growing population in South Asia, the region faces tremendous pressure for land and resources. Due to this growing population the unemployment rates continue to raise resulting in mass poverty. The region accounts for 29% of the people living in extreme poverty worldwide.
- The region also accounts for one of the most poorest health-care systems in the world. Even developing countries like India spend less than 1% of its total GDP on health. Due to growing border tensions India, Pakistan, Bangladesh are forced to spend more on infrastructure and military equipment rather than focusing on health of the population.
- Terrorism is another major challenge surrounding South Asian countries, for years Afghanistan and Pakistan have been the epicentre of terrorist groups. This has not only affected the country's GDP but has affected the growth of countries neighbouring.

8. Central Asia

Countries in this region gained independence in early 1990s after the fall of USSR, since then it has emerged to a hub of developing countries moving from state-controlled economy to a market economy.

World happiness index (mean): 5.47

Central Asia happiness index (mean): 5.70

This region is let down majorly due its economic performance. The strong economic performance is still overshadowed by its widespread dissatisfaction regarding economic policies and corruption. The countries in this region perform from decent to average hence it is difficult to conclude a country is successful in terms of happiness of its population. The ranking ranges from Uzbekistan (38th) to Turkmenistan (95th) in UN World Happiness report.

Table 10. Comparing factors that affect happiness (Central Asia).

	Logged GDP per capita	Health life expectancy (years)	Social support	Freedom to make life choices
World	9.29	72.63	0.80	0.78
Central Asia	8.95	73.20	0.90	0.87

- The countries in this region gained independence in early 1990s, since then the aim has only been to gradually implement market economy to previously state controlled economy. The major hurdle is that structural reforms is needed to increase competitiveness. So far, the progress has only been average, unemployment is still growing and this is coupled with the shortage of skilled workers resulting in significant migration outflow over the past decades.
- The health-care system is another let down for this region. All the five countries in this region inherited a soviet model of healthcare which was focused on universal access to basic care but it had its own drawbacks. Today the health-care system neither meets the current standards nor it is affordable for its citizens. The rural areas are the worst affected, it is almost impossible to find a general practitioner. Advanced and specialized treatments are only limited to prominent hospitals which is a financial burden for its citizens as there is no subsidy on medicines.

9. Sub-Saharan Africa

This region consists of countries that are under-developed and are among the lowest performers in UN World Happiness report, challenges include poor economic growth, high debt, soil erosion, social unrest, poor health care and educational infrastructure.

World happiness index (mean): 5.47

Sub-Saharan Africa happiness index (mean): 4.38

The ranking is this region starts from 49th for Mauritius to 152nd for South Sudan according to UN World Happiness report 2020.

- This region constitutes for the lowest GDP among all regions. The early 2000s saw a good economic growth in this region but this did not reflect back when it comes average income. The GDP per capita is also very low (just under $4000) which is one-fifth of world average. The job market is another concern where the opportunity is next to zero, poor focus on infrastructure and educational institution has led to a lack of skilled workers.

Table 11. Comparing factors that affect happiness (Sub-Saharan Africa).

	Logged GDP per capita	Health life expectancy (years)	Social support	Freedom to make life choices
World	9.29	72.63	0.80	0.78
Sub-Saharan Africa	7.90	61.63	0.68	0.71

- The health-care condition in Sub-Saharan Africa is a global concern. Even the data available is far too less and reliable. The World Health Organization estimates that about 50% of the children who die from pneumonia, diarrhoea, measles are from this region. Poor health-care infrastructure has decreased the health life expectancy of this region.
- This region is also prone to political instability and violence, the situation is better when compared to conflict in 1993 but still stability is fragile also due to the influence of terrorism.
- The freedom experienced by the citizens is also very low, the freedom house rated that only eight countries in this region can be considered free. Half of these eight countries are islands while majority of this region still struggle with repressive laws.

10. Middle East and North Africa

This region has been a long victim of political instability and corruption, ever since the Arab spring in early 2010 the economic growth slowed, crime rates increased and access to basic human necessities vanished.

World happiness index (mean): 5.47

Middle-east and North Africa happiness index (mean): 5.22

Table 12. Comparing factors that affect happiness (Middle-east and North Africa).

	Logged GDP per capita	Health life expectancy (years)	Social support	Freedom to make life choices
World	9.29	72.63	0.80	0.78
Middle-east and North Africa	9.71	64.20	0.79	0.71

Most successful country based on happiness (region-wise): Israel

Even with the rising border tensions of Israel with its neighbours, the country performs well in happiness index. The country ranked 14th in UN World Happiness report 2020.

- Israel stands out in this region in measure of standard of living, the country is often compared among the most developed nation of the world due to its economic achievements. The GDP per capita in 2020 according to IMF is $43,639 which is more compared to developed economies like the UK, Canada, New Zealand. With unemployment rate of just 4.61% in 2020 and a booming job market, the country scores a good score in economic factor.
- The health care system in Israel is also among the most technologically advanced in the world. The citizens enjoy the fundamental right of basic health care, Israel follows universal health care and it is compulsory to get a medical insurance. The focus on health care infrastructure ranked Israel the 3rd most efficient in 2020.

Most unsuccessful country based on happiness (region-wise): Yemen.

Political instability and widespread violence account for the majority of the reasons why Yemen ranked 146th in UN World Happiness report 2020.

- Yemen ranks among one of the poorest countries in this region. The civil war since 2014 has taken a toll on the economy. The country mostly relies on revenues generated by oil and gas which have been declining over the past years and foreign aid for its survival.
- Healthcare system in Yemen is also in the verge of collapse, a majority of the healthcare facilities are either completely destroyed or damaged due to the ongoing civil unrest.

CONCLUSION

Bases on the results, we can be sure that all the four factors put forward have a major role in determining the happiness of a country. The graph show how happiness can be positively related to its GDP per capita, life expectancy, social support and freedom experienced by the population. But since happiness can't be quantified it is difficult to generalize and formulate an equation. The paper was also able to explain the reasons behind the gradient of happiness score experienced by different regions of world by highlighting the problems and successes. One of the major drawbacks is that this paper does not include non-linear factors that a population may experience like political differences, government policies, cross-country relations and many more. It is important to conclude by saying that there is more to explore when it comes to non-linear factors that can determine happiness of a population.

REFERENCES

Abdur Rahman, A., & Veenhoven, R. (2018). Freedom and happiness in nations: A research synthesis. *Applied Research in Quality of Life, 13*(2), 435–456. doi:10.100711482-017-9543-6

Brockmann, H., Delhey, J., Welzel, C., & Yuan, H. (2009). The China puzzle: Falling happiness in a rising economy. *Journal of Happiness Studies, 10*(4), 387–405. doi:10.100710902-008-9095-4

Esmail, H. A. H., & Shili, N. N. J. (2018). The relationship between happiness and economic development in KSA: Study of Jazan region. *Asian Social Science, 14*(3), 78–87. doi:10.5539/ass.v14n3p78

Kasser, T. (2004). The Good Life or the Goods Life? Positive Psychology and Personal Well-Being in the Culture of Consumption. In P. A. Linley & S. Joseph (Eds.), *Positive Psychology in Practice*. doi:10.1002/9780470939338.ch4

Moeini, B., Barati, M., Farhadian, M., & Ara, M. H. (2018). The association between social support and happiness among elderly in Iran. *Korean Journal of Family Medicine, 39*(4), 260–265. doi:10.4082/kjfm.17.0121 PMID:29972894

Oswald, A. (2006). The hippies were right all along about happiness. *Financial Times, 19*. https://www.andrewoswald.com/docs/fthappinessjan96.pdf

Pupavac, D., Delibasic, M., Pupavac, J., & Streimikis, J. (2020). Interdependence of quality of life and happiness of the population in Southeast European Countries. *Montenegrin Journal of Economics, 16*(4), 7-15. http://mnje.com/sites/mnje.com/files/007-015_-pupavac_et_al._-.pdf

Roka, D. (2020). Nexus of Economic Growth on Happiness and Inequality: Re-examine the Paradox. *Asian Journal of Economics, Business and Accounting, 15*(1), 35–49. doi:10.9734/ajeba/2020/v15i130206

Schnittker, J. (2008). Happiness and success: Genes, families, and the psychological effects of socioeconomic position and social support. *American Journal of Sociology, 114*(S1), S233–S259. doi:10.1086/592424 PMID:19569406

Tideman, S. G. (2011). Gross national happiness. In *Ethical principles and economic transformation-A Buddhist approach* (pp. 133–153). Springer. doi:10.1007/978-90-481-9310-3_7

Tofallis, C. (2020). Which formula for national happiness? *Socio-Economic Planning Sciences, 70*, 100688. doi:10.1016/j.seps.2019.02.003

Veenhoven, R. (2008). Healthy happiness: Effects of happiness on physical health and the consequences for preventive health care. *Journal of Happiness Studies, 9*(3), 449–469. doi:10.100710902-006-9042-1

KEY TERMS AND DEFINITIONS

GDP: GDP or gross domestic product refers to the monetary values of final goods and services that is produced in a country in a given period of time.

GDP per Capita: It refers to a country's GDP divided by its population.

GNH: Gross national happiness is a concept by which the Himalayan country of Bhutan measures its economic and moral development.

Health Life Expectancy: It is the expected number of remaining years of life spent in good health from a particular age, typically birth or age sixty-five, assuming current rates of mortality and morbidity.

IMF: The International Monetary Fund (IMF) is an international organization that promotes global economic growth and financial stability, encourages international trade, and reduces poverty.

OECD: The Organisation for Economic Co-operation and Development is an intergovernmental organization with 38 member countries, founded in 1961 to stimulate economic progress and world trade.

Social Support: It is the perception that one is cared for.

Chapter 9
Economic and Societal Inequalities in the Time of COVID-19

Mehtap Isik
https://orcid.org/0000-0002-5210-4480
Bogazici University, Turkey

Arda Can Aktürk
Bogazici University, Turkey

ABSTRACT

In this chapter, the impact of the COVID-19 pandemic on economic and social inequalities is analyzed in five dimensions: health, income, education, gender, and digital inequalities. Cases from developed countries provided as the evidence of the stimulating effects of COVID-19 pandemic on the inequalities. The requirement of emergent transformation of the traditional methods to digital ones put a certain pressure on the social and economic structures. The existing dynamics has been stimulated by the containment and closure policies of the governments. Even in the developed countries, the financial packages couldn't prevent the detrimental effects of the lockdowns on the equities and inequalities. In this chapter, these effects are discussed, and some policy recommendations are offered.

INTRODUCTION

Inequalities have been in a two-way relation with pandemics over the entire modern history. In the past, the Spanish Flu and the HIV pandemics were worsened by the

DOI: 10.4018/978-1-6684-5289-9.ch009

social and economic inequalities in the public. At the same time, the inequalities across income groups within a country and across countries increased after these pandemics. (Farmer, 2001). As of June 2022, some groups look like even more vulnerable to any kind of shocks. Only in 2020, 140 million more people are estimated to be in extreme poverty while most of them are from already poor regions like Africa and South Asia (Laborde et al., 2020). This study questions whether the Covid-19 pandemic made the existing inequalities more visible. Analyzing different cases from different countries, the proper policies are aimed to be investigated.

Covid-19 pandemic created severe acute symptoms not only on humans but on society and the existing economic system and business environment. Some of these symptoms are now permanent. Some income groups and some regions in the world were affected more. Especially, the safety measures to slow down the spread of the virus expanded the negative effects. Social distancing and lockdowns were two of the main strategies used by the policy makers all over the world. Some workers who needed to work physically in-person which were also called essential workers had to face the risk of being infected by the Covid 19 virus.

Almost three years after the first Covid 19 case observed in the world, some group of people have to confront many other economic, social, physical and psychological challenges. Several help packages have been announced and distributed by the most of the governments and non-governmental organizations. However, some economic and non-economic conditions limit the improvements. The major aim of this study is to address the types and roots of the inequalities and identify the groups who are mostly affected from the pandemic related issues. The economic and societal inequalities are analyzed in five dimensions: Health, income, education, gender and digital inequalities. In this purpose, we identify inequities and inequalities in each dimension so that we can correctly diagnose the maladjustments. The role of governmental and non-governmental organizations and institutions are questioned during the pandemic. Based on the cases analyzed, policy recommendations are constructed for a better future.

The chapter surveys the literature for a theoretical framework. Within this framework, cases are analyzed by collecting economic and non-economic data in order to discuss the possible policies that can reduce the existing inequalities. The study shows that even the most developed countries fail to identify the groups to be supported and allocate the aids in an effective way. Although the authorities announce that we are all together in this course, the negative impact of Covid-19 creates deeper economic and social gaps. The picture is even worse for developing countries where already exiting structural problems surfaced and crushed the barely working systems.

In exploring the sources of the inequalities, it is important to identify the existing inequities. Inequalities result from the unbalanced conditions and the lack of equal opportunities. Inequalities may arise due to inequities which are caused by perpetuated biases in the society. Inequity is an important concept while pointing out inequalities since these concepts are supportive of each other and it is necessary to understand them in order to interfere with the inequalities that are already going on.

Healing the inequities and decreasing the inequalities are possible only through inclusive economic policies that are strongly supported by social complementary policies. This chapter discusses possible policy actions from income transformations via taxation system to anti-trust laws that can prevent large-scaled multinational companies' monopolization. While some of the actions are compatible with the existing rules of the game, some requires restructuring of the whole economic distribution.

The rest of the study is organized to analyze the impact of Covid 19 in five dimensions: health, income, education, gender and digital inequalities. Each dimension is analyzed in this order in consecutive sections. In each section, first the literature is reviewed and then, cases from developing and developed countries are analyzed. The sources of inequalities or inequities are identified. Then, policy recommendations for the related dimension of the inequalities are discussed at the end of each section. At the section 7, general findings and limitations of the study are revealed and future research directions are provided. The final section concludes with discussion of the overall coverage of the chapter.

GOVERNMENT RESPONSES TO COVID-19

COVID-19 had a significant effect on the lifestyles of millions of people. Most of the governments took stringent closure policies accompanied by supportive economic and health system policies. The policy change enforced by the COVID-19 was a big shock for some countries' economic and social systems. The impact of policy enforcements caused some unbalanced conditions and triggered the effect of existing inequities on inequalities. There are some systematic attempts to understand the policy responses of the governments to COVID-19. The inequities and inequalities led by the virus is highly related to these policy changes.

IMF tracks 197 countries' policy responses to COVID-19 (IMF, n.d). The reports show that in order to prevent the spread of the virus most of the governments decided on full or partially lockdown of the economy. Especially quarantine of people infected, closure of public places for gathering and the countrywide lockdowns distorted the existing allocation mechanisms. Lockdowns affected different income groups of the society in different ways, causing discrepancies in income, education and job opportunities. These biases caused increased health inequities and accelerated the instabilities in the health system. Being combined with other social factors, inequities caused a dramatic increase in inequalities in general all around the world. However, the degree of inequalities varies across the countries.

In order to make the country wise comparisons more meaningful, Blavatnik School of Government of Oxford University developed a COVID-19 government response tracker by collecting systematic information on policy measures from 150 countries (Oxford University, n.d.). Five policy indices are produced in order to make rigorous analysis: Overall government response index shows the variations of response of governments over the course of the outbreak. Containment and health index combines 'lockdown' restrictions and closures with measures such as health investments. Stringency index reveals strictness of 'lockdown style' policies. Economic support index measures income support and debt relief. Risk of openness index takes World Health Organization (WHO)'s policies.

The index shows a various change regarding policy responses to COVID-19 over time and across countries. As of May 2020, the stringency index of 140 countries were above 60 over 100 with 100 being the strictest. Almost half of the countries had scores between 80 and 90. As the virus changes in nature the containment and closure policies of countries were relaxed. As of April 2022, only 8 countries have scores between 75 and 85 and no countries have score higher than 85. Vanuatu, Solomon Islands and Tonga are the countries having strictest responses, although their initial response was highly relaxed (Oxford University, n.d.)

HEALTH INEQUALITIES

Centers for Disease Control and Prevention (CDC) provides a clear definition to health equity (CDC, n.d): *"Health equity is achieved when every person has the opportunity to attain his or her full health potential and no one is disadvantaged from achieving this potential because of social position or other socially determined circumstances."* Health inequalities that occur from the difference of opportunities stem from unbalanced distribution of health services to citizens. People have to face the inequalities while they are getting health services. Inequity, however, does not rise from lack of health opportunities but the general failures of the governments or the health system and organization of governance (Global Health Europe, 2009). The social factors had a certain impact on an individual's health: Education, the type of employment, income, gender, ethnicity, geography and residency. In that respect, health inequalities generally result from health inequities.

The health system policies of the countries over the course of the pandemic have been varying. In most of the cases, policy changes aimed to provide all of the communities within the country with health services. However, these new policies couldn't prevent rise of the inequities which are caused by different factors. As a result, inequalities increased in both developed and developing countries. In this section, the UK case and supportive evidence from the USA are examined.

Some communities have been going through a harder time with health issues in the time of the pandemic. Lower income earners, migrants or other minorities and senior citizens seems to be the communities that have been experiencing the biggest challenges in the course of the outbreak. Some of these groups experienced health problems, simply because they have to interact with Covid-19-risky situations compared to other groups in the society.

In the case of UK, government has practiced various containment and health policies over the course of the outbreak. The first COVID -19 case was observed on January 31, 2020. As the number of cases increased the first peak was followed by a decline and then the second and third waves of outbreak hit the country. As the initial response, government practiced a set of regulatory measures including school closures, workplace closures, closures of entertainment, social distancing measures and travel bans in March 2020 (IMF, n.d.). The stringency index of the country increased over 80, and stayed above 70 in until April, 2021. The largest economic hit was on the second quarter of 2020, where the GDP decreased almost 20%. The UK economy shrank by 9.8% in 2020. As of March 2022, the pre-crisis economic level still couldn't be recovered. Although the lockdowns and other measures were eased on May 2020, the third lockdown was imposed in response to rapid spread of the virus.

Both monetary and fiscal stimulus packets were released to support the public and the economic activity. National Health Service and public services are additionally funded with £48.5billion. Businesses were supported by £29billion in the form of property tax holidays, direct grants for small firms and firms in the most-affected sectors, and compensation for sick pay leave. The social safety net to support people was strengthened through subsidies of £8 billion. Between March 2020 and March 2021, stimulus packages to protect and create jobs are used being parallel to the restrictiveness of the containment measures. The supports were including direct subsidies given to employees, to local firms that were required to close to businesses in hospitality and leisure sectors. In the fiscal year 2020-2021, COVID-19 measures amounted to £280 billion. This amount was announced to be £55 billion for fiscal year 2021-2022. The monetary expansion in many forms such as decreased interest rates and postponement of the credits for firms supported the fiscal stimulus (IMF, n.d.).

Contradicting to all of the provisions provided by the government, certain groups in UK experienced higher difficulties in health issues. The existing inequalities in UK health system was exaggerated by the COVID-19. The National Health Services (NHS) Equality and Diversity Council of UK works on the health inequalities, promotes the inclusive health services in England. They emphasize the importance of the social determinants of health such as employment, education and housing (NHS, England, n.d.). The health inequalities in England are in life expectancy, accessing to health care, quality of care, related behavioral risks to health, issues related to determinants of health.

COVID-19 increased the health inequalities in England in many respects although a substantial amount of governmental support was provided. Patel et al. (2021) addresses health inequalities through the NHS Health Check Programme in England. Study shows some ethnical differences in the risk factors of getting certain diseases. Also, the geographical variations exist. Patel et al. (2020) reveal another study that emphasizes the impact of COVID-19 on ethnical health inequality in England. They identify ethnic inequalities which are increased in the course of outbreak in mental health, maternal and neo-natal healthcare, genetics, healthcare workforce and digital inclusivity. Low-income groups, migrants and senior citizens were experienced higher health inequalities (Patel et al., 2020). One reason behind the inequalities is the unbalanced conditions regarding the exposure to virus. Low-income groups are more likely to live in crowded places where there is low quality air conditioning which results in more possible exposure to the virus. The disease can easily spread in poorly ventilated places. Individuals in low-income groups also partake in day jobs that mostly prevent the isolation. They have to go to work where their exposure to virus is increased. Especially for those like public transport drivers and retail workers, the risk is even higher since they have to interact with more people in general (Patel et al., 2020).

Inequalities in terms of mental health were also increased especially by the life-standards and workplace conditions altered by COVID-19. The higher stress levels of the individuals who have expose more COVID-19 related conditions harm their immune system in a way that they cannot defend itself against the virus. Because of a lack of guarantee at their workplace and possibility of an income loss increase stress levels of these people to an even more dangerous level. Before the outbreak, low-income earners' access to health care services was subject to inequity concerns. Cookson et al. (2016) show that reception time of low-income earners to health services was longer compared to one of high-income earners (Cookson et al., 2016). Patel et al. (2020) report that the effect of the virus on Black and Asian populations is higher due to the social and biological factors. Also, the low-income groups are more vulnerable to the impacts of the virus. The authors call immediate improvement of the health conditions so that low-income earners and different ethnic groups can get a better treatment at the hospitals.

Other studies from US support the inequality case of UK. Socially and economically vulnerable communities, whether they are a racial minority or low-income, have been at a higher risk of catching the disease or dying from a related cause. A study that compared Covid-19 deaths in the states of the U.S. and the Gini index showed that an increase of the Gini index increases the number of deaths by up to fifty six percent in that state (Oronce et al., 2020). African American communities in the US are also more vulnerable to the disease (Abedi et al., 2020 and Kim and Bostwick, 2020). In another note, African American communities experienced up to six times more mortality risks compared to others in the first waves of Covid-19 (Ali et al., 2020).

Even though, there is no direct evidence of the correlation between the biological impact of the disease and the race of the patients, people of color in developed countries are likely to be affected by the COVID-19 conditions. This is mostly the result of social inequality that these people have already been living through. As the evidence from field studies mentioned above supports, lower income causes individuals to not be able to take good care of themselves against the virus. Moreover, since ethnic minorities consist of mostly low-income earners, they become more vulnerable to health hazards of the pandemic. A dataset from Chicago, US suggests that number of Covid-19 cases are more than doubled in African American citizens compared to white groups while number of deaths caused by Covid-19 are more than tripled, even though population of African Americans and those of White descents are very close in Chicago (Kim and Bostwick, 2020). Geographically in Chicago, in the neighborhood of African American residents are dominant, social vulnerability and the risk factor are significantly higher than in the other parts. This clearly displays the level of difference in risk that disadvantaged people have been put at.

Government facilities, hospitals and some institutions turned into disease hotspots during the course of outbreak even though strict measures are taken into account. Especially at the beginning of pandemic, in some cases, the stuff cannot be equipped with the required protective gear. Some populated places such as prisons, illegal immigrant shelters and other kinds of social network hubs became vulnerable places. Workers, especially healthcare workers were subject to high risk factors. Doctors and other healthcare workers without enough protective gear worked under risky conditions. A lot of losses from healthcare army was another reason behind the overwhelmed healthcare system. In Spain and Italy COVID-19 cases of healthcare workers were more than ten percent of total cases in these countries (Ahmet et al., 2020).

The pandemic with its psychological dimension has also short-run and long-run detrimental effects on the health. In addition to the evidence found on the relation between COVID-19 virus and the brain activity and the increased psychotic disorders (Cowen, 2020), the measures taken to prevent the spread of the virus has a significant effect on the psychological health of the society. While Covid-19 directly threatens the livelihood of humans, another stress source on the society is created by the COVID-19 related containment and closure policies. Davillas and Jones (2020) in UK compares the health level in UK before pandemic and at a peak

Table 1. Distribution of Factors in Stress Sources, Data received from Davillas & Jones, 2020

Sources of Stress during the pandemic	Sample%
Age and gender	18.3
Ethnicity	2.3
Education/qualification	1.03
Housing conditions	21.74
Household Composition	6.28
Employment Status	14.48
COVID-19 related economy	1.72
Financial strain	22.14
Neighborhood characteristics	6.92
Parental occupational Status	5.09
Total	100

of the COVID-19 cases. The questionnaire that they use shows how psychological inequality have increased during the pandemic. Results suggest that psychological burden on the society is increased in general. Share of people that can relate to a psychological problem increased from 18% to 28% in the country. The share of financial strains was higher with 22.14%. Housing conditions were another major source of stress with 21.74%. The share of employment status among other factors was 14.48%. Age and gender were also significant as a stress source. Table 1 reveals the distribution. the However, it has increased even more for a disadvantaged part of the public as main sources of stress were stated to be economic difficulties, keeping a job and accommodating problems (Davillas & Jones, 2020). Since lower income earners had harder times during the course of the outbreak, their stress level was also getting higher than usual and, than other income groups. Another rising stress concern among people was about their age since elder people are affected even more from the disease. Old age has become one of the main sources of psychological problems (Davillas & Jones, 2020).

Health inequalities are preventable inequitable differences in health status between communities, groups or individuals. The unequal distribution of economic, social or environmental resources are the major cause of the health inequalities. As the evidence given above supports, that even in the developed countries where substantial financial support provided to public, the health inequalities were increased with COVID-19 outbreak. The terms of financial supports and governmental regulations and provisions couldn't prevent the exaggerating effect of COVID-19 pandemic on existing inequitable social factors. Especially, low-income groups, migrants and minority ethnic groups who have to live in below the normal standards of life, workers in COVID-19 related industries and elderly people experienced troublesome challenges than the others both in physical and psychological health.

INCOME INEQUALITIES

One of the major safety measures that was proven against the spread of the virus was having a social distance or not having any physical contact at all. Hence, most of the governments imposed very strict contamination and closure policies all around the world (IMF, n.d.) Enforcing these measures helped authorities in some countries keep the pandemic under control for the first couple of waves. However, the policy requirements let only the essential workers to leave their homes. An empirical field study by Adams-Prassl et al. from UK found that just at the very beginning of the outbreak, in March 2020, more than half of the workers had to put in less work hours than in a week before. Especially for the wage group in between £10,000 and £30,000 the working hours are almost halved whereas the higher income groups decreased their working hours with at most 70%. Moreover, almost one in every ten workers have lost their jobs due to Covid-19 restrictions by March 2020. More than one third of the workers feel the pressure of losing their jobs in the upcoming months. In terms of income, while one third of workers anticipate lower earnings in the upcoming quarter, half of them anticipate not being able to pay some of their bills (Adams-Prassl et al., 2020). It is clear that quarantine restrictions put many households at a dangerous financial position and push additional families into poverty line. Palomino et al. (2020) conducted another research to simulate the effects of a complete lockdown where most workers cannot continue to go to their work for European countries. The study revealed overwhelming results. Under two months of quarantine, poverty index for the average of twenty-nine European countries may rise by 4.9 percent. Additionally, lower income earners seem to experience a larger wage loss during this lockdown. While workers across twenty-nine European countries experience an average of 10 percent wage loss during the lockdown, the Gini coefficient can go up by 3.5 percent on average for these countries (Palomino et al., 2020). Another result of the study is also stunning. While inequality inside the countries is expected to increase, the inequality across the European countries is estimated to be increasing as well. In two months of lockdown and 9 months of partial reduction of allowed accommodation, wage inequality between workers in one country increased by 17.9 percent while the number is 4.8 percent in another country in Europe (Palomino et al., 2020). The finding is crucial for the European Union, because the countries' economies are interconnected economies and have to follow connected policies in the Euro zone. Furthermore, EU is one of the biggest economic and social cooperation of the world. If EU policy makers in such a strong network cannot practice fiscal and monetary policies to fight against the heterogonous distributional poverty effects of COVID-19, for the developing part of the world the economic and social recovery after the pandemic may be a hope more than a reality. Rising inequalities in the developing world has to be addressed in national and international level, before it gets too late.

While workers are losing their income due to closure regulations during lockdowns, companies experience difficulties in production and sales operations. Although essential workers such as healthcare workers are allowed to leave their homes during the restrictions, most other workers are restricted. Therefore, many companies started to implement some new models for their labor force. The most popular model became "working from home" or "home office" model. Home office model have been in the agenda of some sectors for many years. Especially, tech companies have been trying out the concept for a couple of years. The model allows workers to work from wherever they want through their digital devices such as computers and pagers, whenever the type of job is appropriate.

Home office concept allowed workers earn their wages as normal. However, this is not an opportunity for any worker as some jobs especially of the blue collars cannot be executed through computers and such. Irlacher and Koch (2021) uses the German Qualifications and Career Survey to explore the effect of COVID-19 on German labor market and the wage differentials. They found a clear positive relationship between higher paying jobs and their capacity of being done from home in German labor market. Similar results are demonstrated for UK labor market. The share of working from home hours in the total working hours increases from 30% to almost 80% as the average income increases from £10,000 to £70,000. Interestingly, over £70,000, the share of working from home hours in total working hours decreases to nearly 70%. The high-level management positions would still ask for more in-office working hours.

As some jobs are compatible with home office models and the employees who perform these jobs can be isolated from the virus-related risks, others cannot. Irlacher and Koch (2021) reveals that in Germany during the Covid-19 lockdowns, the income gap across the income groups only got larger. Moreover, the regional distributions of jobs that are compatible with the home office concept are variant. Average wage in a district is positively correlated with the share of home office jobs in that district. Inequality across regions of the country is also affected by the availability of the remote jobs in the regions. There are already differences in average earnings of the workers. COVID-19 increased the inequalities in Germany during the lockdowns (Irlacher and Koch, 2021).

In another research, Bonaci at al. studies the potential income inequality effects of working from home concept in Italy. Italy has relatively low telecommuting options in its labor market in compared to other European countries (Eurofound and the International Labour Office, 2017). The use of working from home office concept suddenly spread in the Italian businesses with the COVID-19 outbreak. Bonaci at al. (2021) used the Italian Survey of Profession (ICP) to analyze the effect of working from home concept on the labor market. They found that workers who have a better chance of working from home share other characteristics such as being male, experienced, high educated and living in central provinces. Hence, it is found that working from home mostly benefits those who already are in advantage in terms of income, education, gender and older age. The likely future improvements in the feasibility of home office concept might increase the income inequality across certain groups as well as regions (Bonacini et al., 2021).

During the course of the outbreak, these workers who are able to work from home were already in an advantageous position compared others. The cases from Germany, UK and Italy provide evidence on the fact that employees who are working from home create a new class of advantaged workers and new business models based upon home office concept is a new source of inequalities. The income inequalities exacerbated by the working from home models also bring forth the regional income inequalities. Some parts or cities in a country that are more open to new business models become the center of attraction. Hence, the opportunities of working from home concepts can stimulate existing inequity problems caused by center-periphery division of the countries and the world. Precautionary policies should be taken by the policy makers against the upcoming challenges.

EDUCATION INEQUALITY

Already existent inequities in education have also been inflated by the COVID-19 measures. Since the pandemic and lockdowns have started, students from richer regions seem to have crucial advantages compared to students from poorer regions. However, increased inequities cannot be explained only by differences in income inequality. During the pandemic, a spillover effect that shapes the educational opportunities occurred among the other social factors such as technology diffusion in the subject region, existing infrastructural investments, availability of the Information and Communication Technologies (ICT), and trained educators to use the educational technologies. The educational integration of digital technologies is challenging also rom the teacher's perspective. Valverde-Berrocoso et al. (2021) emphasizes the importance of teachers' education to make the flexible education productive. The teacher education model that motivates students to learn everywhere at any time should be provided to the teachers. Otherwise, the investments may not be effective.

The containment and closure policies caused millions of children be out of their classrooms. According to the World Economic Forum (WEF) report written by Li and Lalani in August 2021, 1.2 billion of children in 186 countries were exposed to school closures (WEF, 2020). Lockdown changed the education drastically. New tools were started to be used as the new techniques are enforced to be implemented. In most countries the new method of reaching students became the online classes where classes are done via third party programs that allow teachers to stream their lectures from their computers or smart tablets. Even before the outbreak, the traditional education methods were being tested by the requirements of the post-modern age. The investments on educational technologies were $18.66 billion around the world in 2019 (Metaari, n.d.). As the pandemic pushed the emergency remote education after 2019, the market for online education platforms is forecasted to reach 350 billion by 2025. Online classes required countries to invest on their technological infrastructures. The developed countries and high-income, high-middle income developing countries were more equipped than the middle-income and low-income developing countries to this challenge. Yet, even in the developed countries, existing inequalities were increased by the COVID-19 lockdowns. The picture is even worse for the developing countries.

Against all of the actions taken, a significant part of the students all around the world fall seriously behind their scheduled timeline. Engzell et al., (2020) analyzed the impact of school closures on the learning of students. The national exam results before and after the lockdown were used in the study. Although the Netherlands has a strong technological infrastructure and the lockdown was only 8 weeks which is significantly short in compared to many other countries, the study shows that students couldn't improve in learning during the lockdown. Moreover, learning loss is calculated to be up to fifty-five percent in less-educated parents according to data collected in the Netherlands.

The online streaming services for educational purposes is only possible with internet connection which is unfortunately still not widespread in some of the less developed countries. Besides, the required electronics are not affordable for most of the public. Beyond the hard-ware equipment, students from high-income families in developing countries can access to more privileges such as one-on-one classes. They are provided with better support from their families and also their schools.

In UK Andrew et al. (2020) prepared a comprehensive report for Institute for Fiscal Policies. They have reviewed the students' records. They designed a survey covering 4000 parents of children aged between 5 and 14 on May 2020. Findings of the study is stunning for a developed country like the UK that has a well-prepared technological infrastructure and skilled educational stuff. The study finds that from the children from high-income families are 20% more likely to get online teaching supports from their school in state schools. Students from high-income families are spending 30% more time in learning. The authors conclude that inequalities in education increased certainly because of school closures in UK (Andrew et al., 2020).

The familiarity of using the digital facilities is another factor that enhanced the educational inequalities. In a field study conducted in Denmark, it was shown that, the socioeconomic gradients that affect the families' daily library takeout behavior increased after the lockdown. Those families who used to take out digital materials before the pandemic have higher income and education backgrounds. They keep benefitting from libraries after the lockdown even more. The use of library can be considered as a productive source of learning especially in the period of lockdown, because the online education may not be effective. Therefore, the inequalities in education may rise due to such factors, too (Jæger, & Blaabæk, 2020).

GENDER INEQUALITY

As the aforementioned evidence from developed countries support, Covid-19 pandemic had more destructive effects on people from lower socio-economic classes. Unfortunately, women have also been experiencing unequal negative effects from the pandemic and lockdowns. The unequal living conditions that women have been subject to since the beginning of the known history, are enhanced during the course of the pandemic. Even in the most modern societies, traditional roles are imposed on women. They are expected to get more responsibilities in taking care of their families. Since schools and day care centers were mostly closed during lockdowns, women faced discriminations whether they can work from home or not.

Pandemic lockdowns have tremendous short-term and mid-term effects on households' income. Some workers had to take leaves without payment during the lockdowns. In some cases, after the lockdown some sectors reduce their capacity due to decreased demand and uncertainty created by the Covid-19 pandemic. Workers have been suffering from a stress of losing their jobs or having a cut in their pay checks due to decreased work hours (Davillas & Jones, 2020). However, women have been suffering from job loss stress even more. It was estimated that the probability of losing her job was around twenty percent more in the course of the pandemic. Moreover, the probability of wage cuts due to the pandemic-related reasons were twice compared to men (Dang & Nguyen, 2020). Even though, some can continue to work from their homes, female workers' productivity is lower because of the workload at home that they already have to deal with.

In the case of female academics, Cui et al. (2021) collected data from social sciences produced by more than 75thousand authors across 25 countries. They reported that in the US the total research productivity increased by 35%. However, female academics' research productivity decreased by 13.5% compared to male academics during the lockdown. A similar pattern was found for other 6 countries. The major reason behind the productivity gap is correlated with the unexpected conditions of telecommuting, the housework that increases with the pandemic-related factors and the child-care responsibilities due to the school closures (Cui et al., 2021).

Parenthood is seen as one of the main reasons for the inequalities women face as they are expected to take care of the children in their families even in modern societies. In Germany, a survey on around 4,400 participants was analyzed to test whether the pandemic had positive or negative effects on gender equality. Because most of the essential workers in Germany were females, during the lockdowns, wage increases and improved working conditions would be considered for women. The findings on the collected data revealed that women's responsibilities including childcare and other housework during the restrictions increased. Same participants reported lower fulfillment with their family and work life compared to their male partners (Hipp & Bünning, 2020).

In the UK case, 1500 respondents' data analyzed to test the gender inequality in the time of COVID-19. The study found that women's mental health was more affected by the pandemic. Women were more anxious about the health effects of the virus. They were more pessimistic about the long-term effects of the virus on the economy. Women had to deal with the childcare and housework more than men. As a result of all the disadvantages females have to experience during this pandemic, women prone to higher stress than men regarding the future social and economic effects of the virus (Oreffice & Quintana-Domeque, 2020).

DIGITAL INEQUALITY

Digital equity represents people's ability to participate in societies and economies through utilizing information technologies (NDIA). Thus, digital equity is necessary for people to have similar opportunities in their lives especially right after the outbreak emphasized the importance of digital technologies. However, the pandemic has also created additional digital inequalities through increased inequity in digital communications which have affected people in many ways.

Since restrictions and complete lockdowns restrict people from physical contact and meetings in person, communication methods through digital channels became quite popular and widely used by crowds. However, not everyone has the necessary equipment and the skills to use these devices and to benefit from them at the same level. Using data of 2,925 participants from US, Nguyen et al. observed that people from better socio-economic backgrounds have higher technological know-how in using internet. They increased their time on digital communication platforms during the course of the outbreak. Therefore, they overcome most of the challenges created by the pandemic by using digital solutions. This situation enhanced the inequality that the disadvantaged groups already face (Nguyen et al., 2021).

Internet access have become an essential need for most people as it has nowadays been playing a major role in most of the daily life activities. Therefore, it is essential to have access to high quality internet during the pandemic. Otherwise, people would be put behind the others in participating the remote activities. As people also have been spending their free time on the internet besides of fulfilling their other responsibilities, internet access can also be an important incentive for people to stay at their homes. Moreover, it seems that even the speed of their internet may affect a person's willingness to stay at their home. Chiou and Tucker (2020) conduct a study in which they followed 20 million of the mobile devices that have access to internet during lockdown measures. They found that even though income is a major indicator in explaining the difference in time of staying home between different economic regions, access to higher speed internet has a significant biggest impact on staying home during the pandemics. High speed internet and high income is the better combination to not leave homes (Chiou & Tucker, 2020). The result of the study emphasizes the inequality that high income group who had qualified digital facilities are more likely to prevent themselves from virus-related troubles.

DISCUSSIONS AND POLICY IMPLICATIONS OF THE STUDY

Covid-19 pandemic caused the systematic problems that are suppressed under the normal conditions to surface. Malfunctioning institutions, governments failures in providing equitable services, weak civil society networks exaggerated the impact of the virus on the society by increasing the existing inequities. Moreover, the cases that we have analyzed in this chapter show that probable new pandemics or other disasters caused by climate change will increase the existing societal problems especially in terms of inequalities. The policy makers should take economic, social, political and climate policies into consideration at the same time to design and implement the appropriate plannings.

As the pandemic created new groups of vulnerable individuals or increased the severity of already vulnerable people, many governments and other related organizations have tried to address these individuals and help them through financial packages. Even though the supports give relief in some cases, they still are not adequate in reaching out people to decrease the inequalities. Solutions should be more fundamentally planned towards socially accepted active administrative results. Authorities can encourage people to use the public services that they can benefit from during hard times such as pandemics in order to decrease the negative effects of the crisis on the society.

Ashford et al. (2020) suggest a comprehensive approach to achieve a more equal society. In this approach the solution focus on nine dimensions. The capital relocations can create more equal purchasing power. The share of workers in the production profit and the property of capital can be increased through different firm structures. Adjustments should be made so that the basic needs to survive can be provided to every person in the society. The climate actions and environmentally friendly production and consumption should be encouraged. The required safety nets can be provided so that strengthened job market can achieve higher labor productivities with higher employment rates. The jobs can be protected in that sense. Through functioning and efficient anti-trust laws, a creative competition environment should be supported. Education and healthcare are vital services in the creation of a more equal society. The governments' support is identified as a must. Especially in the developing countries, army expenditures can provide some basic needs to a part of the society which otherwise cannot reach these services. Therefore, the military expenses can be planned for social causes. Developing countries should be supported financially.

The adjustments proposed by Ashford et al. (2020) can be reviewed under the necessary paradigm shift of the economic production of countries. Furceri et ala (2021) discusses the effectiveness of fiscal policies to mitigate the effects of pandemic on the inequalities. They show that the lack of strong fiscal policies causes increased inequalities in the society. Therefore, well-planned fiscal policies that are balanced in terms of their share in GDP are vital. Such policies should complement the other economic, social and environmental concerns and publicly acceptable. Zahariadis et al. (2022) discusses different policy making approaches across the world. The policy styles are an important in shaping the society after the crisis. COVID-19 is a major problem on its own for countries to deal with. However, it can be considered as just a part of the giant iceberg namely climate change. The alarming forecasts regarding the near future effects of climate change constitutes real threats with the COVID-19 pandemic. Together with the technological and digital transformation that we are passing through, migration and aging issues enforces the policy makers to leave the traditional approaches.

As of 2022, the acute symptoms of COVID 19 have passed. The society hurt in many ways. In that respect, the policy makers should review that severe pandemic as a signal of future troubles. A set of comprehensive structural changes has to be designed and implemented to cure the existing vulnerabilities of the society. So that the future social and economic effects of possible disasters and pandemic can be prevented. These changes require governmental planning as well as international institutions' involvement. The existing inequalities across the countries and across different groups within a country can be prevented only through cooperatively coordinated actions of the countries. The capital relocations through efficient taxation systems is crucial. The military expenses should be planned for peaceful environments so that social causes can be prioritized. Multinational companies are an important part of the economic system. Yet, the small and medium enterprises and the entrepreneurial activities should be supported. Most importantly, a new economic system where the natural degradation is minimized has to be constructed. The cases we analyze show that the technology diffusion rate of the societies is the most important determinant regarding the social impacts of any probable disaster or pandemic. In that respect, the education should be provided properly. Either though public system or through efficiently regulated private system, education system must be designed efficiently and fairly. Cases show that health system is better to be regulated through central authority so that services can be provided equally.

At least, adaptation of the traditional systems with the new approaches are inevitable. In that respect, inequalities and inequities are deepened by the challenges such as pandemic, climate change, automatization, migration, international trade etc.... Therefore, they have to be the first topic in the agenda of the policy makers. From environmentally concerned city plans to country development plans, policies in every level should be taking the reduction of inequalities and removal of inequities into consideration.

CONCLUSION

This paper brings several studies that focus on the disadvantaged groups in the aftermath of the Covid-19 lockdowns and other new normal applications. The cases that we analyzed show that some groups experienced difficulties more than others. Especially, low-income groups, women and migrants were affected from the social impacts of the pandemic even though the governmental financial supports are provided during the course of the pandemic. As well as the existing income inequality, the technology diffusion is one of the most important determinants of the inequalities. The working from home/telecommuting concept that took flight during the course of the pandemic puts a real pressure on the labor markets as well as the future of the businesses. As the remote working or education become the new normal, the familiarity of using digital facilities becomes a new source of inequities. The differences in being used to get the digital public services caused the inequalities to increase after the outbreak.

Moreover, though the notion has been promoted by many spokespersons and authorities that we are all in this together and harmed all the same, it has not been the case. Some socio-economic groups, ethnic minorities, women and migrants have been more vulnerable during the catastrophe. Unfortunately, in most of the cases, initiatives that are taken to make up for the loss of these groups did not work properly. Hence increased inequalities are observed in both developed and developing countries. Even the most developed countries seem to fail to concentrate their aids at the groups that most need them.

As of June 2022, the worst days of COVID 19 seems to be over. However, the course of pandemic should be reviewed as a signal of upcoming various disasters that are probable results of climate change. Each and every shock to our traditional living standards are about to exaggerate already existing systematic problems. A comprehensive set of policy changes are obligatory to prepare the society for the future. Policy makers should run more serious examinations to come up with structural solutions to address problems rather than just releasing help packages which only seems to feed the problem in the long run. Moreover, transition into more social administrations should also be considered as these kinds of shocks are too costly to be ignored by the public.

The cases analyzed in this chapter provide evidences that even in the developed countries where monetary and fiscal policies are provided to support vulnerable groups, the inequalities are worsened during the course of the outbreak. The analysis should be extended to the developing countries as one can expect worse cases than the ones in the developed countries. The future works can focus on adaptation or mitigation strategies for the future disasters and pandemics. The economic, financial and social systems should be transformed to prepare the society for a better future.

KEY TERMS

Equity, Inequality, Policy Responses to COVID-19

ACKNOWLEDGMENT

This research received no specific grant from any funding agency in the public, commercial, or not-for-profit sectors.

REFERENCES

Abedi, V., Olulana, O., Avula, V., Chaudhary, D., Khan, A., Shahjouei, S., ... Zand, R. (2020). Racial, economic, and health inequality and COVID-19 infection in the United States. *Journal of Racial and Ethnic Health Disparities*, 1–11. PMID:32875535

Adams-Prassl, A., Boneva, T., Golin, M., & Rauh, C. (2020). *Inequality in the impact of the coronavirus shock: new survey evidence for the UK*. Academic Press.

Ahmed, F., Ahmed, N. E., Pissarides, C., & Stiglitz, J. (2020). Why inequality could spread COVID-19. *The Lancet. Public Health*, *5*(5), e240. doi:10.1016/S2468-2667(20)30085-2 PMID:32247329

Andrew, A., Cattan, S., Costa-Dias, M., Farquharson, C., Kraftman, L., Krutikova, S., ... Sevilla, A. (2020). *Learning during the lockdown: real-time data on children's experiences during home learning*. Institute for Fiscal Studies, IFS Briefing Note BN288.

Ashford, N. A., Hall, R. P., Arango-Quiroga, J., Metaxas, K. A., & Showalter, A. L. (2020). Addressing inequality: The first step beyond COVID-19 and Towards Sustainability. *Sustainability*, *12*(13), 5404. doi:10.3390u12135404

Bonacini, L., Gallo, G., & Scicchitano, S. (2021). Working from home and income inequality: Risks of a 'new normal' with COVID-19. *Journal of Population Economics*, *34*(1), 303–360. doi:10.100700148-020-00800-7 PMID:32952308

CDC. (n.d.). *Health Equity*. Retrieved on April, 9 2022, from https://www.cdc.gov/chronicdisease/healthequity/index.htm

Chiou, L., & Tucker, C. (2020). Social distancing, internet access and inequality (No. w26982). National Bureau of Economic Research.

Cookson, R., Propper, C., Asaria, M., & Raine, R. (2016). Socio-economic inequalities in health care in England. *Fiscal Studies*, *37*(3-4), 371–403. doi:10.1111/j.1475-5890.2016.12109

Cowan, H. R. (2020). Is schizophrenia research relevant during the COVID-19 pandemic? *Schizophrenia Research*, *220*, 271–272. doi:10.1016/j.schres.2020.04.002 PMID:32345478

Cui, R., Ding, H., & Zhu, F. (2021). Gender inequality in research productivity during the COVID-19 pandemic. *Manufacturing & Service Operations Management*.

Dang, H. A. H., & Nguyen, C. V. (2021). Gender inequality during the COVID-19 pandemic: Income, expenditure, savings, and job loss. *World Development*, *140*, 105296. doi:10.1016/j.worlddev.2020.105296 PMID:34548740

Davillas, A., & Jones, A. M. (2020). *The COVID-19 pandemic and its impact on inequality of opportunity in psychological distress in the UK*. Academic Press.

Elgar, F. J., Stefaniak, A., & Wohl, M. J. (2020). The trouble with trust: Time-series analysis of social capital, income inequality, and COVID-19 deaths in 84 countries. *Social Science & Medicine, 263*, 113365. doi:10.1016/j.socscimed.2020.113365 PMID:32981770

Engzell, P., Frey, A., & Verhagen, M. D. (2020). Learning inequality during the COVID-19 pandemic. *SocArXiv*.

Eurofound and the International Labour Office. (2017). *Working anytime, anywhere: the effects on the world of work*. Publications Office of the European Union, Luxembourg, and the International Labour Office.

Farmer, P. (2001). *Infections and inequalities: The modern plagues*. Univ of California Press.

Furceri, D., Loungani, P., Ostry, J. D., & Pizzuto, P. (2021). The rise in inequality after pandemics: Can fiscal support play a mitigating role? *Industrial and Corporate Change, 30*(2), 445–457. doi:10.1093/icc/dtab031

Hipp, L., & Bünning, M. (2020). Parenthood as a driver of increased gender inequality during COVID-19? Exploratory evidence from Germany. *European Societies*, 1–16.

IMF. (n.d.). *Policy Responses to COVID 19*. Retrieved on April 9, 2022, from https://www.imf.org/en/Topics/imf-and-covid19/Policy-Responses-to-COVID-19

Irlacher, M., & Koch, M. (2021). Working from home, wages, and regional inequality in the light of Covid-19. *Jahrbucher fur Nationalokonomie und Statistik, 241*(3), 1. doi:10.1515/jbnst-2020-0030

Jæger, M. M., & Blaabæk, E. H. (2020). Inequality in learning opportunities during Covid-19: Evidence from library takeout. *Research in Social Stratification and Mobility, 68*, 100524. doi:10.1016/j.rssm.2020.100524 PMID:32834345

Kim, S. J., & Bostwick, W. (2020). Social Vulnerability and Racial Inequality in COVID-19 Deaths in Chicago. *Health Education & Behavior, 47*(4), 509–513. doi:10.1177/1090198120929677 PMID:32436405

Metaari. (n.d.). *Free Metaari Whitepapers on the Learning Technology Industry*. Retrieved on April 11, 2022 from http://www.metaari.com/whitepapers.html

Nguyen, M. H., Hargittai, E., & Marler, W. (2021). Digital inequality in communication during a time of physical distancing: The case of COVID-19. *Computers in Human Behavior, 120*, 106717. doi:10.1016/j.chb.2021.106717 PMID:34751201

NHS England. (n.d.). *Resources*. Retrieved on April 9, 2022, from https://www.england.nhs.uk/about/equality/equality-hub/resources/

Oreffice, S., & Quintana-Domeque, C. (2021). Gender inequality in COVID-19 times: Evidence from UK prolific participants. *Journal of Demographic Economics*, *87*(2), 261–287. doi:10.1017/dem.2021.2

Oronce, C. I. A., Scannell, C. A., Kawachi, I., & Tsugawa, Y. (2020). Association between state-level income inequality and COVID-19 cases and mortality in the USA. *Journal of General Internal Medicine*, *35*(9), 2791–2793. doi:10.100711606-020-05971-3 PMID:32583336

Oxford University. (n.d.). *COVID-19 Government Response Tracker*. Retrieved on April 9, 2022, from https://www.bsg.ox.ac.uk/research/research-projects/covid-19-government-response-tracker

Palomino, J. C., Rodriguez, J. G., & Sebastian, R. (2020). *Wage inequality and poverty effects of lockdown and social distancing in Europe*. Academic Press.

Patel, K. C., & Hanif, W. (2022). Ethnic health inequalities in the NHS. *BMJ (Clinical Research Ed.)*, 376.

PatelR.BarnardS.LagordC.ThompsonK.HughesA.FoxS.DeanfieldJ. (2021). *Addressing Health Inequalities Through the NHS Health Check Programme in England*. doi:10.2139/ssrn.3937909

Valverde-Berrocoso, J., Fernández-Sánchez, M. R., Revuelta Dominguez, F. I., & Sosa-Díaz, M. J. (2021). The educational integration of digital technologies preCovid-19: Lessons for teacher education. *PLoS One*, *16*(8), e0256283. doi:10.1371/journal.pone.0256283 PMID:34411161

Vos, R., Martin, W., & Laborde, D. (2020). How much will global poverty increase because of COVID-19. International Food Policy Research Institute.

WEF. (2020, April 29). *The COVID-19 pandemic has changed education forever. This is how*. https://www.weforum.org/agenda/2020/04/coronavirus-education-global-covid19-online-digital-learning/

Zahariadis, N., Petridou, E., Exadaktylos, T., & Sparf, J. (2022). Policy Styles and Policymaking During Times of Crisis. In Policy Styles and Trust in the Age of Pandemics (pp. 17-38). Routledge. doi:10.4324/9781003137399-3

Conclusion

Currently, the world economies seem to have been trapped in several socio-economic and political problems at the same time. The global supply chain disruptions, declining demand due to the spread of the COVID 19 pandemic, geopolitical tensions, and stagflationary tendencies have been mainly causing uncertainty about the future growth of the economies. These problems can further result in aggravating socioeconomic and other forms of inequalities. Hence, this book enables us to understand the past and present scenarios w.r.t the global economic inequalities, the devastating influence that COVID 19 has on worsening the inequalities, the dire need to tackle the sectoral inequalities with the help of more context-specific policies, the interrelationship between inequalities and macroeconomic indicators and the cumulative role played by them in influencing the economic positions of the countries.

Chapter one presents the historical overview of the role played by major global crises like the Great Depression, East Asian Economic Crisis, the Great Recession, and the COVID 19 pandemic in changing economic inequalities of mainly affected countries viz., USA, Malaysia, Indonesia, Korea, Thailand, and the Philippines. The World Inequality Database has been utilized to present the analysis. However, within-country inequalities and inequalities other than economic have not been discussed in this chapter. The affected sectors' economies can emerge from crises and move closer to sustainable development if certain welfare measures are provided, including improved access to high-quality education and health care services at affordable rates, cash transfers to the needy for predetermined time periods, unemployment benefits, and skill up-gradation with changing times, to name a few.

The second chapter focuses on the pervasive disparities that exist in all countries among various demographic groups like inequalities in public revenue and expenses, gender disparity, carbon emissions, education, and housing to name a few. The data from different nations have undergone scrutiny. It looks at how various forms of inequality converge to prevent the economy from growing in the face of the pandemic. Globalization has reduced inter-country inequality and opened the door for advancement and development, but the dissemination of this growth is uneven.

The development of computers and the internet resulted in the rise of technologically advanced businesses that pondered ways to conduct business considerably more successfully. Automation and trade liberalization have significantly changed labor markets in industrialized nations, benefiting highly educated and talented people disproportionately. However, the responsibility for putting new ideas into action doesn't just fall on policymakers, economists, the government, corporate leaders, etc.; it also falls on each of us who wants to live in a society that is better. Equality will undoubtedly be experienced because of combining ideas for improved sustainable development and working with various stakeholders.

Several causes of post-pandemic situations like regional patterns, skilled worker migration, the effect of policy, climate mitigation and adoption policies, etc., and the measures to overcome them for eradicating global inequalities have been discussed in chapter 3. It also emphasizes the after-effects of the pandemic like increasing deaths and infected people, growing inflation, increasing inequality w.r.t opportunity, access to vaccines, incomes, credit availability, etc. It suggests several policy recommendations like more investments in the health, education, and social insurance sectors, boosting employment opportunities, and enhancing access to digital financial services.

The tourism industry has been one of the hardest hit sectors due to the spread of the COVID 19 pandemic. This issue has been addressed in chapter 4 which highlights the economic impact of the pandemic on the tourism industry in Turkey. There are dozens of employees in each of the sector's numerous and diverse business segments. As a result, every negative aspect of the process from an economic standpoint was evident at every point in the industry. Accelerating the vaccination program is necessary for the sector to recover, but there has been a decline in confidence in travel because of limited access to the vaccine in developing nations, frequent changes to travel restrictions in developed nations, and a lack of intergovernmental coordination. This study was conducted to evaluate how travel companies, one of the most significant components of Turkey's tourist industry, handled this situation and how much the Covid-19 global financial crisis affected them. Marketing, governmental backing, human resources, and protection were identified as the four elements that best described crisis management techniques in the survey with 322 participants. According to the data analysis findings, the marketing factor's total variance explanation rate was 57,291 percent, the human resources factor's total variance explanation rate was 10,132 percent, the government support factor's total variance explanation rate was 7,937 percent, and the maintenance factor's total variance explanation rate was 5,286 percent. It is essential for the tourism sector and all other sectors to take decisions together, assure normalization, and receive support from policymakers. Additionally, it is essential to carefully choose the policies and put them into practice to get the greatest benefits. Examples of these include the rights of sector employees, financial losses, applicable loans and assistance, and innovations in the process management of employers.

Chapter 5 depicts the adoption of the fourth industrial revolution as an approach to reducing inequality. It must be understood and utilized in conjunction with sound corporate entrepreneurship. If managers and business leaders employ the tools that the fourth industrial revolution gives properly, they are invaluable. Many nations are still working to adjust to the fourth industrial revolution, which is still very much in its infancy. If inequality is to be eliminated, governments must ensure that the fourth industrial revolution is ushered in and that firms are encouraged to adapt to it. Assistance can be provided to local businesses, colleges, and schools so they can prepare the next generation to benefit from the industrial revolution. They will be more prepared for the future, and people from all walks of life may start using those tools to raise the standard of living for those around them. All businesses and organizations should be sure to hire qualified people, especially those in developing nations. These workers must be equipped with the necessary abilities to instruct and prepare future generations to make greater use of the advantages that the industrial revolution affords.

The farming community, especially the small farmers, has also been bearing the brunt of increasing inequalities. Chapter 6 throws light on the limited usage of technology by the farmers in Indonesia which widens this gap. According to several studies, the digitalization of agriculture can improve the efficacy and efficiency of agricultural products. So, improving agricultural output will also increase farmers' well-being. Therefore, especially in agriculture, farmers must be able to master and benefit from technological advancements. Technology-savvy farmers are referred to as millennial farmers. Farmers in Indonesia will benefit with the help of millennial farmers who can make use of current technological advancements in agricultural enterprises. Hence, the government must inform farmers, especially young farmers, about newly developed breakthroughs like Agriculture 4.0 so that they may access and use the research. It must also offer advice, training, and support in relation to the usage of digital agriculture technologies. Universities must also work closely with farmers and the agricultural sector to develop innovations that will hasten the digitization of agriculture.

The countries in the African continent have been experiencing various forms of inequalities. Hence, chapter 7 has been devoted to understanding the interlinkages between savings, consumption, and inequality in 24 African nations. The economic fortune of the continent has had an equal impact on household consumption and saving rates across Africa. The policymakers must recognize that for the continent to experience sustained economic growth, key macroeconomic factors like consumption and saving must be balanced. Policies that raise consumption should be supported, such as those that increase government spending, decrease inequality, and provide economic prospects for residents while simultaneously lowering dependency ratios Policies that promote saving, such as financial development, are equally vital and have a good impact on saving. Due to the catastrophic consequences of global crises like COVID-19 and the global financial crisis of 2008, African economies must construct their economies to be resilient and absorb shocks whenever they arrive to prepare themselves for future crises. For the African economy to be less affected by any future crises, there must be strong economic growth and development. As the largest employer on the continent and to prevent the spread of food insecurity, nations in this region of the world must support initiatives that further expand their agricultural industries.

In chapter 8, the factors determining happiness and influencing inequality have been explored. The GDP per capita, life expectancy, social support, and level of freedom enjoyed by the people are all positively associated with happiness. The inability to measure happiness makes it challenging to generalize and create an equation. One of the main flaws of this study is that it leaves out many non-linear aspects that a population could encounter, like political tensions, governmental regulations, international ties, and many more.

The COVID 19 pandemic has acted as a divider in the economies, influencing different sectors differently. Chapter 9 incorporates a range of studies that focus on underprivileged groups in the wake of the Covid-19 lock-downs and other new normal applications. The cases analyzed in the paper demonstrate that some groups encountered challenges more frequently than others. Even though the government provided financial support throughout the pandemic, low-income groups, women, and migrants were particularly impacted by its social effects. One of the most significant factors of the inequalities, in addition to the current income inequality, is the dissemination of technology. The rise of telecommuting and working from home during the pandemic has had a significant impact on both the labor markets and the outlook for businesses. The expertise in using digital tools has become a new source of disparities as remote employment or schooling become the new standard. After the epidemic, disparities grew due to the variations in methods utilized to access digital public services. Instead of simply delivering temporary financial packages that ultimately seem to feed the problem, policymakers should do more thorough investigations to develop structural answers to problems. Additionally, since these kinds of shocks are too expensive for the general population to ignore, a shift to more social administrations should also be considered.

Therefore, this book revolves around the pressing issue of widening economic inequalities and the factors determining them. It captures the role played by past crises, COVID 19 pandemic, and several macroeconomic indicators like consumption, saving, GDP per capita, freedom, life expectancy, and social support. It specifically highlights the disastrous impact that COVID-19 had on the tourism sector in Turkey thereby widening the inequalities over there. It distinctly covers the limited usage of technology by farmers in Indonesia that keeps them amongst the have-nots. A wide-ranging study covering 24 African countries has been incorporated that emphasizes the inequalities in that region. In every chapter, policy recommendations have been shared with the help of which economic inequality can be reduced constructively. One chapter has been devoted to highlighting the need for increasing the adoption of the fourth industrial revolution for decreasing the gap between haves and have-nots. The current challenges that are being experienced around the world like the Sri Lankan crisis, Pakistan's downfall, depreciation of currencies due to the adoption of monetary tightening policies, global supply chain disruptions, stagflation, and the Russia – Ukraine war may further widen the socio-economic inequalities calling out the need for immediate action. One of the Sustainable Development Goals is to reduce inequality within and among the countries by 2030. This book can certainly be highly beneficial for researchers and policymakers in making decisions regarding optimal utilization of resources and reducing inequalities to make the world a better place to live in.

Compilation of References

Abdur Rahman, A., & Veenhoven, R. (2018). Freedom and happiness in nations: A research synthesis. *Applied Research in Quality of Life*, *13*(2), 435–456. doi:10.100711482-017-9543-6

Abedi, V., Olulana, O., Avula, V., Chaudhary, D., Khan, A., Shahjouei, S., ... Zand, R. (2020). Racial, economic, and health inequality and COVID-19 infection in the United States. *Journal of Racial and Ethnic Health Disparities*, 1–11. PMID:32875535

Abiwodo. (2021). Digitalisasi Pertanian dan Peran Bank Negara Indonesia dalam Ketahanan Pangan Paska Adaptasi Kebiasaan Baru. *Jurnal Kajian Lembaga Ketahanan Nasional Republik Indonesia, 8*(3), 227–243.

Adams-Prassl, A., Boneva, T., Golin, M., & Rauh, C. (2020). *Inequality in the impact of the coronavirus shock: new survey evidence for the UK*. Academic Press.

Adams, R., Pienaar, G., Gastrow, M., Olorunju, N., Gaffley, M., & Ramkissoon, Y. (2021). *Human rights and the Fourth Industrial Revolution in South Africa*. HSRC Press.

Adams, S. (2009). Foreign Direct investment, domestic investment, and economic growth in Sub-Saharan Africa. *Journal of Policy Modeling*, *31*(6), 939–949. doi:10.1016/j.jpolmod.2009.03.003

Adewuyi, A. O., Bankole, A. S., & Arawomo, D. F. (n.d.). what determines saving in the Economic Community of West African State (ECOWAS)? *Journal of Monetary and Economic Integration*, *10*(2), 71–100.

Aguiar, M., & Bils, M. (2015). Has Consumption Inequality Mirrored Income Inequality? *The American Economic Review*, *105*(9), 2725–2756. doi:10.1257/aer.20120599

Ahmed, F., Ahmed, N. E., Pissarides, C., & Stiglitz, J. (2020). Why inequality could spread COVID-19. *The Lancet. Public Health*, *5*(5), e240. doi:10.1016/S2468-2667(20)30085-2 PMID:32247329

Ahuja, V., Bidani, B., Ferreira, F., & Walton, M. (Eds.). (1997). *Everyone's Miracle? Revisiting poverty and inequality in East Asia*. World Bank Publications. doi:10.1596/0-8213-3979-6

Akadiri, S. S., & Akadiri, A. C. (2018). Growth and Inequality in Africa: Reconsideration. *Academic Journal of Economic Studies*, *4*(3), 76–86.

Alexander, B., & Adam, B. (2020). *Real time labor market estimates during the 2020 coronavirus outbreak*. Technical report, Arizona State University. https://papers.ssrn.com/sol3/papers.cfm?abstract_id=3692425

Ali, S., Asaria, M., & Stranges, S. (2020). COVID-19 and inequality: Are we all in this together? *Canadian Journal of Public Health*, *111*(3), 415–416. doi:10.1726941997-020-00351-0 PMID:32578185

Alvarez-Cuadrado, F., & Vilalta, M. E. (2018). Income inequality and saving. *Oxford Bulletin of Economics and Statistics*, *80*(6), 1029–1061. doi:10.1111/obes.12236

Amalia, N. (2019). 5G Siap Hadirkan Teknologi Canggih pada Ranah Pertanian. *whiteboard Journal*. https://www.whiteboardjournal.com/ideas/media/5g-siap-hadirkan-teknologi-canggih-pada-ranah-pertanian/

Andrew, A., Cattan, S., Costa-Dias, M., Farquharson, C., Kraftman, L., Krutikova, S., ... Sevilla, A. (2020). *Learning during the lockdown: real-time data on children's experiences during home learning*. Institute for Fiscal Studies, IFS Briefing Note BN288.

Aryeetey & Udry.(1999). *Rural Household Asset Choice in Ghana*. ISSER and Yale.

Aryeetey, E., & Udry, C. (2000). *Saving in Sub-Saharan Africa*. Center for International Development, Working Paper no. 38.

Ashford, N. A., Hall, R. P., Arango-Quiroga, J., Metaxas, K. A., & Showalter, A. L. (2020). Addressing inequality: The first step beyond COVID-19 and Towards Sustainability. *Sustainability*, *12*(13), 5404. doi:10.3390u12135404

Aspachs, O., Durante, R., Graziano, A., Mestres, J., Reynal-Querol, M., & Montalvo, J. G. (2021, March 31). Tracking the impact of COVID-19 on economic inequality at high frequency. *PLoS One*, *16*(3), e0249121. Advance online publication. doi:10.1371/journal.pone.0249121 PMID:33788886

Autor, D., Cho, D., Crane, L., Goldar, M., Lutz, B., & Montes, J. (2020, July). *An evaluation of the paycheck protection program using administrative payroll microdata*. Technical report, MIT WP. https://blueprintlabs.mit.edu/research/an-evaluation-of-the-paycheck-protection-program-using-administrative-payroll-microdata/

Baarsch, F., Granadillos, J. R., Hare, W., Knaus, M., Krapp, M., Schaeffer, M., & Lotze-Campen, H. (2020). The impact of climate change on incomes and convergence in Africa. *World Development*, *126*, 104699. https://doi.org/10.1016/j.worlddev.2019.104699

Baltagi, B. H. (2005). *Econometric Analysis of Panel Data* (3rd ed.). John Wiley & Sons Ltd.

Banerjee, A., Niehaus, P., & Suri, T. (2019). *Universal basic income in the developing world*. NBER Working Paper No. 25598. National Bureau of Economic Research. https://www.nber.org/system/files/working_papers/w25598/w25598.pdf

Bappeda Jawa Timur. (2021). *Rencana Kerja Pemerintah Daerah Provinsi Jawa Timur*. Author.

Bashizi Bashige Murhula, P., & Nunlall, R. (2022). Covid-19 and the Ban of Alcohol Sales in South Africa: A Critical Overview. *Acta Criminological: African Journal of Criminology & Victimology, 34*(3).

Baxter, M., & Crucini, M. J. (1993). Explaining Saving—Investment Correlations. *The American Economic Review, 83*(3), 416–436.

Belitski, M., Guenther, C., Kritikos, A., & Thurik, R. (2021). Economic effects of the COVID-19 pandemic on entrepreneurship and small businesses. *Small Business Economics, 58*(2), 593–609. doi:10.100711187-021-00544-y

Berkhout, E., Galasso, N., Lawson, M., Pablo, A. R. M., Taneja, A., & Diego, A. V. P. (2021, January). *The Inequality Virus*. OXFAM Briefing Paper. https://www.oxfam.org/en/research/inequality-virus

BioNTech. (2020). *A Phase 1/2/3 Study to Evaluate the Safety, Tolerability, Immunogenicity, and Efficacy of RNA Vaccine Candidates Against COVID-19 in Healthy Individuals*. Pfizer. Retrieved from https://cdn.pfizer.com/pfizercom/2020-11/C4591001_Clinical_Protocol_Nov2020.pdf

Bonacini, L., Gallo, G., & Scicchitano, S. (2021). Working from home and income inequality: Risks of a 'new normal'with COVID-19. *Journal of Population Economics, 34*(1), 303–360. doi:10.100700148-020-00800-7 PMID:32952308

Botta, A., Bruno, P., Chaudhuri, R., Nadeau, M. C., Taya, G., & Trascasa, C. (2020). *The 2020 McKinsey Global Payments Report*. McKinsey Global.

Bouchard, V., & Fayolle, A. (2018). *Corporate entrepreneurship*. Routledge.

BPS. (2020). *Statistik Pemuda Indonesia*. Badan Pusat Statistik (BPS). https://www.bps.go.id/publication/2020/12/21/4a39564b84a1c4e7a615f28b/statistik-pemuda-indonesia-2020.html

Brockmann, H., Delhey, J., Welzel, C., & Yuan, H. (2009). The China puzzle: Falling happiness in a rising economy. *Journal of Happiness Studies, 10*(4), 387–405. doi:10.100710902-008-9095-4

Burns, P. (2020). *Corporate entrepreneurship and innovation*. Red Globe Press.

Carroll, C., Weil, D., & Summers, L. H. (1993). *Savings and Growth: A reinterpretation*. Paper Presented at the Carnegie-Rochester Public Policy Conference, Bradley Policy Research Centre. 10.3386/w4470

Carvalho, V. M., Stephen, H., Alvaro, O., Ramon, G. J., Tomasa, R., & Rodriguez, M. S. (2020). Tracking the covid-19 crisis with high-resolution transaction data, Technical report. *CEPR, DP14642*. Advance online publication. doi:10.1098/rsos.210218

Caya, B. A. (2020). Strategi Digitalisasi Pelatihan Pertanian Berbasis Online di Era Revolusi Industri 4.0: Laporan Proyek Perubahan. In *Kementerian Pertanian Republik Indonesia*. PPMKP. http://repository.pertanian.go.id/handle/123456789/12648

CDC. (n.d.). *Health Equity*. Retrieved on April, 9 2022, from https://www.cdc.gov/chronicdisease/healthequity/index.htm

Champernowne, D. G., & Cowell, F. A. (1998). *Economic inequality and income distribution*. Cambridge University Press.

Chancel, L., Piketty, T., Saez, E., Zucman, G., Duflo, E., & Banerjee, A. (2021). *World Inequality Report 2022*. World Inequality Lab.

Chiou, L., & Tucker, C. (2020). Social distancing, internet access and inequality (No. w26982). National Bureau of Economic Research.

Cingano, F. (2014). *Trends in Income Inequality and its Impact on Economic Growth*. OECD Social, Employment and Migration Working Papers, No. 163. OECD Publishing. doi:10.1787/1815199X

Clark, A., D'Ambrosio, C., & Lepinteur, A. (2020). *The Fall in Income Inequality during COVID-19 in Five European Countries. ECINEQ Working Paper 2020-565*. Society for the Study of Economic Inequality. http://www.ecineq.org/milano/WP/ECINEQ2020-565.pdf

Clemens, M. A., & Pritchett, L. (2019, May). The new economic cases for migration restrictions: An assessment. *Journal of Development Economics*, *138*, 153–164. https://doi.org/10.1016/j.jdeveco.2018.12.003

Cookson, R., Propper, C., Asaria, M., & Raine, R. (2016). Socio-economic inequalities in health care in England. *Fiscal Studies*, *37*(3-4), 371–403. doi:10.1111/j.1475-5890.2016.12109

Cowan, H. R. (2020). Is schizophrenia research relevant during the COVID-19 pandemic? *Schizophrenia Research*, *220*, 271–272. doi:10.1016/j.schres.2020.04.002 PMID:32345478

Cserháti, I. (2020). "Business is unusual" – Remote work after COVID-19. *Köz-Gazdaság, 2*. doi:10.14267/RETP2020.02.04

Cugat, G., & Narita, F. (2020). How COVID-19 will increase inequality in emerging markets and developing economies. *IMFBlog*. Retrieved from https://blogs.imf.org/2020/10/29/how-covid-19-will-increase-inequality-in-emerging-markets-and-developing-economies/

Cui, R., Ding, H., & Zhu, F. (2021). Gender inequality in research productivity during the COVID-19 pandemic. *Manufacturing & Service Operations Management*.

Cynamon, B. Z., & Fazzari, S. M. (2016). Inequality, the Great Recession and slow recovery. *Cambridge Journal of Economics*, *40*(2), 373–399. doi:10.1093/cje/bev016

Dabla-Norris, E., Kochhar, K., Suphaphiphat, N., Ricka, F., & Tsounta, E. (2015). *Causes and Consequences of Income Inequality: A Global Perspective*. International Monetary Fund Discussion Note, SDN/15/13.

Dang, H. A. H., & Nguyen, C. V. (2021). Gender inequality during the COVID-19 pandemic: Income, expenditure, savings, and job loss. *World Development*, *140*, 105296. doi:10.1016/j.worlddev.2020.105296 PMID:34548740

Davillas, A., & Jones, A. M. (2020). *The COVID-19 pandemic and its impact on inequality of opportunity in psychological distress in the UK.* Academic Press.

De Nardi, M., & Fella, G. (2017). Saving and wealth inequality. *Review of Economic Dynamics*. doi:10.1016/j.red.2017.06.002

Deaton, A. (2021). *Covid-19 and global income inequality*. NBER working paper no. w28392. National Bureau of Economic Research. Retrieved from https://www.nber.org/system/files/working_papers/w28392/w28392.pdf

Deaton, A. (2021). *COVID-19 and Global Income Inequality. NBER Working Paper 28392*. National Bureau of Economic Research. https://www.nber.org/papers/w28392

Diagne, A., & Cabral, F. J. (2017). *Agricultural Transformation in Senegal: Impact of an Integrated Program*. Policy Analysis on Growth and Employment.

Edy. (2009). *Analisis Keberagaman Usaha Rumah Tangga Pertanian Lahan Kering di Kabupaten Banyumas*. Universitas Jenderal Soedirman.

Ekawati, I. (2019). Smart Farming: Teknologi PGPR untuk Keberlanjutan Pertanian Lahan Kering. *Seminar Nasional Optimalisasi Sumberdaya Lokal di Era Revolusi Industri*, *4*(0), 615–622.

Elgar, F. J., Stefaniak, A., & Wohl, M. J. (2020). The trouble with trust: Time-series analysis of social capital, income inequality, and COVID-19 deaths in 84 countries. *Social Science & Medicine*, *263*, 113365. doi:10.1016/j.socscimed.2020.113365 PMID:32981770

Engzell, P., Frey, A., & Verhagen, M. D. (2020). Learning inequality during the COVID-19 pandemic. *SocArXiv*.

Esmail, H. A. H., & Shili, N. N. J. (2018). The relationship between happiness and economic development in KSA: Study of Jazan region. *Asian Social Science*, *14*(3), 78–87. doi:10.5539/ass.v14n3p78

Espinoza Revollo, P. (2021). *The Inequality Virus: Methodology note*. Oxfam. https://oxfamilibrary.openrepository.com/bitstream/handle/10546/621149/bp-the-inequality-virus-summ-250121-en.pdf

Eurofound and the International Labour Office. (2017). *Working anytime, anywhere: the effects on the world of work*. Publications Office of the European Union, Luxembourg, and the International Labour Office.

FAO. (1992). *Final Report of the International Conference on Nutrition*. FAO.

Farmer, P. (2001). *Infections and inequalities: The modern plagues*. Univ of California Press.

Feldstein, M., & Horioka, C. (1980). Domestic Saving and International Capital Flow. *Economic Journal (London)*, *90*(358), 314–329. doi:10.2307/2231790

Ferreira, F. (2019). *Inequality of opportunity: New measurements reveal the consequences of unequal life chances.* The World Bank. Retrieved from https://www.worldbank.org/en/news/feature/2019/03/28/inequality-of-opportunity-new-measurements-reveal-the-consequences-of-unequal-life-chances

Ferreira, F. H. G. (2021, June). Inequality in the time of COVID-19. *Finance & Development*, 20–23. https://www.imf.org/external/pubs/ft/fandd/2021/06/inequality-and-covid-19-ferreira.htm

Ferreira, F., & Ravallion, M. (2009). Poverty and Inequality: The Global Context. In *The Oxford Handbook of Economic Inequality* (pp. 599–636). Oxford University Press.

Ferreira, F., Sterck, O., Mahler, D., & Decerf, B. (2021). Death and Destitution: The Global Distribution of Welfare Losses from the COVID-19 Pandemic, LSE Public. *Policy Review*, *1*(4), 2. http://hdl.handle.net/10986/35634

Flassbeck, H. (2008). *Savings, investment and growth: theory and reality.* G-24 Policy Brief No. 35.

Furceri, D., Loungani, P., Ostry, J. D., & Pizzuto, P. (2020). Will Covid-19 affect inequality? Evidence from past pandemics. *Covid Economics*, *12*(1), 138–157.

Furceri, D., Loungani, P., Ostry, J. D., & Pizzuto, P. (2021). The rise in inequality after pandemics: Can fiscal support play a mitigating role? *Industrial and Corporate Change*, *30*(2), 445–457. doi:10.1093/icc/dtab031

Geda, A., & Kebret, H. (2006). Aggregate Saving Behavior in Africa: A Review of the Theory and the ExistingEvidence with a New Empirical Results. *Ethiopian Journal of Economics*, *12*(1), 13–42.

Georgieva, K. (2020). No lost generation: can poor countries avoid the Covid trap? *The Guardian*. https://www.theguardian.com/business/2020/sep/29/covid-pandemic-imf-kristalina-georgieva

Gift Makgamatha, M., & Maureen Makgato-Khunou, P. (2021). Coronavirus (COVID-19) A Severe Push to the Fourth Industrial Revolution (4IR) Whether Ready or Not: African Realities. *CCSE, 12*, 62-74. Retrieved from https://static1.squarespace.com/static/5f2e7663885b2571f33c3d52/t/622e19dc9359524fc74b4f21/1647188448201/Conference+Proceeding+Final+Version_2022-03-14.pdf

Global Economic Prospects. (2022). *Impact of COVID-19 on Global income inequality*. Author.

Godoy, A., & Reich, M. (2019, July). *Minimum wage effects in low-wage areas*. Institute for Research on Labour and Employment Working Paper No. 106-19. https://irle.berkeley.edu/files/2019/07/Godoy-Reich.pdf

Goldin, I., & Muggah, R. (2020). *COVID-19 is increasing multiple kinds of inequality. Here's what we can do about it.* World Economic Forum. Retrieved from https://www.weforum.org/agenda/2020/10/covid-19-is-increasing-multiple-kinds-of-inequality-here-s-what-we-can-do-about-it/

Goldin, I., & Muggah, R. (2020, October 9). *COVID-19 is increasing multiple kinds of inequality*. Word Economic Forum. https://www.weforum.org/agenda/2020/10/covid-19-is-increasing-multiple-kinds-of-inequality-here-s-what-we-can-do-about-it/

Gopalkrishnan, V., Wadhwa, D., Haddad, S., & Blake, P. (2021, December 21). *2021 Year in Review in 11 charts: The Inequality Pandemic, Feature Story*. https://www.worldbank.org/en/news/feature/2021/12/20/year-2021-in-review-the-inequality-pandemic

Gourinchas, P. O. (Ed.). (2020). *Flattening the Pandemic and Recession Curves in Mitigating the COVID Economic Crisis: Act Fast and Do Whatever*. CEPR Press. https://voxeu.org/content/mitigating-covid-economic-crisis-act-fast-and-do-whatever-it-takes

Gray, R. (2017). Could the fourth industrial revolution combat inequality? *Horizon Magazine*. Retrieved 9 May 2022, from https://ec.europa.eu/research-and-innovation/en/horizon-magazine/could-fourth-industrial-revolution-combat-inequality

Guarda, D., & Hussin, R. (2019). *4IR AI Blockchain Fintech IoT - Reinventing a Nation*. EMIR Research.

Gui-Diby, S. L. (2014). Impact of foreign direct investments on economic growth in Africa: Evidence from three decades of panel data analyses. *Research in Economics*, *68*(3), 248–256. doi:10.1016/j.rie.2014.04.003

Gujarati, D. N. (2004). Basic Econometrics (4th ed.). The McGraw–Hill.

Guterres. (2020). *World Social Report 2020: Inequality in a Rapidly Changing World*. United Nations Publication.

Gwagwa, A., Kazim, E., Kachidza, P., Hilliard, A., Siminyu, K., Smith, M., & Shawe-Taylor, J. (2021). Road map for research on responsible artificial intelligence for development (AI4D) in African countries: The case study of agriculture. *Patterns*, *2*(12), 100381. doi:10.1016/j.patter.2021.100381 PMID:34950903

Hakim, M. (2014). *Memperkuat Ketahanan Pangan Demi Masa Depan Indonesia 2015-2025*. CV Rumah Buku.

Hanson, J. L. (1978). *Monetary theory and practice*. Macdonald and Evans.

Hassana, M. K., Sanchezb, B., & Yu, J. (2011). Financial development and economic growth: New evidence from panel data. *The Quarterly Review of Economics and Finance*, *51*(1), 88–104. doi:10.1016/j.qref.2010.09.001

Hill, R., & Narayan, A. (2021, January 7). *What COVID-19 can mean for long term inequality in developing countries*. Voices. https://blogs.worldbank.org/voices/what-covid-19-can-mean-long-term-inequality-developing-countries

Hillbom, E., Bolt, J., Haas, M., & Tadei, F. (2021). *Measuring historical inequality in Africa: What can we learn from social tables?* African Economic History Working Paper Series No. 63/2021.

Hill, H. (2021). What's Happened to Poverty and Inequality in Indonesia over Half a Century? *Asian Development Review, 38*(1), 68–97. doi:10.1162/adev_a_00158

Hipp, L., & Bünning, M. (2020). Parenthood as a driver of increased gender inequality during COVID-19? Exploratory evidence from Germany. *European Societies*, 1–16.

Hsiao, C. (2003). Analysis of Panel Data (2nd ed.). Econometric Society Monograph No. 34. Cambridge University Press. doi:10.1017/CBO9780511754203

IMF. (n.d.). *Policy Responses to COVID 19.* Retrieved on April 9, 2022, from https://www.imf.org/en/Topics/imf-and-covid19/Policy-Responses-to-COVID-19

Im, K. S., Pesaran, M. H., & Shin, Y. (2003). Testing for Unit Roots in Heterogeneous Panels. *Journal of Econometrics, 115*(1), 53–74. doi:10.1016/S0304-4076(03)00092-7

International Monetary Fund. (1998). The Asian Crisis: Causes and Cures. *Finance & Development, 35*(2).

International Monetary Fund. (2022). *The IMF and income inequality: Introduction to inequality*. Retrieved from https://www.imf.org/en/Topics/Inequality/introduction-to-inequality

Irandoust, M. (2019). Saving and investment causality: Implications for financial integration in transition countries of Eastern Europe. *International Economics and Economic Policy, 16*(2), 397–416. doi:10.100710368-017-0390-6

Irlacher, M., & Koch, M. (2021). Working from home, wages, and regional inequality in the light of Covid-19. *Jahrbucher fur Nationalokonomie und Statistik, 241*(3), 1. doi:10.1515/jbnst-2020-0030

Ishikawa, S., & Vorranikulkij, W. (2019). Korea: Tackling inequality with new economic policy for inclusive growth. *AMRO*. Retrieved from https://www.amro-asia.org/korea-tackling-inequality-with-new-economic-policy-for-inclusive-growth/

Jæger, M. M., & Blaabæk, E. H. (2020). Inequality in learning opportunities during Covid-19: Evidence from library takeout. *Research in Social Stratification and Mobility, 68*, 100524. doi:10.1016/j.rssm.2020.100524 PMID:32834345

Kafile, M. (2022). A framework of intrapreneurship development for corporate entrepreneurship: A case study of organisational development. *Educor Multidisciplinary Journal, 2*(1). Retrieved from https://journals.co.za/doi/abs/10.10520/EJC-13d336741d#

Kaldor, N. (1957). A model of economic growth. *Economic Journal (London)*, •••, 57.

Kang, S. (2016). Inequality and crime revisited: Effects of local inequality and economic segregation on crime. *Journal of Population Economics, 29*(2), 593–626. doi:10.100700148-015-0579-3

Kasser, T. (2004). The Good Life or the Goods Life? Positive Psychology and Personal Well-Being in the Culture of Consumption. In P. A. Linley & S. Joseph (Eds.), *Positive Psychology in Practice*. doi:10.1002/9780470939338.ch4

Kementerian Pertanian, R. I. (2019). *Kementerian Pertanian - Pertanian 4.0 Efisiensi Waktu dan Peningkatan Produktivitas*. https://www.pertanian.go.id/home/?show=news&act=view&id=3819

Kim, D., Trimi, S., Hong, S., & Lim, S. (2020). Effects of co-creation on organizational performance of small and medium manufacturers. *Journal of Business Research*, *109*, 574–584. doi:10.1016/j.jbusres.2019.03.055

Kim, S. J., & Bostwick, W. (2020). Social Vulnerability and Racial Inequality in COVID-19 Deaths in Chicago. *Health Education & Behavior*, *47*(4), 509–513. doi:10.1177/1090198120929677 PMID:32436405

Koh, S. (2019). Inequality. In A. Kobayashi (Ed.), *International encyclopedia of human geography*. Elsevier.

Koo, J., & Song, Y. (2016). The relationship between income inequality and aggregate saving: An empirical analysis using cross-country panel data. *Applied Economics*, *48*(10), 892–901. do i:10.1080/00036846.2015.1090548

Krueger, D., & Perri, F. (2005). *Does Income Inequality Lead to Consumption Equality? Evidence and Theory*. Federal Reserve Bank of Minneapolis Research Department Staff Report 363.

Kuper, S. (2020). This economist has a radical plan to solve wealth inequality. *Wired*. Retrieved from https://www.wired.co.uk/article/thomas-piketty-capital-ideology

Kuznets, S. (1955). Economic growth and income inequality. *The American Economic Review*, *45*(1), 1–28.

Layton-Matthews, S., & Landsberg, C. (2022). The Fourth Industrial Revolution (4IR) and its Effects on Public Service Delivery in South Africa. *Special Focus, 90*. Retrieved from https://journals.uj.ac.za/index.php/The_Thinker/article/download/1173/752

Lee, S., & Trimi, S. (2021). Convergence innovation in the digital age and in the COVID-19 pandemic crisis. *Journal of Business Research*, *123*, 14–22. doi:10.1016/j.jbusres.2020.09.041 PMID:33012897

Levin, A., Lin, C., & Chu, C. J. (2002). Unit Root Test in Panel Data: Asymptotic and Finite Sample Properties. *Journal of Econometrics*, *108*(1), 1–24. doi:10.1016/S0304-4076(01)00098-7

Lewis, W. A. (1954). Economic development with unlimited supplies of labor. *Manchester School*, *22*(2), 139–191. doi:10.1111/j.1467-9957.1954.tb00021.x

Li, J., Zhang, Y., & Cui, B. (2018). Internet +" is used to promote the upgrading of agricultural technology extension mode. *Agriculture Technology Extension*, *6*(1), 7–8.

Lotz, H., & van der Merwe, S. (2018). An assessment of selected organizational-based factors on the perceived success of agribusinesses: A corporate entrepreneurship perspective. *Southern African Business Review*, *17*(13). Retrieved May 10, 2022, from http://hdl.handle.net/10394/16625

Makamase, M. (2022). *The Fourth Industrial Revolution: Impact on unemployment and inequality in South Africa*. Retrieved 10 May 2022, from https://www.igd.org.za/infocus/12080-the-fourth-industrial-revolution-impact-on-unemployemnet-and-inequality-in-south-africa

Maloney, C. B., & Schumer, C. E. (2010). *Income inequality and the great recession*. US Congress Joint Economic Committee.

Manalu, L. P. (2013). Aplikasi Kontrol Digital untuk Pemupukan Secara Variable Rate pada Sistem Pertanian Presisi. *Jurnal Sains dan Teknologi, 15*(3), 31–28.

Mankiw, N. G. (2007). *Macroeconomics*. Worth publishers.

Martins, N. (2010). Globalisation, Inequality and the Economic Crisis. *New Political Economy*.

Marwala, T. (2020). *Closing the Gap: The Fourth Industrial Revolution in Africa*. Pan MacMillan.

McGreal, C. (2020). The inequality virus: how the pandemic hit America's poorest. *The Guardian*. Retrieved from https://www.theguardian.com/world/2020/apr/09/america-inequality-laid-bare-coronavirus

Metaari. (n.d.). *Free Metaari Whitepapers on the Learning Technology Industry*. Retrieved on April 11, 2022 from http://www.metaari.com/whitepapers.html

Meyer, B. D., & Sullivan, J. X. (2013). Consumption and income inequality and the great recession. *The American Economic Review, 103*(3), 178–183. doi:10.1257/aer.103.3.178

Mhlanga, D., & Moloi, T. (2020). COVID-19 and the Digital Transformation of Education: What Are We Learning on 4IR in South Africa? *Education Sciences, 10*(180), 180. Advance online publication. Retrieved May 12, 2022, from. doi:10.3390/educsci10070180

Moeini, B., Barati, M., Farhadian, M., & Ara, M. H. (2018). The association between social support and happiness among elderly in Iran. *Korean Journal of Family Medicine, 39*(4), 260–265. doi:10.4082/kjfm.17.0121 PMID:29972894

Morris, M., Kuratko, D., & Covin, J. (2019). *Corporate entrepreneurship and innovation*. South-Western Cengage Learning.

Ndambiri, Ritho, Ng'ang'a, Kubowon, & Mairura, Nyangweso, Muiruri, & Cherotwo. (2012). Determinants of Economic growth in sub-Saharan Africa: A Panel Data Approach. *International Journal of Economics and Management Sciences*, *2*(2), 18–24.

Ndikumana, L. (2000). Financial Determinants of Domestic Investment in Sub-Saharan Africa: Evidence from Panel Data. *World Development, 28*(2), 381–400. doi:10.1016/S0305-750X(99)00129-1

Nel, P. (2018). Inequality in Africa. In T. Binns, K. Lynch, & E. Nel (Eds.), *Routledge Handbook of African Development*. Routledge.

Nguyen, M. H., Hargittai, E., & Marler, W. (2021). Digital inequality in communication during a time of physical distancing: The case of COVID-19. *Computers in Human Behavior, 120*, 106717. doi:10.1016/j.chb.2021.106717 PMID:34751201

NHS England. (n.d.). *Resources.* Retrieved on April 9, 2022, from https://www.england.nhs.uk/about/equality/equality-hub/resources/

O'Brien, M. (2015). This chart explains everything you need to know about inequality. *The Washington Post*. Retrieved from https://www.washingtonpost.com/news/wonk/wp/2015/04/20/this-chart-explains-everything-you-need-to-know-about-inequality/

Ogunlela, O., & Tengeh, R. (2021). The fourth industrial revolution and the future of the entrepreneurial university in South Africa. *International Journal of Research in Business and Social Science, 10*(3), 91-100. doi:10.20525/ijrbs.v10i3.1103

Olagbaju, I. O., & Akinlo, A. E. (2018). FDI And Economic Growth Relationship In Sub-Saharan Africa: Is The Domestic Financial System A Significant Intermediator? *Archives of Business Research*, *6*(5), 90–112. doi:10.14738/abr.65.4540

Olaitan, O., Issah, M., & Wayi, N. (2021). A framework to test South Africa's readiness for the Fourth Industrial Revolution. *South African Journal of Information Management*, *23*(1). Advance online publication. doi:10.4102ajim.v23i1.1284

Onu, P., & Mbohwa, C. (2021). Industry 4.0 opportunities in manufacturing SMEs: Sustainability outlook. *Materials Today: Proceedings*, *44*, 1925–1930. doi:10.1016/j.matpr.2020.12.095

Onwuka, C. E. (2022). Poverty, Income Inequality and Economic Growth in Nigeria (1981-2019). *J Eco Res & Rev*, *2*(2), 92–100.

Oreffice, S., & Quintana-Domeque, C. (2021). Gender inequality in COVID-19 times: Evidence from UK prolific participants. *Journal of Demographic Economics*, *87*(2), 261–287. doi:10.1017/dem.2021.2

Oronce, C. I. A., Scannell, C. A., Kawachi, I., & Tsugawa, Y. (2020). Association between state-level income inequality and COVID-19 cases and mortality in the USA. *Journal of General Internal Medicine*, *35*(9), 2791–2793. doi:10.100711606-020-05971-3 PMID:32583336

Oswald, A. (2006). The hippies were right all along about happiness. *Financial Times, 19*. https://www.andrewoswald.com/docs/fthappinessjan96.pdf

Oxford University. (n.d.). *COVID-19 Government Response Tracker.* Retrieved on April 9, 2022, from https://www.bsg.ox.ac.uk/research/research-projects/covid-19-government-response-tracker

Palomino, J. C., Rodriguez, J. G., & Sebastian, R. (2020). *Wage inequality and poverty effects of lockdown and social distancing in Europe*. Academic Press.

Pasinetti, L. (1962). Rate of profit and income distribution in relation to the rate of economic Growth. *The Review of Economic Studies*, *29*(4), 267–279. doi:10.2307/2296303

Patel, J. A., Nielsen, F. B. H., Badiani, A. A., Assi, S., Unadkat, V. A., Patel, B., Ravindrane, R., & Wardle, H. (2020). Poverty, inequality and COVID-19: The forgotten vulnerable. *Public Health, 183*, 110–111. doi:10.1016/j.puhe.2020.05.006 PMID:32502699

Patel, K. C., & Hanif, W. (2022). Ethnic health inequalities in the NHS. *BMJ (Clinical Research Ed.)*, 376.

PatelR.BarnardS.LagordC.ThompsonK.HughesA.FoxS.DeanfieldJ. (2021). *Addressing Health Inequalities Through the NHS Health Check Programme in England.* doi:10.2139/ssrn.3937909

Pedroni, P. (2000). Fully Modified OLS For Heterogeneous Cointegrated Panels, Nonstationary Panels, Panel Cointegration, and Dynamic Panels. *Advances in Econometrics, 15*, 93–130. doi:10.1016/S0731-9053(00)15004-2

Perri, F., & Steinberg, J. (2012). Inequality and redistribution during the Great Recession. *Economic Policy Paper*, 1.

Pesaran, M. H., & Smith, R. (1995). Estimating long-run relationships from dynamic heterogeneous Panels. *Journal of Economics, 68*(1), 79–113. doi:10.1016/0304-4076(94)01644-F

Piketty, T., & Saez, E. (2003). Income inequality in the United States, 1913–1998. *The Quarterly Journal of Economics, 118*(1), 1–41. doi:10.1162/00335530360535135

Poppe, K., Wolfert, J., Verdouw, C., & Renwick, A. (2015). A European Perpective on The Economics of Big Data. *Farm Policy Journal, 12*, 11–19.

Pupavac, D., Delibasic, M., Pupavac, J., & Streimikis, J. (2020). Interdependence of quality of life and happiness of the population in Southeast European Countries. *Montenegrin Journal of Economics, 16*(4), 7-15. http://mnje.com/sites/mnje.com/files/007-015_-pupavac_et_al._-.pdf

Purwantini, T. B., & Suhaeti, R. N. (2017). Irigasi Kecil: Kinerja, Masalah, dan Solusinya. *Forum Penelitian Agro Ekonomi, 35*(2), 91–105.

Raj, C., Friedman, J. N., Nathaniel, H., & Michael, S. (2020). *Real-time economics: A new platform to track the impacts of covid-19 on people, businesses, and communities using private sector data.* Technical report, NBER WP 27431. https://opportunityinsights.org/wp-content/uploads/2020/06/Short_Covid_Paper.pdf

Rao, V. B. (1999). East Asian economies: Trends in poverty and income inequality. *Economic and Political Weekly*, 1029–1039.

Ratten, V. (2021). *COVID-19 and entrepreneurship: Challenges and Opportunities for Small Business.* Routledge. doi:10.4324/9781003149248

Raut, L. K., & Virmani, A. (1989). Determinants of Consumption and Savings Behavior in Developing Countries. *The World Bank Economic Review, 3*(3), 379–393. doi:10.1093/wber/3.3.379

Ravjee, B., & Mamabolo, M. (2019). The impact of corporate entrepreneurship on service innovation: A case of a South African banking institution. *The Southern African Journal of Entrepreneurship and Small Business Management, 11*(1). Advance online publication. doi:10.4102ajesbm.v11i1.155

Republic of Kiribati. (2019, May 1). *Tebunginako Village*. Office of the President. https://www.climate.gov.ki/case-studies/abaiang/

Roka, D. (2020). Nexus of Economic Growth on Happiness and Inequality: Re-examine the Paradox. *Asian Journal of Economics, Business and Accounting, 15*(1), 35–49. doi:10.9734/ajeba/2020/v15i130206

Romer, D. (2005). *Advanced Macroeconomic* (3rd ed.). University of California.

Sakhdari, K. (2016). Corporate Entrepreneurship: A Review and Future Research Agenda. *Technology Innovation Management Review, 6*(8), 1–18. doi:10.22215/timreview/1007

Sanchez-Paramo, C., & Malgioglio, S. (2022). *Here's a remedy for COVID's legacy of growing inequality*. The World Bank. Retrieved from https://blogs.worldbank.org/voices/heres-remedy-covids-legacy-growing-inequality

Sander, F. (2015). *How can Malaysia reduce inequality?* World Economic Forum. Retrieved from https://www.weforum.org/agenda/2015/02/how-can-malaysia-reduce-inequality/

Santo, S. Q. (2021). Digitalisasi Pertanian di Indonesia, Strategi Di Masa Pandemi dan New Normal. *Jurnal Teknologi dan Industri Pertanian Indonesia, 8*(10).

Schmidt-Hebbel, K., & Serven, L. (2000). Does income inequality raise aggregate saving? *Journal of Development Economics, 61*(2), 417–446. doi:10.1016/S0304-3878(00)00063-8

Schmitt, J. (2009). Inequality as policy. *Real Word Economics Review, 51*(1), 2–9.

Schnittker, J. (2008). Happiness and success: Genes, families, and the psychological effects of socioeconomic position and social support. *American Journal of Sociology, 114*(S1), S233–S259. doi:10.1086/592424 PMID:19569406

Schwab, K. (2018). *The fourth industrial revolution*. Currency.

Seale, J. L., & Regmi, A. (2006). Modeling international consumption patterns. *Review of Income and Wealth Series, 52*(4), 603–624. doi:10.1111/j.1475-4991.2006.00204.x

Selvia, S., Hos, J., & Moita, S. (2019). Dampak Modernisasi Pertanian terhadap Kondisi Sosial Ekonomi Masyarakat Petani Sawah (Studi di Desa Masagena Kecamatan Konda Kabupaten Konawe Selatan). *Neo Societal, 4*(2), 767–776.

Sembene, D. (2015). *Poverty, Growth, and Inequality in Sub-Saharan Africa: Did the Walk Match the Talk under the PRSP Approach?* IMF Working Paper, WP/15/122.

Sen, A. K. (1997). From income inequality to economic inequality. *Southern Economic Journal, 64*(2), 384–401. doi:10.1002/j.2325-8012.1997.tb00063.x

Setiana, L., Nuskhi, M., & Hidayat, S. (2021). Kompetensi Penyuluh Pertanian dalam Revolusi Industri 4.0 Menuju Pertanian Modern. *Prosiding Seminar Teknologi Agribisnis Peternakan (STAP) Fakultas Peternakan Universitas Jenderal Soedirman, 8*, 602–607. http://jnp.fapet.unsoed.ac.id/index.php/psv/article/view/1225

Shawa, K. C. (2016). Drivers of private saving in sub-Saharan Africancountries. *Journal of Economic Development, 41*(2), 77–110. doi:10.35866/caujed.2016.41.2.004

Shimeles, A., & Nabassaga, T. (2017). *Why is inequality high in Africa?* Working Paper Series N° 246. African Development Bank.

Shinta, N. (2014). *Pemetaan Ketahanan Pangan di Indonesia: Pendekatan TFP dan Indeks Ketahanan Pangan* (No. 4). Academic Press.

Sima, V., Georgiana Gheorghe, I., Subi'c, J., & Nancu, D. (2020). Influences of the Industry 4.0 Revolution on the Human Capital Development and Consumer Behavior: A Systematic Review. *Sustainability, 12*(43), 4035. Advance online publication. doi:10.3390u12104035

Sobrosa Neto, R., Sobrosa Maia, J., de Silva Neiva, S., Scalia, M., & de Andrade Guerra, J. (2020). The fourth industrial revolution and the coronavirus: A new era catalyzed by a virus. *Research In Globalization, 2*, 100024. Advance online publication. doi:10.1016/j.resglo.2020.100024

Soltanifar, M., Hughes, M., & Göcke, L. (2021). *Digital Entrepreneurship Impact on Business and Society*. Springer. doi:10.1007/978-3-030-53914-6

Sonka, S. (2015). Big Data; from hype to agricultural tool. *Farm Policy Journal, 12*, 1–9.

Sophia, C., Deniz, I., Nicola, P., & Presbitero, A. F. (2020). *Tracking the economic impact of covid-19 and mitigation policies in Europe and the United States*. Technical report, IMF WP/20/125. https://www.imf.org/en/Publications/WP/Issues/2020/07/10/Tracking-the-Economic-Impact-of-COVID-19-and-Mitigation-Policies-in-Europe-and-the-United-49553

Steve, C. (2020). *Early economic impacts of covid-19 in europe: A view from the grid*. Technical report, University of Chicago. https://epic.uchicago.edu/research/early-economic-impacts-of-covid-19-in-europe-a-view-from-the-grid/

Stiglitz, J. (2020). *Conquering the great divide*. International Monetary Fund. Retrieved from https://www.imf.org/Publications/fandd/issues/2020/09/COVID19-and-global-inequality-joseph-stiglitz

Telukdarie, A., Buhulaiga, E., Bag, S., Gupta, S., & Luo, Z. (2018). Industry 4.0 implementation for multinationals. *Process Safety and Environmental Protection, 118*, 316–329. doi:10.1016/j.psep.2018.06.030

The World Bank. (1998). What effect will East Asia's crisis have on developing countries? *PREM Notes*, (1).

Thompson, J. P., & Smeeding, T. M. T. (2013). *Inequality and poverty in the United States: the aftermath of the Great Recession*. FEDS Working paper no. 2013-51. doi:10.2139/ssrn.2340665

Thorbecke, E., & Charumilind, C. (2002). Economic inequality and its socioeconomic impact. *World Development*, *30*(9), 1477–1495. doi:10.1016/S0305-750X(02)00052-9

Tideman, S. G. (2011). Gross national happiness. In *Ethical principles and economic transformation-A Buddhist approach* (pp. 133–153). Springer. doi:10.1007/978-90-481-9310-3_7

Tofallis, C. (2020). Which formula for national happiness? *Socio-Economic Planning Sciences*, *70*, 100688. doi:10.1016/j.seps.2019.02.003

UN. (2020). *Tackling the Inequality Pandemic: A New Social Contract for a New Era.* UN Secretary - General's Lecture for Nelson Mandela's International Day. https://www.un.org/sg/en/content/sg/statement/2020-07-18/secretary-generals-nelson-mandela-lecture-%E2%80%9Ctackling-the-inequality-pandemic-new-social-contract-for-new-era%E2%80%9D-delivered

Utomo, S. H., Mukhlis, I., & Yusida, E. (n.d.). A Model for Predicting Food Security Status Among Indonesian Farmer's Households During Covid-19 Pandemic. *Pertanika. Journal of Tropical Agricultural Science*, 1–17.

Valverde-Berrocoso, J., Fernández-Sánchez, M. R., Revuelta Dominguez, F. I., & Sosa-Díaz, M. J. (2021). The educational integration of digital technologies preCovid-19: Lessons for teacher education. *PLoS One*, *16*(8), e0256283. doi:10.1371/journal.pone.0256283 PMID:34411161

van Tonder, C., Schachtebeck, C., Nieuwenhuizen, C., & Bossink, B. (2021). Business Model Innovation Success in the Fourth Industrial Revolution. *Research Gate*, *21*. Advance online publication. doi:10.34190/EIE.21.038

Veenhoven, R. (2008). Healthy happiness: Effects of happiness on physical health and the consequences for preventive health care. *Journal of Happiness Studies*, *9*(3), 449–469. doi:10.100710902-006-9042-1

Vizitiu, C., Agapie, A., Paiusan, R., Hadad, S., & Nastase, M. (2018). Adapting corporate entrepreneurship assessment instrument for Romania. *South African Journal of Business Management*, *49*(1). Advance online publication. doi:10.4102ajbm.v49i1.8

Vos, R., Martin, W., & Laborde, D. (2020). How much will global poverty increase because of COVID-19. International Food Policy Research Institute.

Wansbeek, T.J. (2001). GMM Estimation in Panel Data Models with Measurement error. *Journal of Econoimetrics*, 104.

WEF. (2020, April 29). *The COVID-19 pandemic has changed education forever. This is how.* https://www.weforum.org/agenda/2020/04/coronavirus-education-global-covid19-online-digital-learning/

Wibowo, D. S., & Dairoh, D. (2018). Sistem Digitalisasi Pemetaan Lahan Pertanian Di Kabupaten Brebes. *Sinkron : Jurnal dan Penelitian Teknik Informatika, 3*(1), 20–30. https://www.polgan.ac.id/jurnal/index.php/sinkron/article/view/157

WID. (n.d.). Retrieved August 30, 2022, from https://wid.world

World Bank. (1993). *The East Asian miracle: Economic growth and public policy*. Oxford University Press.

World Bank. (n.d.). *Overview*. Retrieved August 30, 2022, from https://www.worldbank.org/en/country/malaysia/overview#1

Yasin, M. (n.d.). *Public spending and economic growth: empirical investigation of Sub-Sahara Africa. Southwestern Economic Review.*

Yin, R., Luo, X., Li, R., & Huang, Y. (2018). Under the background of informatization, why do farmers favor agricultural technicians to carry out agricultural technology extension in the field? *Nongye Xiandaihua Yanjiu*, *39*(4), 576–583.

Yonzan, N., Lakner, C., & Mahler, D. (2021). *Is COVID-19 increasing global inequality?* World Bank. Retrieved from https://blogs.worldbank.org/opendata/covid-19-increasing-global-inequality

Yusida, E. (2021). The Digital Agriculture Model For Sustainable Food System: An Analysis of Agricultural Technology Adoption in Jawa Timur, Indonesia. *Journal of Sustainability Science and Management.*

Zahariadis, N., Petridou, E., Exadaktylos, T., & Sparf, J. (2022). Policy Styles and Policymaking During Times of Crisis. In Policy Styles and Trust in the Age of Pandemics (pp. 17-38). Routledge. doi:10.4324/9781003137399-3

Related References

To continue our tradition of advancing information science and technology research, we have compiled a list of recommended IGI Global readings. These references will provide additional information and guidance to further enrich your knowledge and assist you with your own research and future publications.

Abdul Razak, R., & Mansor, N. A. (2021). Instagram Influencers in Social Media-Induced Tourism: Rethinking Tourist Trust Towards Tourism Destination. In M. Dinis, L. Bonixe, S. Lamy, & Z. Breda (Eds.), *Impact of New Media in Tourism* (pp. 135-144). IGI Global. https://doi.org/10.4018/978-1-7998-7095-1.ch009

Abir, T., & Khan, M. Y. (2022). Importance of ICT Advancement and Culture of Adaptation in the Tourism and Hospitality Industry for Developing Countries. In C. Ramos, S. Quinteiro, & A. Gonçalves (Eds.), *ICT as Innovator Between Tourism and Culture* (pp. 30–41). IGI Global. https://doi.org/10.4018/978-1-7998-8165-0.ch003

Abtahi, M. S., Behboudi, L., & Hasanabad, H. M. (2017). Factors Affecting Internet Advertising Adoption in Ad Agencies. *International Journal of Innovation in the Digital Economy*, *8*(4), 18–29. doi:10.4018/IJIDE.2017100102

Afenyo-Agbe, E., & Mensah, I. (2022). Principles, Benefits, and Barriers to Community-Based Tourism: Implications for Management. In I. Mensah & E. Afenyo-Agbe (Eds.), *Prospects and Challenges of Community-Based Tourism and Changing Demographics* (pp. 1–29). IGI Global. doi:10.4018/978-1-7998-7335-8.ch001

Agbo, V. M. (2022). Distributive Justice Issues in Community-Based Tourism. In I. Mensah & E. Afenyo-Agbe (Eds.), *Prospects and Challenges of Community-Based Tourism and Changing Demographics* (pp. 107–129). IGI Global. https://doi.org/10.4018/978-1-7998-7335-8.ch005

Agrawal, S. (2017). The Impact of Emerging Technologies and Social Media on Different Business(es): Marketing and Management. In O. Rishi & A. Sharma (Eds.), *Maximizing Business Performance and Efficiency Through Intelligent Systems* (pp. 37–49). Hershey, PA: IGI Global. doi:10.4018/978-1-5225-2234-8.ch002

Ahmad, A., & Johari, S. (2022). Georgetown as a Gastronomy Tourism Destination: Visitor Awareness Towards Revisit Intention of Nasi Kandar Restaurant. In M. Valeri (Ed.), *New Governance and Management in Touristic Destinations* (pp. 71–83). IGI Global. https://doi.org/10.4018/978-1-6684-3889-3.ch005

Alkhatib, G., & Bayouq, S. T. (2021). A TAM-Based Model of Technological Factors Affecting Use of E-Tourism. *International Journal of Tourism and Hospitality Management in the Digital Age*, *5*(2), 50–67. https://doi.org/10.4018/IJTHMDA.20210701.oa1

Altinay Ozdemir, M. (2021). Virtual Reality (VR) and Augmented Reality (AR) Technologies for Accessibility and Marketing in the Tourism Industry. In C. Eusébio, L. Teixeira, & M. Carneiro (Eds.), *ICT Tools and Applications for Accessible Tourism* (pp. 277-301). IGI Global. https://doi.org/10.4018/978-1-7998-6428-8.ch013

Anantharaman, R. N., Rajeswari, K. S., Angusamy, A., & Kuppusamy, J. (2017). Role of Self-Efficacy and Collective Efficacy as Moderators of Occupational Stress Among Software Development Professionals. *International Journal of Human Capital and Information Technology Professionals*, *8*(2), 45–58. doi:10.4018/IJHCITP.2017040103

Aninze, F., El-Gohary, H., & Hussain, J. (2018). The Role of Microfinance to Empower Women: The Case of Developing Countries. *International Journal of Customer Relationship Marketing and Management*, *9*(1), 54–78. doi:10.4018/IJCRMM.2018010104

Antosova, G., Sabogal-Salamanca, M., & Krizova, E. (2021). Human Capital in Tourism: A Practical Model of Endogenous and Exogenous Territorial Tourism Planning in Bahía Solano, Colombia. In V. Costa, A. Moura, & M. Mira (Eds.), *Handbook of Research on Human Capital and People Management in the Tourism Industry* (pp. 282–302). IGI Global. https://doi.org/10.4018/978-1-7998-4318-4.ch014

Arsenijević, O. M., Orčić, D., & Kastratović, E. (2017). Development of an Optimization Tool for Intangibles in SMEs: A Case Study from Serbia with a Pilot Research in the Prestige by Milka Company. In M. Vemić (Ed.), *Optimal Management Strategies in Small and Medium Enterprises* (pp. 320–347). Hershey, PA: IGI Global. doi:10.4018/978-1-5225-1949-2.ch015

Aryanto, V. D., Wismantoro, Y., & Widyatmoko, K. (2018). Implementing Eco-Innovation by Utilizing the Internet to Enhance Firm's Marketing Performance: Study of Green Batik Small and Medium Enterprises in Indonesia. *International Journal of E-Business Research, 14*(1), 21–36. doi:10.4018/IJEBR.2018010102

Asero, V., & Billi, S. (2022). New Perspective of Networking in the DMO Model. In M. Valeri (Ed.), *New Governance and Management in Touristic Destinations* (pp. 105–118). IGI Global. https://doi.org/10.4018/978-1-6684-3889-3.ch007

Atiku, S. O., & Fields, Z. (2017). Multicultural Orientations for 21st Century Global Leadership. In N. Baporikar (Ed.), *Management Education for Global Leadership* (pp. 28–51). Hershey, PA: IGI Global. doi:10.4018/978-1-5225-1013-0.ch002

Atiku, S. O., & Fields, Z. (2018). Organisational Learning Dimensions and Talent Retention Strategies for the Service Industries. In N. Baporikar (Ed.), *Global Practices in Knowledge Management for Societal and Organizational Development* (pp. 358–381). Hershey, PA: IGI Global. doi:10.4018/978-1-5225-3009-1.ch017

Atsa'am, D. D., & Kuset Bodur, E. (2021). Pattern Mining on How Organizational Tenure Affects the Psychological Capital of Employees Within the Hospitality and Tourism Industry: Linking Employees' Organizational Tenure With PsyCap. *International Journal of Tourism and Hospitality Management in the Digital Age, 5*(2), 17–28. https://doi.org/10.4018/IJTHMDA.2021070102

Ávila, L., & Teixeira, L. (2018). The Main Concepts Behind the Dematerialization of Business Processes. In M. Khosrow-Pour, D.B.A. (Ed.), Encyclopedia of Information Science and Technology, Fourth Edition (pp. 888-898). Hershey, PA: IGI Global. https://doi.org/ doi:10.4018/978-1-5225-2255-3.ch076

Ayorekire, J., Mugizi, F., Obua, J., & Ampaire, G. (2022). Community-Based Tourism and Local People's Perceptions Towards Conservation: The Case of Queen Elizabeth Conservation Area, Uganda. In I. Mensah & E. Afenyo-Agbe (Eds.), *Prospects and Challenges of Community-Based Tourism and Changing Demographics* (pp. 56–82). IGI Global. https://doi.org/10.4018/978-1-7998-7335-8.ch003

Baleiro, R. (2022). Tourist Literature and the Architecture of Travel in Olga Tokarczuk and Patti Smith. In R. Baleiro & R. Pereira (Eds.), *Global Perspectives on Literary Tourism and Film-Induced Tourism* (pp. 202-216). IGI Global. https://doi.org/10.4018/978-1-7998-8262-6.ch011

Barat, S. (2021). Looking at the Future of Medical Tourism in Asia. *International Journal of Tourism and Hospitality Management in the Digital Age, 5*(1), 19–33. https://doi.org/10.4018/IJTHMDA.2021010102

Barbosa, C. A., Magalhães, M., & Nunes, M. R. (2021). Travel Instagramability: A Way of Choosing a Destination? In M. Dinis, L. Bonixe, S. Lamy, & Z. Breda (Eds.), *Impact of New Media in Tourism* (pp. 173-190). IGI Global. https://doi.org/10.4018/978-1-7998-7095-1.ch011

Bari, M. W., & Khan, Q. (2021). Pakistan as a Destination of Religious Tourism. In E. Alaverdov & M. Bari (Eds.), *Global Development of Religious Tourism* (pp. 1-10). IGI Global. https://doi.org/10.4018/978-1-7998-5792-1.ch001

Bartens, Y., Chunpir, H. I., Schulte, F., & Voß, S. (2017). Business/IT Alignment in Two-Sided Markets: A COBIT 5 Analysis for Media Streaming Business Models. In S. De Haes & W. Van Grembergen (Eds.), *Strategic IT Governance and Alignment in Business Settings* (pp. 82–111). Hershey, PA: IGI Global. doi:10.4018/978-1-5225-0861-8.ch004

Bashayreh, A. M. (2018). Organizational Culture and Organizational Performance. In W. Lee & F. Sabetzadeh (Eds.), *Contemporary Knowledge and Systems Science* (pp. 50–69). Hershey, PA: IGI Global. doi:10.4018/978-1-5225-5655-8.ch003

Bechthold, L., Lude, M., & Prügl, R. (2021). Crisis Favors the Prepared Firm: How Organizational Ambidexterity Relates to Perceptions of Organizational Resilience. In A. Zehrer, G. Glowka, K. Schwaiger, & V. Ranacher-Lackner (Eds.), *Resiliency Models and Addressing Future Risks for Family Firms in the Tourism Industry* (pp. 178–205). IGI Global. https://doi.org/10.4018/978-1-7998-7352-5.ch008

Bedford, D. A. (2018). Sustainable Knowledge Management Strategies: Aligning Business Capabilities and Knowledge Management Goals. In N. Baporikar (Ed.), *Global Practices in Knowledge Management for Societal and Organizational Development* (pp. 46–73). Hershey, PA: IGI Global. doi:10.4018/978-1-5225-3009-1.ch003

Bekjanov, D., & Matyusupov, B. (2021). Influence of Innovative Processes in the Competitiveness of Tourist Destination. In J. Soares (Ed.), *Innovation and Entrepreneurial Opportunities in Community Tourism* (pp. 243–263). IGI Global. https://doi.org/10.4018/978-1-7998-4855-4.ch014

Bharwani, S., & Musunuri, D. (2018). Reflection as a Process From Theory to Practice. In M. Khosrow-Pour, D.B.A. (Ed.), Encyclopedia of Information Science and Technology, Fourth Edition (pp. 1529-1539). Hershey, PA: IGI Global. doi:10.4018/978-1-5225-2255-3.ch132

Bhatt, G. D., Wang, Z., & Rodger, J. A. (2017). Information Systems Capabilities and Their Effects on Competitive Advantages: A Study of Chinese Companies. *Information Resources Management Journal, 30*(3), 41–57. doi:10.4018/IRMJ.2017070103

Bhushan, M., & Yadav, A. (2017). Concept of Cloud Computing in ESB. In R. Bhadoria, N. Chaudhari, G. Tomar, & S. Singh (Eds.), *Exploring Enterprise Service Bus in the Service-Oriented Architecture Paradigm* (pp. 116–127). Hershey, PA: IGI Global. doi:10.4018/978-1-5225-2157-0.ch008

Bhushan, S. (2017). System Dynamics Base-Model of Humanitarian Supply Chain (HSCM) in Disaster Prone Eco-Communities of India: A Discussion on Simulation and Scenario Results. *International Journal of System Dynamics Applications*, *6*(3), 20–37. doi:10.4018/IJSDA.2017070102

Binder, D., & Miller, J. W. (2021). A Generations' Perspective on Employer Branding in Tourism. In V. Costa, A. Moura, & M. Mira (Eds.), *Handbook of Research on Human Capital and People Management in the Tourism Industry* (pp. 152–174). IGI Global. https://doi.org/10.4018/978-1-7998-4318-4.ch008

Birch Freeman, A. A., Mensah, I., & Antwi, K. B. (2022). Smiling vs. Frowning Faces: Community Participation for Sustainable Tourism in Ghanaian Communities. In I. Mensah & E. Afenyo-Agbe (Eds.), *Prospects and Challenges of Community-Based Tourism and Changing Demographics* (pp. 83–106). IGI Global. https://doi.org/10.4018/978-1-7998-7335-8.ch004

Biswas, A., & De, A. K. (2017). On Development of a Fuzzy Stochastic Programming Model with Its Application to Business Management. In S. Trivedi, S. Dey, A. Kumar, & T. Panda (Eds.), *Handbook of Research on Advanced Data Mining Techniques and Applications for Business Intelligence* (pp. 353–378). Hershey, PA: IGI Global. doi:10.4018/978-1-5225-2031-3.ch021

Boragnio, A., & Faracce Macia, C. (2021). "Taking Care of Yourself at Home": Use of E-Commerce About Food and Care During the COVID-19 Pandemic in the City of Buenos Aires. In M. Korstanje (Ed.), *Socio-Economic Effects and Recovery Efforts for the Rental Industry: Post-COVID-19 Strategies* (pp. 45–71). IGI Global. https://doi.org/10.4018/978-1-7998-7287-0.ch003

Borges, V. D. (2021). Happiness: The Basis for Public Policy in Tourism. In A. Perinotto, V. Mayer, & J. Soares (Eds.), *Rebuilding and Restructuring the Tourism Industry: Infusion of Happiness and Quality of Life* (pp. 1–25). IGI Global. https://doi.org/10.4018/978-1-7998-7239-9.ch001

Bücker, J., & Ernste, K. (2018). Use of Brand Heroes in Strategic Reputation Management: The Case of Bacardi, Adidas, and Daimler. In A. Erdemir (Ed.), *Reputation Management Techniques in Public Relations* (pp. 126–150). Hershey, PA: IGI Global. doi:10.4018/978-1-5225-3619-2.ch007

Buluk Eşitti, B. (2021). COVID-19 and Alternative Tourism: New Destinations and New Tourism Products. In M. Demir, A. Dalgıç, & F. Ergen (Eds.), *Handbook of Research on the Impacts and Implications of COVID-19 on the Tourism Industry* (pp. 786–805). IGI Global. https://doi.org/10.4018/978-1-7998-8231-2.ch038

Bureš, V. (2018). Industry 4.0 From the Systems Engineering Perspective: Alternative Holistic Framework Development. In R. Brunet-Thornton & F. Martinez (Eds.), *Analyzing the Impacts of Industry 4.0 in Modern Business Environments* (pp. 199–223). Hershey, PA: IGI Global. doi:10.4018/978-1-5225-3468-6.ch011

Buzady, Z. (2017). Resolving the Magic Cube of Effective Case Teaching: Benchmarking Case Teaching Practices in Emerging Markets – Insights from the Central European University Business School, Hungary. In D. Latusek (Ed.), *Case Studies as a Teaching Tool in Management Education* (pp. 79–103). Hershey, PA: IGI Global. doi:10.4018/978-1-5225-0770-3.ch005

Camillo, A. (2021). *Legal Matters, Risk Management, and Risk Prevention: From Forming a Business to Legal Representation.* IGI Global. doi:10.4018/978-1-7998-4342-9.ch004

Căpusneanu, S., & Topor, D. I. (2018). Business Ethics and Cost Management in SMEs: Theories of Business Ethics and Cost Management Ethos. In I. Oncioiu (Ed.), *Ethics and Decision-Making for Sustainable Business Practices* (pp. 109–127). Hershey, PA: IGI Global. doi:10.4018/978-1-5225-3773-1.ch007

Chan, R. L., Mo, P. L., & Moon, K. K. (2018). Strategic and Tactical Measures in Managing Enterprise Risks: A Study of the Textile and Apparel Industry. In K. Strang, M. Korstanje, & N. Vajjhala (Eds.), *Research, Practices, and Innovations in Global Risk and Contingency Management* (pp. 1–19). Hershey, PA: IGI Global. doi:10.4018/978-1-5225-4754-9.ch001

Charlier, S. D., Burke-Smalley, L. A., & Fisher, S. L. (2018). Undergraduate Programs in the U.S: A Contextual and Content-Based Analysis. In J. Mendy (Ed.), *Teaching Human Resources and Organizational Behavior at the College Level* (pp. 26–57). Hershey, PA: IGI Global. doi:10.4018/978-1-5225-2820-3.ch002

Chumillas, J., Güell, M., & Quer, P. (2022). The Use of ICT in Tourist and Educational Literary Routes: The Role of the Guide. In C. Ramos, S. Quinteiro, & A. Gonçalves (Eds.), *ICT as Innovator Between Tourism and Culture* (pp. 15–29). IGI Global. https://doi.org/10.4018/978-1-7998-8165-0.ch002

Dahlberg, T., Kivijärvi, H., & Saarinen, T. (2017). IT Investment Consistency and Other Factors Influencing the Success of IT Performance. In S. De Haes & W. Van Grembergen (Eds.), *Strategic IT Governance and Alignment in Business Settings* (pp. 176–208). Hershey, PA: IGI Global. doi:10.4018/978-1-5225-0861-8.ch007

Damnjanović, A. M. (2017). Knowledge Management Optimization through IT and E-Business Utilization: A Qualitative Study on Serbian SMEs. In M. Vemić (Ed.), *Optimal Management Strategies in Small and Medium Enterprises* (pp. 249–267). Hershey, PA: IGI Global. doi:10.4018/978-1-5225-1949-2.ch012

Daneshpour, H. (2017). Integrating Sustainable Development into Project Portfolio Management through Application of Open Innovation. In M. Vemić (Ed.), *Optimal Management Strategies in Small and Medium Enterprises* (pp. 370–387). Hershey, PA: IGI Global. doi:10.4018/978-1-5225-1949-2.ch017

Daniel, A. D., & Reis de Castro, V. (2018). Entrepreneurship Education: How to Measure the Impact on Nascent Entrepreneurs. In A. Carrizo Moreira, J. Guilherme Leitão Dantas, & F. Manuel Valente (Eds.), *Nascent Entrepreneurship and Successful New Venture Creation* (pp. 85–110). Hershey, PA: IGI Global. doi:10.4018/978-1-5225-2936-1.ch004

David, R., Swami, B. N., & Tangirala, S. (2018). Ethics Impact on Knowledge Management in Organizational Development: A Case Study. In N. Baporikar (Ed.), *Global Practices in Knowledge Management for Societal and Organizational Development* (pp. 19–45). Hershey, PA: IGI Global. doi:10.4018/978-1-5225-3009-1.ch002

De Uña-Álvarez, E., & Villarino-Pérez, M. (2022). Fostering Ecocultural Resources, Identity, and Tourism in Inland Territories (Galicia, NW Spain). In G. Fernandes (Ed.), *Challenges and New Opportunities for Tourism in Inland Territories: Ecocultural Resources and Sustainable Initiatives* (pp. 1-16). IGI Global. https://doi.org/10.4018/978-1-7998-7339-6.ch001

Delias, P., & Lakiotaki, K. (2018). Discovering Process Horizontal Boundaries to Facilitate Process Comprehension. *International Journal of Operations Research and Information Systems*, *9*(2), 1–31. doi:10.4018/IJORIS.2018040101

Denholm, J., & Lee-Davies, L. (2018). Success Factors for Games in Business and Project Management. In *Enhancing Education and Training Initiatives Through Serious Games* (pp. 34–68). Hershey, PA: IGI Global. doi:10.4018/978-1-5225-3689-5.ch002

Deshpande, M. (2017). Best Practices in Management Institutions for Global Leadership: Policy Aspects. In N. Baporikar (Ed.), *Management Education for Global Leadership* (pp. 1–27). Hershey, PA: IGI Global. doi:10.4018/978-1-5225-1013-0.ch001

Deshpande, M. (2018). Policy Perspectives for SMEs Knowledge Management. In N. Baporikar (Ed.), *Knowledge Integration Strategies for Entrepreneurship and Sustainability* (pp. 23–46). Hershey, PA: IGI Global. doi:10.4018/978-1-5225-5115-7.ch002

Dezdar, S. (2017). ERP Implementation Projects in Asian Countries: A Comparative Study on Iran and China. *International Journal of Information Technology Project Management, 8*(3), 52–68. doi:10.4018/IJITPM.2017070104

Domingos, D., Respício, A., & Martinho, R. (2017). Reliability of IoT-Aware BPMN Healthcare Processes. In C. Reis & M. Maximiano (Eds.), *Internet of Things and Advanced Application in Healthcare* (pp. 214–248). Hershey, PA: IGI Global. doi:10.4018/978-1-5225-1820-4.ch008

Dosumu, O., Hussain, J., & El-Gohary, H. (2017). An Exploratory Study of the Impact of Government Policies on the Development of Small and Medium Enterprises in Developing Countries: The Case of Nigeria. *International Journal of Customer Relationship Marketing and Management, 8*(4), 51–62. doi:10.4018/IJCRMM.2017100104

Durst, S., Bruns, G., & Edvardsson, I. R. (2017). Retaining Knowledge in Smaller Building and Construction Firms. *International Journal of Knowledge and Systems Science, 8*(3), 1–12. doi:10.4018/IJKSS.2017070101

Edvardsson, I. R., & Durst, S. (2017). Outsourcing, Knowledge, and Learning: A Critical Review. *International Journal of Knowledge-Based Organizations, 7*(2), 13–26. doi:10.4018/IJKBO.2017040102

Edwards, J. S. (2018). Integrating Knowledge Management and Business Processes. In M. Khosrow-Pour, D.B.A. (Ed.), Encyclopedia of Information Science and Technology, Fourth Edition (pp. 5046-5055). Hershey, PA: IGI Global. doi:10.4018/978-1-5225-2255-3.ch437

Eichelberger, S., & Peters, M. (2021). Family Firm Management in Turbulent Times: Opportunities for Responsible Tourism. In A. Zehrer, G. Glowka, K. Schwaiger, & V. Ranacher-Lackner (Eds.), *Resiliency Models and Addressing Future Risks for Family Firms in the Tourism Industry* (pp. 103–124). IGI Global. https://doi.org/10.4018/978-1-7998-7352-5.ch005

Eide, D., Hjalager, A., & Hansen, M. (2022). Innovative Certifications in Adventure Tourism: Attributes and Diffusion. In R. Augusto Costa, F. Brandão, Z. Breda, & C. Costa (Eds.), *Planning and Managing the Experience Economy in Tourism* (pp. 161-175). IGI Global. https://doi.org/10.4018/978-1-7998-8775-1.ch009

Ejiogu, A. O. (2018). Economics of Farm Management. In *Agricultural Finance and Opportunities for Investment and Expansion* (pp. 56–72). Hershey, PA: IGI Global. doi:10.4018/978-1-5225-3059-6.ch003

Ekanem, I., & Abiade, G. E. (2018). Factors Influencing the Use of E-Commerce by Small Enterprises in Nigeria. *International Journal of ICT Research in Africa and the Middle East*, *7*(1), 37–53. doi:10.4018/IJICTRAME.2018010103

Ekanem, I., & Alrossais, L. A. (2017). Succession Challenges Facing Family Businesses in Saudi Arabia. In P. Zgheib (Ed.), *Entrepreneurship and Business Innovation in the Middle East* (pp. 122–146). Hershey, PA: IGI Global. doi:10.4018/978-1-5225-2066-5.ch007

El Faquih, L., & Fredj, M. (2017). Ontology-Based Framework for Quality in Configurable Process Models. *Journal of Electronic Commerce in Organizations*, *15*(2), 48–60. doi:10.4018/JECO.2017040104

Faisal, M. N., & Talib, F. (2017). Building Ambidextrous Supply Chains in SMEs: How to Tackle the Barriers? *International Journal of Information Systems and Supply Chain Management*, *10*(4), 80–100. doi:10.4018/IJISSCM.2017100105

Fernandes, T. M., Gomes, J., & Romão, M. (2017). Investments in E-Government: A Benefit Management Case Study. *International Journal of Electronic Government Research*, *13*(3), 1–17. doi:10.4018/IJEGR.2017070101

Figueira, L. M., Honrado, G. R., & Dionísio, M. S. (2021). Human Capital Management in the Tourism Industry in Portugal. In V. Costa, A. Moura, & M. Mira (Eds.), *Handbook of Research on Human Capital and People Management in the Tourism Industry* (pp. 1–19). IGI Global. doi:10.4018/978-1-7998-4318-4.ch001

Gao, S. S., Oreal, S., & Zhang, J. (2018). Contemporary Financial Risk Management Perceptions and Practices of Small-Sized Chinese Businesses. In I. Management Association (Ed.), Global Business Expansion: Concepts, Methodologies, Tools, and Applications (pp. 917-931). Hershey, PA: IGI Global. doi:10.4018/978-1-5225-5481-3.ch041

Garg, R., & Berning, S. C. (2017). Indigenous Chinese Management Philosophies: Key Concepts and Relevance for Modern Chinese Firms. In B. Christiansen & G. Koc (Eds.), *Transcontinental Strategies for Industrial Development and Economic Growth* (pp. 43–57). Hershey, PA: IGI Global. doi:10.4018/978-1-5225-2160-0.ch003

Gencer, Y. G. (2017). Supply Chain Management in Retailing Business. In U. Akkucuk (Ed.), *Ethics and Sustainability in Global Supply Chain Management* (pp. 197–210). Hershey, PA: IGI Global. doi:10.4018/978-1-5225-2036-8.ch011

Gera, R., Arora, S., & Malik, S. (2021). Emotional Labor in the Tourism Industry: Strategies, Antecedents, and Outcomes. In V. Costa, A. Moura, & M. Mira (Eds.), *Handbook of Research on Human Capital and People Management in the Tourism Industry* (pp. 73–91). IGI Global. https://doi.org/10.4018/978-1-7998-4318-4.ch004

Giacosa, E. (2018). The Increasing of the Regional Development Thanks to the Luxury Business Innovation. In L. Carvalho (Ed.), *Handbook of Research on Entrepreneurial Ecosystems and Social Dynamics in a Globalized World* (pp. 260–273). Hershey, PA: IGI Global. doi:10.4018/978-1-5225-3525-6.ch011

Glowka, G., Tusch, M., & Zehrer, A. (2021). The Risk Perception of Family Business Owner-Manager in the Tourism Industry: A Qualitative Comparison of the Intra-Firm Senior and Junior Generation. In A. Zehrer, G. Glowka, K. Schwaiger, & V. Ranacher-Lackner (Eds.), *Resiliency Models and Addressing Future Risks for Family Firms in the Tourism Industry* (pp. 126–153). IGI Global. https://doi.org/10.4018/978-1-7998-7352-5.ch006

Glykas, M., & George, J. (2017). Quality and Process Management Systems in the UAE Maritime Industry. *International Journal of Productivity Management and Assessment Technologies*, *5*(1), 20–39. doi:10.4018/IJPMAT.2017010102

Glykas, M., Valiris, G., Kokkinaki, A., & Koutsoukou, Z. (2018). Banking Business Process Management Implementation. *International Journal of Productivity Management and Assessment Technologies*, *6*(1), 50–69. doi:10.4018/IJPMAT.2018010104

Gomes, J., & Romão, M. (2017). The Balanced Scorecard: Keeping Updated and Aligned with Today's Business Trends. *International Journal of Productivity Management and Assessment Technologies*, *5*(2), 1–15. doi:10.4018/IJPMAT.2017070101

Gomes, J., & Romão, M. (2017). Aligning Information Systems and Technology with Benefit Management and Balanced Scorecard. In S. De Haes & W. Van Grembergen (Eds.), *Strategic IT Governance and Alignment in Business Settings* (pp. 112–131). Hershey, PA: IGI Global. doi:10.4018/978-1-5225-0861-8.ch005

Goyal, A. (2021). Communicating and Building Destination Brands With New Media. In M. Dinis, L. Bonixe, S. Lamy, & Z. Breda (Eds.), *Impact of New Media in Tourism* (pp. 1-20). IGI Global. https://doi.org/10.4018/978-1-7998-7095-1.ch001

Grefen, P., & Turetken, O. (2017). Advanced Business Process Management in Networked E-Business Scenarios. *International Journal of E-Business Research, 13*(4), 70–104. doi:10.4018/IJEBR.2017100105

Guasca, M., Van Broeck, A. M., & Vanneste, D. (2021). Tourism and the Social Reintegration of Colombian Ex-Combatants. In J. da Silva, Z. Breda, & F. Carbone (Eds.), *Role and Impact of Tourism in Peacebuilding and Conflict Transformation* (pp. 66-86). IGI Global. https://doi.org/10.4018/978-1-7998-5053-3.ch005

Haider, A., & Saetang, S. (2017). Strategic IT Alignment in Service Sector. In S. Rozenes & Y. Cohen (Eds.), *Handbook of Research on Strategic Alliances and Value Co-Creation in the Service Industry* (pp. 231–258). Hershey, PA: IGI Global. doi:10.4018/978-1-5225-2084-9.ch012

Hajilari, A. B., Ghadaksaz, M., & Fasghandis, G. S. (2017). Assessing Organizational Readiness for Implementing ERP System Using Fuzzy Expert System Approach. *International Journal of Enterprise Information Systems, 13*(1), 67–85. doi:10.4018/IJEIS.2017010105

Haldorai, A., Ramu, A., & Murugan, S. (2018). Social Aware Cognitive Radio Networks: Effectiveness of Social Networks as a Strategic Tool for Organizational Business Management. In H. Bansal, G. Shrivastava, G. Nguyen, & L. Stanciu (Eds.), *Social Network Analytics for Contemporary Business Organizations* (pp. 188–202). Hershey, PA: IGI Global. doi:10.4018/978-1-5225-5097-6.ch010

Hall, O. P. Jr. (2017). Social Media Driven Management Education. *International Journal of Knowledge-Based Organizations, 7*(2), 43–59. doi:10.4018/IJKBO.2017040104

Hanifah, H., Halim, H. A., Ahmad, N. H., & Vafaei-Zadeh, A. (2017). Innovation Culture as a Mediator Between Specific Human Capital and Innovation Performance Among Bumiputera SMEs in Malaysia. In N. Ahmad, T. Ramayah, H. Halim, & S. Rahman (Eds.), *Handbook of Research on Small and Medium Enterprises in Developing Countries* (pp. 261–279). Hershey, PA: IGI Global. doi:10.4018/978-1-5225-2165-5.ch012

Hartlieb, S., & Silvius, G. (2017). Handling Uncertainty in Project Management and Business Development: Similarities and Differences. In Y. Raydugin (Ed.), *Handbook of Research on Leveraging Risk and Uncertainties for Effective Project Management* (pp. 337–362). Hershey, PA: IGI Global. doi:10.4018/978-1-5225-1790-0.ch016

Hass, K. B. (2017). Living on the Edge: Managing Project Complexity. In Y. Raydugin (Ed.), *Handbook of Research on Leveraging Risk and Uncertainties for Effective Project Management* (pp. 177–201). Hershey, PA: IGI Global. doi:10.4018/978-1-5225-1790-0.ch009

Hawking, P., & Carmine Sellitto, C. (2017). Developing an Effective Strategy for Organizational Business Intelligence. In M. Tavana (Ed.), *Enterprise Information Systems and the Digitalization of Business Functions* (pp. 222–237). Hershey, PA: IGI Global. doi:10.4018/978-1-5225-2382-6.ch010

Hawking, P., & Sellitto, C. (2017). A Fast-Moving Consumer Goods Company and Business Intelligence Strategy Development. *International Journal of Enterprise Information Systems*, *13*(2), 22–33. doi:10.4018/IJEIS.2017040102

Hawking, P., & Sellitto, C. (2017). Business Intelligence Strategy: Two Case Studies. *International Journal of Business Intelligence Research*, *8*(2), 17–30. doi:10.4018/IJBIR.2017070102

Hee, W. J., Jalleh, G., Lai, H., & Lin, C. (2017). E-Commerce and IT Projects: Evaluation and Management Issues in Australian and Taiwanese Hospitals. *International Journal of Public Health Management and Ethics*, *2*(1), 69–90. doi:10.4018/IJPHME.2017010104

Hernandez, A. A. (2018). Exploring the Factors to Green IT Adoption of SMEs in the Philippines. *Journal of Cases on Information Technology*, *20*(2), 49–66. doi:10.4018/JCIT.2018040104

Hollman, A., Bickford, S., & Hollman, T. (2017). Cyber InSecurity: A Post-Mortem Attempt to Assess Cyber Problems from IT and Business Management Perspectives. *Journal of Cases on Information Technology*, *19*(3), 42–70. doi:10.4018/JCIT.2017070104

Ibrahim, F., & Zainin, N. M. (2021). Exploring the Technological Impacts: The Case of Museums in Brunei Darussalam. *International Journal of Tourism and Hospitality Management in the Digital Age*, *5*(1), 1–18. https://doi.org/10.4018/IJTHMDA.2021010101

Igbinakhase, I. (2017). Responsible and Sustainable Management Practices in Developing and Developed Business Environments. In Z. Fields (Ed.), *Collective Creativity for Responsible and Sustainable Business Practice* (pp. 180–207). Hershey, PA: IGI Global. doi:10.4018/978-1-5225-1823-5.ch010

Iwata, J. J., & Hoskins, R. G. (2017). Managing Indigenous Knowledge in Tanzania: A Business Perspective. In P. Jain & N. Mnjama (Eds.), *Managing Knowledge Resources and Records in Modern Organizations* (pp. 198–214). Hershey, PA: IGI Global. doi:10.4018/978-1-5225-1965-2.ch012

Jain, P. (2017). Ethical and Legal Issues in Knowledge Management Life-Cycle in Business. In P. Jain & N. Mnjama (Eds.), *Managing Knowledge Resources and Records in Modern Organizations* (pp. 82–101). Hershey, PA: IGI Global. doi:10.4018/978-1-5225-1965-2.ch006

James, S., & Hauli, E. (2017). Holistic Management Education at Tanzanian Rural Development Planning Institute. In N. Baporikar (Ed.), *Management Education for Global Leadership* (pp. 112–136). Hershey, PA: IGI Global. doi:10.4018/978-1-5225-1013-0.ch006

Janošková, M., Csikósová, A., & Čulková, K. (2018). Measurement of Company Performance as Part of Its Strategic Management. In R. Leon (Ed.), *Managerial Strategies for Business Sustainability During Turbulent Times* (pp. 309–335). Hershey, PA: IGI Global. doi:10.4018/978-1-5225-2716-9.ch017

Jean-Vasile, A., & Alecu, A. (2017). Theoretical and Practical Approaches in Understanding the Influences of Cost-Productivity-Profit Trinomial in Contemporary Enterprises. In A. Jean Vasile & D. Nicolò (Eds.), *Sustainable Entrepreneurship and Investments in the Green Economy* (pp. 28–62). Hershey, PA: IGI Global. doi:10.4018/978-1-5225-2075-7.ch002

Joia, L. A., & Correia, J. C. (2018). CIO Competencies From the IT Professional Perspective: Insights From Brazil. *Journal of Global Information Management, 26*(2), 74–103. doi:10.4018/JGIM.2018040104

Juma, A., & Mzera, N. (2017). Knowledge Management and Records Management and Competitive Advantage in Business. In P. Jain & N. Mnjama (Eds.), *Managing Knowledge Resources and Records in Modern Organizations* (pp. 15–28). Hershey, PA: IGI Global. doi:10.4018/978-1-5225-1965-2.ch002

K., I., & A, V. (2018). Monitoring and Auditing in the Cloud. In K. Munir (Ed.), *Cloud Computing Technologies for Green Enterprises* (pp. 318-350). Hershey, PA: IGI Global. https://doi.org/ doi:10.4018/978-1-5225-3038-1.ch013

Kabra, G., Ghosh, V., & Ramesh, A. (2018). Enterprise Integrated Business Process Management and Business Intelligence Framework for Business Process Sustainability. In A. Paul, D. Bhattacharyya, & S. Anand (Eds.), *Green Initiatives for Business Sustainability and Value Creation* (pp. 228–238). Hershey, PA: IGI Global. doi:10.4018/978-1-5225-2662-9.ch010

Kaoud, M. (2017). Investigation of Customer Knowledge Management: A Case Study Research. *International Journal of Service Science, Management, Engineering, and Technology*, *8*(2), 12–22. doi:10.4018/IJSSMET.2017040102

Katuu, S. (2018). A Comparative Assessment of Enterprise Content Management Maturity Models. In N. Gwangwava & M. Mutingi (Eds.), *E-Manufacturing and E-Service Strategies in Contemporary Organizations* (pp. 93–118). Hershey, PA: IGI Global. doi:10.4018/978-1-5225-3628-4.ch005

Khan, M. Y., & Abir, T. (2022). The Role of Social Media Marketing in the Tourism and Hospitality Industry: A Conceptual Study on Bangladesh. In C. Ramos, S. Quinteiro, & A. Gonçalves (Eds.), *ICT as Innovator Between Tourism and Culture* (pp. 213–229). IGI Global. https://doi.org/10.4018/978-1-7998-8165-0.ch013

Kinnunen, S., Ylä-Kujala, A., Marttonen-Arola, S., Kärri, T., & Baglee, D. (2018). Internet of Things in Asset Management: Insights from Industrial Professionals and Academia. *International Journal of Service Science, Management, Engineering, and Technology*, *9*(2), 104–119. doi:10.4018/IJSSMET.2018040105

Klein, A. Z., Sabino de Freitas, A., Machado, L., Freitas, J. C. Jr, Graziola, P. G. Jr, & Schlemmer, E. (2017). Virtual Worlds Applications for Management Education. In L. Tomei (Ed.), *Exploring the New Era of Technology-Infused Education* (pp. 279–299). Hershey, PA: IGI Global. doi:10.4018/978-1-5225-1709-2.ch017

Kővári, E., Saleh, M., & Steinbachné Hajmásy, G. (2022). The Impact of Corporate Digital Responsibility (CDR) on Internal Stakeholders' Satisfaction in Hungarian Upscale Hotels. In M. Valeri (Ed.), *New Governance and Management in Touristic Destinations* (pp. 35–51). IGI Global. https://doi.org/10.4018/978-1-6684-3889-3.ch003

Kożuch, B., & Jabłoński, A. (2017). Adopting the Concept of Business Models in Public Management. In M. Lewandowski & B. Kożuch (Eds.), *Public Sector Entrepreneurship and the Integration of Innovative Business Models* (pp. 10–46). Hershey, PA: IGI Global. doi:10.4018/978-1-5225-2215-7.ch002

Kumar, J., Adhikary, A., & Jha, A. (2017). Small Active Investors' Perceptions and Preferences Towards Tax Saving Mutual Fund Schemes in Eastern India: An Empirical Note. *International Journal of Asian Business and Information Management*, *8*(2), 35–45. doi:10.4018/IJABIM.2017040103

Latusi, S., & Fissore, M. (2021). Pilgrimage Routes to Happiness: Comparing the Camino de Santiago and Via Francigena. In A. Perinotto, V. Mayer, & J. Soares (Eds.), *Rebuilding and Restructuring the Tourism Industry: Infusion of Happiness and Quality of Life* (pp. 157–182). IGI Global. https://doi.org/10.4018/978-1-7998-7239-9.ch008

Lavassani, K. M., & Movahedi, B. (2017). Applications Driven Information Systems: Beyond Networks toward Business Ecosystems. *International Journal of Innovation in the Digital Economy*, *8*(1), 61–75. doi:10.4018/IJIDE.2017010104

Lazzareschi, V. H., & Brito, M. S. (2017). Strategic Information Management: Proposal of Business Project Model. In G. Jamil, A. Soares, & C. Pessoa (Eds.), *Handbook of Research on Information Management for Effective Logistics and Supply Chains* (pp. 59–88). Hershey, PA: IGI Global. doi:10.4018/978-1-5225-0973-8.ch004

Lechuga Sancho, M. P., & Martín Navarro, A. (2022). Evolution of the Literature on Social Responsibility in the Tourism Sector: A Systematic Literature Review. In G. Fernandes (Ed.), *Challenges and New Opportunities for Tourism in Inland Territories: Ecocultural Resources and Sustainable Initiatives* (pp. 169–186). IGI Global. https://doi.org/10.4018/978-1-7998-7339-6.ch010

Lederer, M., Kurz, M., & Lazarov, P. (2017). Usage and Suitability of Methods for Strategic Business Process Initiatives: A Multi Case Study Research. *International Journal of Productivity Management and Assessment Technologies*, *5*(1), 40–51. doi:10.4018/IJPMAT.2017010103

Lee, I. (2017). A Social Enterprise Business Model and a Case Study of Pacific Community Ventures (PCV). In V. Potocan, M. Üngan, & Z. Nedelko (Eds.), *Handbook of Research on Managerial Solutions in Non-Profit Organizations* (pp. 182–204). Hershey, PA: IGI Global. doi:10.4018/978-1-5225-0731-4.ch009

Leon, L. A., Seal, K. C., Przasnyski, Z. H., & Wiedenman, I. (2017). Skills and Competencies Required for Jobs in Business Analytics: A Content Analysis of Job Advertisements Using Text Mining. *International Journal of Business Intelligence Research*, *8*(1), 1–25. doi:10.4018/IJBIR.2017010101

Levy, C. L., & Elias, N. I. (2017). SOHO Users' Perceptions of Reliability and Continuity of Cloud-Based Services. In M. Moore (Ed.), *Cybersecurity Breaches and Issues Surrounding Online Threat Protection* (pp. 248–287). Hershey, PA: IGI Global. doi:10.4018/978-1-5225-1941-6.ch011

Levy, M. (2018). Change Management Serving Knowledge Management and Organizational Development: Reflections and Review. In N. Baporikar (Ed.), *Global Practices in Knowledge Management for Societal and Organizational Development* (pp. 256–270). Hershey, PA: IGI Global. doi:10.4018/978-1-5225-3009-1.ch012

Lewandowski, M. (2017). Public Organizations and Business Model Innovation: The Role of Public Service Design. In M. Lewandowski & B. Kożuch (Eds.), *Public Sector Entrepreneurship and the Integration of Innovative Business Models* (pp. 47–72). Hershey, PA: IGI Global. doi:10.4018/978-1-5225-2215-7.ch003

Lhannaoui, H., Kabbaj, M. I., & Bakkoury, Z. (2017). A Survey of Risk-Aware Business Process Modelling. *International Journal of Risk and Contingency Management, 6*(3), 14–26. doi:10.4018/IJRCM.2017070102

Li, J., Sun, W., Jiang, W., Yang, H., & Zhang, L. (2017). How the Nature of Exogenous Shocks and Crises Impact Company Performance?: The Effects of Industry Characteristics. *International Journal of Risk and Contingency Management, 6*(4), 40–55. doi:10.4018/IJRCM.2017100103

Lopez-Fernandez, M., Perez-Perez, M., Serrano-Bedia, A., & Cobo-Gonzalez, A. (2021). Small and Medium Tourism Enterprise Survival in Times of Crisis: "El Capricho de Gaudí. In D. Toubes & N. Araújo-Vila (Eds.), *Risk, Crisis, and Disaster Management in Small and Medium-Sized Tourism Enterprises* (pp. 103–129). IGI Global. doi:10.4018/978-1-7998-6996-2.ch005

Mahajan, A., Maidullah, S., & Hossain, M. R. (2022). Experience Toward Smart Tour Guide Apps in Travelling: An Analysis of Users' Reviews on Audio Odigos and Trip My Way. In R. Augusto Costa, F. Brandão, Z. Breda, & C. Costa (Eds.), *Planning and Managing the Experience Economy in Tourism* (pp. 255-273). IGI Global. https://doi.org/10.4018/978-1-7998-8775-1.ch014

Malega, P. (2017). Small and Medium Enterprises in the Slovak Republic: Status and Competitiveness of SMEs in the Global Markets and Possibilities of Optimization. In M. Vemić (Ed.), *Optimal Management Strategies in Small and Medium Enterprises* (pp. 102–124). Hershey, PA: IGI Global. doi:10.4018/978-1-5225-1949-2.ch006

Malewska, K. M. (2017). Intuition in Decision-Making on the Example of a Non-Profit Organization. In V. Potocan, M. Üngan, & Z. Nedelko (Eds.), *Handbook of Research on Managerial Solutions in Non-Profit Organizations* (pp. 378–399). Hershey, PA: IGI Global. doi:10.4018/978-1-5225-0731-4.ch018

Maroofi, F. (2017). Entrepreneurial Orientation and Organizational Learning Ability Analysis for Innovation and Firm Performance. In N. Baporikar (Ed.), *Innovation and Shifting Perspectives in Management Education* (pp. 144–165). Hershey, PA: IGI Global. doi:10.4018/978-1-5225-1019-2.ch007

Marques, M., Moleiro, D., Brito, T. M., & Marques, T. (2021). Customer Relationship Management as an Important Relationship Marketing Tool: The Case of the Hospitality Industry in Estoril Coast. In M. Dinis, L. Bonixe, S. Lamy, & Z. Breda (Eds.), Impact of New Media in Tourism (pp. 39-56). IGI Global. https://doi.org/doi:10.4018/978-1-7998-7095-1.ch003

Martins, P. V., & Zacarias, M. (2017). A Web-based Tool for Business Process Improvement. *International Journal of Web Portals*, *9*(2), 68–84. doi:10.4018/IJWP.2017070104

Matthies, B., & Coners, A. (2017). Exploring the Conceptual Nature of e-Business Projects. *Journal of Electronic Commerce in Organizations*, *15*(3), 33–63. doi:10.4018/JECO.2017070103

Mayer, V. F., Fraga, C. C., & Silva, L. C. (2021). Contributions of Neurosciences to Studies of Well-Being in Tourism. In A. Perinotto, V. Mayer, & J. Soares (Eds.), *Rebuilding and Restructuring the Tourism Industry: Infusion of Happiness and Quality of Life* (pp. 108–128). IGI Global. https://doi.org/10.4018/978-1-7998-7239-9.ch006

McKee, J. (2018). Architecture as a Tool to Solve Business Planning Problems. In M. Khosrow-Pour, D.B.A. (Ed.), Encyclopedia of Information Science and Technology, Fourth Edition (pp. 573-586). Hershey, PA: IGI Global. doi:10.4018/978-1-5225-2255-3.ch050

McMurray, A. J., Cross, J., & Caponecchia, C. (2018). The Risk Management Profession in Australia: Business Continuity Plan Practices. In N. Bajgoric (Ed.), *Always-On Enterprise Information Systems for Modern Organizations* (pp. 112–129). Hershey, PA: IGI Global. doi:10.4018/978-1-5225-3704-5.ch006

Meddah, I. H., & Belkadi, K. (2018). Mining Patterns Using Business Process Management. In R. Hamou (Ed.), *Handbook of Research on Biomimicry in Information Retrieval and Knowledge Management* (pp. 78–89). Hershey, PA: IGI Global. doi:10.4018/978-1-5225-3004-6.ch005

Melian, A. G., & Camprubí, R. (2021). The Accessibility of Museum Websites: The Case of Barcelona. In C. Eusébio, L. Teixeira, & M. Carneiro (Eds.), *ICT Tools and Applications for Accessible Tourism* (pp. 234–255). IGI Global. https://doi.org/10.4018/978-1-7998-6428-8.ch011

Mendes, L. (2017). TQM and Knowledge Management: An Integrated Approach Towards Tacit Knowledge Management. In D. Jaziri-Bouagina & G. Jamil (Eds.), *Handbook of Research on Tacit Knowledge Management for Organizational Success* (pp. 236–263). Hershey, PA: IGI Global. doi:10.4018/978-1-5225-2394-9.ch009

Menezes, V. D., & Cavagnaro, E. (2021). Communicating Sustainable Initiatives in the Hotel Industry: The Case of the Hotel Jakarta Amsterdam. In F. Brandão, Z. Breda, R. Costa, & C. Costa (Eds.), *Handbook of Research on the Role of Tourism in Achieving Sustainable Development Goals* (pp. 224-234). IGI Global. https://doi.org/10.4018/978-1-7998-5691-7.ch013

Menezes, V. D., & Cavagnaro, E. (2021). Communicating Sustainable Initiatives in the Hotel Industry: The Case of the Hotel Jakarta Amsterdam. In F. Brandão, Z. Breda, R. Costa, & C. Costa (Eds.), *Handbook of Research on the Role of Tourism in Achieving Sustainable Development Goals* (pp. 224-234). IGI Global. https://doi.org/10.4018/978-1-7998-5691-7.ch013

Mitas, O., Bastiaansen, M., & Boode, W. (2022). If You're Happy, I'm Happy: Emotion Contagion at a Tourist Information Center. In R. Augusto Costa, F. Brandão, Z. Breda, & C. Costa (Eds.), *Planning and Managing the Experience Economy in Tourism* (pp. 122-140). IGI Global. https://doi.org/10.4018/978-1-7998-8775-1.ch007

Mnjama, N. M. (2017). Preservation of Recorded Information in Public and Private Sector Organizations. In P. Jain & N. Mnjama (Eds.), *Managing Knowledge Resources and Records in Modern Organizations* (pp. 149–167). Hershey, PA: IGI Global. doi:10.4018/978-1-5225-1965-2.ch009

Mokoqama, M., & Fields, Z. (2017). Principles of Responsible Management Education (PRME): Call for Responsible Management Education. In Z. Fields (Ed.), *Collective Creativity for Responsible and Sustainable Business Practice* (pp. 229–241). Hershey, PA: IGI Global. doi:10.4018/978-1-5225-1823-5.ch012

Monteiro, A., Lopes, S., & Carbone, F. (2021). Academic Mobility: Bridging Tourism and Peace Education. In J. da Silva, Z. Breda, & F. Carbone (Eds.), *Role and Impact of Tourism in Peacebuilding and Conflict Transformation* (pp. 275-301). IGI Global. https://doi.org/10.4018/978-1-7998-5053-3.ch016

Muniapan, B. (2017). Philosophy and Management: The Relevance of Vedanta in Management. In P. Ordóñez de Pablos (Ed.), *Managerial Strategies and Solutions for Business Success in Asia* (pp. 124–139). Hershey, PA: IGI Global. doi:10.4018/978-1-5225-1886-0.ch007

Murad, S. E., & Dowaji, S. (2017). Using Value-Based Approach for Managing Cloud-Based Services. In A. Turuk, B. Sahoo, & S. Addya (Eds.), *Resource Management and Efficiency in Cloud Computing Environments* (pp. 33–60). Hershey, PA: IGI Global. doi:10.4018/978-1-5225-1721-4.ch002

Mutahar, A. M., Daud, N. M., Thurasamy, R., Isaac, O., & Abdulsalam, R. (2018). The Mediating of Perceived Usefulness and Perceived Ease of Use: The Case of Mobile Banking in Yemen. *International Journal of Technology Diffusion*, *9*(2), 21–40. doi:10.4018/IJTD.2018040102

Naidoo, V. (2017). E-Learning and Management Education at African Universities. In N. Baporikar (Ed.), *Management Education for Global Leadership* (pp. 181–201). Hershey, PA: IGI Global. doi:10.4018/978-1-5225-1013-0.ch009

Naidoo, V., & Igbinakhase, I. (2018). Opportunities and Challenges of Knowledge Retention in SMEs. In N. Baporikar (Ed.), *Knowledge Integration Strategies for Entrepreneurship and Sustainability* (pp. 70–94). Hershey, PA: IGI Global. doi:10.4018/978-1-5225-5115-7.ch004

Naumov, N., & Costandachi, G. (2021). Creativity and Entrepreneurship: Gastronomic Tourism in Mexico. In J. Soares (Ed.), *Innovation and Entrepreneurial Opportunities in Community Tourism* (pp. 90–108). IGI Global. https://doi.org/10.4018/978-1-7998-4855-4.ch006

Nayak, S., & Prabhu, N. (2017). Paradigm Shift in Management Education: Need for a Cross Functional Perspective. In N. Baporikar (Ed.), *Management Education for Global Leadership* (pp. 241–255). Hershey, PA: IGI Global. doi:10.4018/978-1-5225-1013-0.ch012

Nedelko, Z., & Potocan, V. (2017). Management Solutions in Non-Profit Organizations: Case of Slovenia. In V. Potocan, M. Üngan, & Z. Nedelko (Eds.), *Handbook of Research on Managerial Solutions in Non-Profit Organizations* (pp. 1–22). Hershey, PA: IGI Global. doi:10.4018/978-1-5225-0731-4.ch001

Nedelko, Z., & Potocan, V. (2017). Priority of Management Tools Utilization among Managers: International Comparison. In V. Wang (Ed.), *Encyclopedia of Strategic Leadership and Management* (pp. 1083–1094). Hershey, PA: IGI Global. doi:10.4018/978-1-5225-1049-9.ch075

Nedelko, Z., Raudeliūnienė, J., & Črešnar, R. (2018). Knowledge Dynamics in Supply Chain Management. In N. Baporikar (Ed.), *Knowledge Integration Strategies for Entrepreneurship and Sustainability* (pp. 150–166). Hershey, PA: IGI Global. doi:10.4018/978-1-5225-5115-7.ch008

Nguyen, H. T., & Hipsher, S. A. (2018). Innovation and Creativity Used by Private Sector Firms in a Resources-Constrained Environment. In S. Hipsher (Ed.), *Examining the Private Sector's Role in Wealth Creation and Poverty Reduction* (pp. 219–238). Hershey, PA: IGI Global. doi:10.4018/978-1-5225-3117-3.ch010

Obicci, P. A. (2017). Risk Sharing in a Partnership. In *Risk Management Strategies in Public-Private Partnerships* (pp. 115–152). Hershey, PA: IGI Global. doi:10.4018/978-1-5225-2503-5.ch004

Obidallah, W. J., & Raahemi, B. (2017). Managing Changes in Service Oriented Virtual Organizations: A Structural and Procedural Framework to Facilitate the Process of Change. *Journal of Electronic Commerce in Organizations, 15*(1), 59–83. doi:10.4018/JECO.2017010104

Ojo, O. (2017). Impact of Innovation on the Entrepreneurial Success in Selected Business Enterprises in South-West Nigeria. *International Journal of Innovation in the Digital Economy*, *8*(2), 29–38. doi:10.4018/IJIDE.2017040103

Okdinawati, L., Simatupang, T. M., & Sunitiyoso, Y. (2017). Multi-Agent Reinforcement Learning for Value Co-Creation of Collaborative Transportation Management (CTM). *International Journal of Information Systems and Supply Chain Management, 10*(3), 84–95. doi:10.4018/IJISSCM.2017070105

Olivera, V. A., & Carrillo, I. M. (2021). Organizational Culture: A Key Element for the Development of Mexican Micro and Small Tourist Companies. In J. Soares (Ed.), *Innovation and Entrepreneurial Opportunities in Community Tourism* (pp. 227–242). IGI Global. doi:10.4018/978-1-7998-4855-4.ch013

Ossorio, M. (2022). Corporate Museum Experiences in Enogastronomic Tourism. In R. Augusto Costa, F. Brandão, Z. Breda, & C. Costa (Eds.), Planning and Managing the Experience Economy in Tourism (pp. 107-121). IGI Global. https://doi.org/doi:10.4018/978-1-7998-8775-1.ch006

Ossorio, M. (2022). Enogastronomic Tourism in Times of Pandemic. In G. Fernandes (Ed.), *Challenges and New Opportunities for Tourism in Inland Territories: Ecocultural Resources and Sustainable Initiatives* (pp. 241–255). IGI Global. https://doi.org/10.4018/978-1-7998-7339-6.ch014

Özekici, Y. K. (2022). ICT as an Acculturative Agent and Its Role in the Tourism Context: Introduction, Acculturation Theory, Progress of the Acculturation Theory in Extant Literature. In C. Ramos, S. Quinteiro, & A. Gonçalves (Eds.), *ICT as Innovator Between Tourism and Culture* (pp. 42–66). IGI Global. https://doi.org/10.4018/978-1-7998-8165-0.ch004

Pal, K. (2018). Building High Quality Big Data-Based Applications in Supply Chains. In A. Kumar & S. Saurav (Eds.), *Supply Chain Management Strategies and Risk Assessment in Retail Environments* (pp. 1–24). Hershey, PA: IGI Global. doi:10.4018/978-1-5225-3056-5.ch001

Palos-Sanchez, P. R., & Correia, M. B. (2018). Perspectives of the Adoption of Cloud Computing in the Tourism Sector. In J. Rodrigues, C. Ramos, P. Cardoso, & C. Henriques (Eds.), *Handbook of Research on Technological Developments for Cultural Heritage and eTourism Applications* (pp. 377–400). Hershey, PA: IGI Global. doi:10.4018/978-1-5225-2927-9.ch018

Papadopoulou, G. (2021). Promoting Gender Equality and Women Empowerment in the Tourism Sector. In F. Brandão, Z. Breda, R. Costa, & C. Costa (Eds.), Handbook of Research on the Role of Tourism in Achieving Sustainable Development Goals (pp. 152-174). IGI Global. https://doi.org/ doi:10.4018/978-1-7998-5691-7.ch009

Papp-Váry, Á. F., & Tóth, T. Z. (2022). Analysis of Budapest as a Film Tourism Destination. In R. Baleiro & R. Pereira (Eds.), *Global Perspectives on Literary Tourism and Film-Induced Tourism* (pp. 257-279). IGI Global. https://doi.org/10.4018/978-1-7998-8262-6.ch014

Patiño, B. E. (2017). New Generation Management by Convergence and Individual Identity: A Systemic and Human-Oriented Approach. In N. Baporikar (Ed.), *Innovation and Shifting Perspectives in Management Education* (pp. 119–143). Hershey, PA: IGI Global. doi:10.4018/978-1-5225-1019-2.ch006

Patro, C. S. (2021). Digital Tourism: Influence of E-Marketing Technology. In M. Dinis, L. Bonixe, S. Lamy, & Z. Breda (Eds.), *Impact of New Media in Tourism* (pp. 234-254). IGI Global. https://doi.org/10.4018/978-1-7998-7095-1.ch014

Pawliczek, A., & Rössler, M. (2017). Knowledge of Management Tools and Systems in SMEs: Knowledge Transfer in Management. In A. Bencsik (Ed.), *Knowledge Management Initiatives and Strategies in Small and Medium Enterprises* (pp. 180–203). Hershey, PA: IGI Global. doi:10.4018/978-1-5225-1642-2.ch009

Pejic-Bach, M., Omazic, M. A., Aleksic, A., & Zoroja, J. (2018). Knowledge-Based Decision Making: A Multi-Case Analysis. In R. Leon (Ed.), *Managerial Strategies for Business Sustainability During Turbulent Times* (pp. 160–184). Hershey, PA: IGI Global. doi:10.4018/978-1-5225-2716-9.ch009

Perano, M., Hysa, X., & Calabrese, M. (2018). Strategic Planning, Cultural Context, and Business Continuity Management: Business Cases in the City of Shkoder. In A. Presenza & L. Sheehan (Eds.), *Geopolitics and Strategic Management in the Global Economy* (pp. 57–77). Hershey, PA: IGI Global. doi:10.4018/978-1-5225-2673-5.ch004

Pereira, R., Mira da Silva, M., & Lapão, L. V. (2017). IT Governance Maturity Patterns in Portuguese Healthcare. In S. De Haes & W. Van Grembergen (Eds.), *Strategic IT Governance and Alignment in Business Settings* (pp. 24–52). Hershey, PA: IGI Global. doi:10.4018/978-1-5225-0861-8.ch002

Pérez-Uribe, R. I., Torres, D. A., Jurado, S. P., & Prada, D. M. (2018). Cloud Tools for the Development of Project Management in SMEs. In R. Perez-Uribe, C. Salcedo-Perez, & D. Ocampo-Guzman (Eds.), *Handbook of Research on Intrapreneurship and Organizational Sustainability in SMEs* (pp. 95–120). Hershey, PA: IGI Global. doi:10.4018/978-1-5225-3543-0.ch005

Petrisor, I., & Cozmiuc, D. (2017). Global Supply Chain Management Organization at Siemens in the Advent of Industry 4.0. In L. Saglietto & C. Cezanne (Eds.), *Global Intermediation and Logistics Service Providers* (pp. 123–142). Hershey, PA: IGI Global. doi:10.4018/978-1-5225-2133-4.ch007

Pierce, J. M., Velliaris, D. M., & Edwards, J. (2017). A Living Case Study: A Journey Not a Destination. In N. Silton (Ed.), *Exploring the Benefits of Creativity in Education, Media, and the Arts* (pp. 158–178). Hershey, PA: IGI Global. doi:10.4018/978-1-5225-0504-4.ch008

Pipia, S., & Pipia, S. (2021). Challenges of Religious Tourism in the Conflict Region: An Example of Jerusalem. In E. Alaverdov & M. Bari (Eds.), *Global Development of Religious Tourism* (pp. 135-148). IGI Global. https://doi.org/10.4018/978-1-7998-5792-1.ch009

Poulaki, P., Kritikos, A., Vasilakis, N., & Valeri, M. (2022). The Contribution of Female Creativity to the Development of Gastronomic Tourism in Greece: The Case of the Island of Naxos in the South Aegean Region. In M. Valeri (Ed.), *New Governance and Management in Touristic Destinations* (pp. 246–258). IGI Global. https://doi.org/10.4018/978-1-6684-3889-3.ch015

Radosavljevic, M., & Andjelkovic, A. (2017). Multi-Criteria Decision Making Approach for Choosing Business Process for the Improvement: Upgrading of the Six Sigma Methodology. In J. Stanković, P. Delias, S. Marinković, & S. Rochhia (Eds.), *Tools and Techniques for Economic Decision Analysis* (pp. 225–247). Hershey, PA: IGI Global. doi:10.4018/978-1-5225-0959-2.ch011

Radovic, V. M. (2017). Corporate Sustainability and Responsibility and Disaster Risk Reduction: A Serbian Overview. In M. Camilleri (Ed.), *CSR 2.0 and the New Era of Corporate Citizenship* (pp. 147–164). Hershey, PA: IGI Global. doi:10.4018/978-1-5225-1842-6.ch008

Raghunath, K. M., Devi, S. L., & Patro, C. S. (2018). Impact of Risk Assessment Models on Risk Factors: A Holistic Outlook. In K. Strang, M. Korstanje, & N. Vajjhala (Eds.), *Research, Practices, and Innovations in Global Risk and Contingency Management* (pp. 134–153). Hershey, PA: IGI Global. doi:10.4018/978-1-5225-4754-9.ch008

Raman, A., & Goyal, D. P. (2017). Extending IMPLEMENT Framework for Enterprise Information Systems Implementation to Information System Innovation. In M. Tavana (Ed.), *Enterprise Information Systems and the Digitalization of Business Functions* (pp. 137–177). Hershey, PA: IGI Global. doi:10.4018/978-1-5225-2382-6.ch007

Rao, Y., & Zhang, Y. (2017). The Construction and Development of Academic Library Digital Special Subject Databases. In L. Ruan, Q. Zhu, & Y. Ye (Eds.), *Academic Library Development and Administration in China* (pp. 163–183). Hershey, PA: IGI Global. doi:10.4018/978-1-5225-0550-1.ch010

Ravasan, A. Z., Mohammadi, M. M., & Hamidi, H. (2018). An Investigation Into the Critical Success Factors of Implementing Information Technology Service Management Frameworks. In K. Jakobs (Ed.), *Corporate and Global Standardization Initiatives in Contemporary Society* (pp. 200–218). Hershey, PA: IGI Global. doi:10.4018/978-1-5225-5320-5.ch009

Rezaie, S., Mirabedini, S. J., & Abtahi, A. (2018). Designing a Model for Implementation of Business Intelligence in the Banking Industry. *International Journal of Enterprise Information Systems, 14*(1), 77–103. doi:10.4018/IJEIS.2018010105

Richards, V., Matthews, N., Williams, O. J., & Khan, Z. (2021). The Challenges of Accessible Tourism Information Systems for Tourists With Vision Impairment: Sensory Communications Beyond the Screen. In C. Eusébio, L. Teixeira, & M. Carneiro (Eds.), *ICT Tools and Applications for Accessible Tourism* (pp. 26–54). IGI Global. https://doi.org/10.4018/978-1-7998-6428-8.ch002

Rodrigues de Souza Neto, V., & Marques, O. (2021). Rural Tourism Fostering Welfare Through Sustainable Development: A Conceptual Approach. In A. Perinotto, V. Mayer, & J. Soares (Eds.), *Rebuilding and Restructuring the Tourism Industry: Infusion of Happiness and Quality of Life* (pp. 38–57). IGI Global. https://doi.org/10.4018/978-1-7998-7239-9.ch003

Romano, L., Grimaldi, R., & Colasuonno, F. S. (2017). Demand Management as a Success Factor in Project Portfolio Management. In L. Romano (Ed.), *Project Portfolio Management Strategies for Effective Organizational Operations* (pp. 202–219). Hershey, PA: IGI Global. doi:10.4018/978-1-5225-2151-8.ch008

Rubio-Escuderos, L., & García-Andreu, H. (2021). Competitiveness Factors of Accessible Tourism E-Travel Agencies. In C. Eusébio, L. Teixeira, & M. Carneiro (Eds.), *ICT Tools and Applications for Accessible Tourism* (pp. 196–217). IGI Global. https://doi.org/10.4018/978-1-7998-6428-8.ch009

Rucci, A. C., Porto, N., Darcy, S., & Becka, L. (2021). Smart and Accessible Cities?: Not Always – The Case for Accessible Tourism Initiatives in Buenos Aries and Sydney. In C. Eusébio, L. Teixeira, & M. Carneiro (Eds.), *ICT Tools and Applications for Accessible Tourism* (pp. 115–145). IGI Global. https://doi.org/10.4018/978-1-7998-6428-8.ch006

Ruhi, U. (2018). Towards an Interdisciplinary Socio-Technical Definition of Virtual Communities. In M. Khosrow-Pour, D.B.A. (Ed.), Encyclopedia of Information Science and Technology, Fourth Edition (pp. 4278-4295). Hershey, PA: IGI Global. doi:10.4018/978-1-5225-2255-3.ch371

Ryan, L., Catena, M., Ros, P., & Stephens, S. (2021). Designing Entrepreneurial Ecosystems to Support Resource Management in the Tourism Industry. In V. Costa, A. Moura, & M. Mira (Eds.), *Handbook of Research on Human Capital and People Management in the Tourism Industry* (pp. 265–281). IGI Global. https://doi.org/10.4018/978-1-7998-4318-4.ch013

Sabuncu, I. (2021). Understanding Tourist Perceptions and Expectations During Pandemic Through Social Media Big Data. In M. Demir, A. Dalgıç, & F. Ergen (Eds.), *Handbook of Research on the Impacts and Implications of COVID-19 on the Tourism Industry* (pp. 330–350). IGI Global. https://doi.org/10.4018/978-1-7998-8231-2.ch016

Safari, M. R., & Jiang, Q. (2018). The Theory and Practice of IT Governance Maturity and Strategies Alignment: Evidence From Banking Industry. *Journal of Global Information Management*, *26*(2), 127–146. doi:10.4018/JGIM.2018040106

Sahoo, J., Pati, B., & Mohanty, B. (2017). Knowledge Management as an Academic Discipline: An Assessment. In B. Gunjal (Ed.), *Managing Knowledge and Scholarly Assets in Academic Libraries* (pp. 99–126). Hershey, PA: IGI Global. doi:10.4018/978-1-5225-1741-2.ch005

Saini, D. (2017). Relevance of Teaching Values and Ethics in Management Education. In N. Baporikar (Ed.), *Management Education for Global Leadership* (pp. 90–111). Hershey, PA: IGI Global. doi:10.4018/978-1-5225-1013-0.ch005

Sambhanthan, A. (2017). Assessing and Benchmarking Sustainability in Organisations: An Integrated Conceptual Model. *International Journal of Systems and Service-Oriented Engineering*, *7*(4), 22–43. doi:10.4018/IJSSOE.2017100102

Sambhanthan, A., & Potdar, V. (2017). A Study of the Parameters Impacting Sustainability in Information Technology Organizations. *International Journal of Knowledge-Based Organizations*, *7*(3), 27–39. doi:10.4018/IJKBO.2017070103

Sánchez-Fernández, M. D., & Manríquez, M. R. (2018). The Entrepreneurial Spirit Based on Social Values: The Digital Generation. In P. Isaias & L. Carvalho (Eds.), *User Innovation and the Entrepreneurship Phenomenon in the Digital Economy* (pp. 173–193). Hershey, PA: IGI Global. doi:10.4018/978-1-5225-2826-5.ch009

Sanchez-Ruiz, L., & Blanco, B. (2017). Process Management for SMEs: Barriers, Enablers, and Benefits. In M. Vemić (Ed.), *Optimal Management Strategies in Small and Medium Enterprises* (pp. 293–319). Hershey, PA: IGI Global. doi:10.4018/978-1-5225-1949-2.ch014

Sanz, L. F., Gómez-Pérez, J., & Castillo-Martinez, A. (2018). Analysis of the European ICT Competence Frameworks. In V. Ahuja & S. Rathore (Eds.), *Multidisciplinary Perspectives on Human Capital and Information Technology Professionals* (pp. 225–245). Hershey, PA: IGI Global. doi:10.4018/978-1-5225-5297-0.ch012

Sarvepalli, A., & Godin, J. (2017). Business Process Management in the Classroom. *Journal of Cases on Information Technology*, *19*(2), 17–28. doi:10.4018/JCIT.2017040102

Saxena, G. G., & Saxena, A. (2021). Host Community Role in Medical Tourism Development. In M. Singh & S. Kumaran (Eds.), *Growth of the Medical Tourism Industry and Its Impact on Society: Emerging Research and Opportunities* (pp. 105–127). IGI Global. https://doi.org/10.4018/978-1-7998-3427-4.ch006

Saygili, E. E., Ozturkoglu, Y., & Kocakulah, M. C. (2017). End Users' Perceptions of Critical Success Factors in ERP Applications. *International Journal of Enterprise Information Systems*, *13*(4), 58–75. doi:10.4018/IJEIS.2017100104

Saygili, E. E., & Saygili, A. T. (2017). Contemporary Issues in Enterprise Information Systems: A Critical Review of CSFs in ERP Implementations. In M. Tavana (Ed.), *Enterprise Information Systems and the Digitalization of Business Functions* (pp. 120–136). Hershey, PA: IGI Global. doi:10.4018/978-1-5225-2382-6.ch006

Schwaiger, K. M., & Zehrer, A. (2021). The COVID-19 Pandemic and Organizational Resilience in Hospitality Family Firms: A Qualitative Approach. In A. Zehrer, G. Glowka, K. Schwaiger, & V. Ranacher-Lackner (Eds.), *Resiliency Models and Addressing Future Risks for Family Firms in the Tourism Industry* (pp. 32–49). IGI Global. https://doi.org/10.4018/978-1-7998-7352-5.ch002

Scott, N., & Campos, A. C. (2022). Cognitive Science of Tourism Experiences. In R. Augusto Costa, F. Brandão, Z. Breda, & C. Costa (Eds.), Planning and Managing the Experience Economy in Tourism (pp. 1-21). IGI Global. https://doi.org/ doi:10.4018/978-1-7998-8775-1.ch001

Seidenstricker, S., & Antonino, A. (2018). Business Model Innovation-Oriented Technology Management for Emergent Technologies. In M. Khosrow-Pour, D.B.A. (Ed.), Encyclopedia of Information Science and Technology, Fourth Edition (pp. 4560-4569). Hershey, PA: IGI Global. doi:10.4018/978-1-5225-2255-3.ch396

Selvi, M. S. (2021). Changes in Tourism Sales and Marketing Post COVID-19. In M. Demir, A. Dalgıç, & F. Ergen (Eds.), *Handbook of Research on the Impacts and Implications of COVID-19 on the Tourism Industry* (pp. 437–460). IGI Global. doi:10.4018/978-1-7998-8231-2.ch021

Senaratne, S., & Gunarathne, A. D. (2017). Excellence Perspective for Management Education from a Global Accountants' Hub in Asia. In N. Baporikar (Ed.), *Management Education for Global Leadership* (pp. 158–180). Hershey, PA: IGI Global. doi:10.4018/978-1-5225-1013-0.ch008

Sensuse, D. I., & Cahyaningsih, E. (2018). Knowledge Management Models: A Summative Review. *International Journal of Information Systems in the Service Sector*, *10*(1), 71–100. doi:10.4018/IJISSS.2018010105

Seth, M., Goyal, D., & Kiran, R. (2017). Diminution of Impediments in Implementation of Supply Chain Management Information System for Enhancing its Effectiveness in Indian Automobile Industry. *Journal of Global Information Management*, *25*(3), 1–20. doi:10.4018/JGIM.2017070101

Seyal, A. H., & Rahman, M. N. (2017). Investigating Impact of Inter-Organizational Factors in Measuring ERP Systems Success: Bruneian Perspectives. In M. Tavana (Ed.), *Enterprise Information Systems and the Digitalization of Business Functions* (pp. 178–204). Hershey, PA: IGI Global. doi:10.4018/978-1-5225-2382-6.ch008

Shaqrah, A. A. (2018). Analyzing Business Intelligence Systems Based on 7s Model of McKinsey. *International Journal of Business Intelligence Research*, *9*(1), 53–63. doi:10.4018/IJBIR.2018010104

Sharma, A. J. (2017). Enhancing Sustainability through Experiential Learning in Management Education. In N. Baporikar (Ed.), *Management Education for Global Leadership* (pp. 256–274). Hershey, PA: IGI Global. doi:10.4018/978-1-5225-1013-0.ch013

Shetty, K. P. (2017). Responsible Global Leadership: Ethical Challenges in Management Education. In N. Baporikar (Ed.), *Innovation and Shifting Perspectives in Management Education* (pp. 194–223). Hershey, PA: IGI Global. doi:10.4018/978-1-5225-1019-2.ch009

Sinthupundaja, J., & Kohda, Y. (2017). Effects of Corporate Social Responsibility and Creating Shared Value on Sustainability. *International Journal of Sustainable Entrepreneurship and Corporate Social Responsibility*, *2*(1), 27–38. doi:10.4018/IJSECSR.2017010103

Škarica, I., & Hrgović, A. V. (2018). Implementation of Total Quality Management Principles in Public Health Institutes in the Republic of Croatia. *International Journal of Productivity Management and Assessment Technologies*, *6*(1), 1–16. doi:10.4018/IJPMAT.2018010101

Skokic, V. (2021). How Small Hotel Owners Practice Resilience: Longitudinal Study Among Small Family Hotels in Croatia. In A. Zehrer, G. Glowka, K. Schwaiger, & V. Ranacher-Lackner (Eds.), *Resiliency Models and Addressing Future Risks for Family Firms in the Tourism Industry* (pp. 50–73). IGI Global. doi:10.4018/978-1-7998-7352-5.ch003

Smuts, H., Kotzé, P., Van der Merwe, A., & Loock, M. (2017). Framework for Managing Shared Knowledge in an Information Systems Outsourcing Context. *International Journal of Knowledge Management*, *13*(4), 1–30. doi:10.4018/IJKM.2017100101

Sousa, M. J., Cruz, R., Dias, I., & Caracol, C. (2017). Information Management Systems in the Supply Chain. In G. Jamil, A. Soares, & C. Pessoa (Eds.), *Handbook of Research on Information Management for Effective Logistics and Supply Chains* (pp. 469–485). Hershey, PA: IGI Global. doi:10.4018/978-1-5225-0973-8.ch025

Spremic, M., Turulja, L., & Bajgoric, N. (2018). Two Approaches in Assessing Business Continuity Management Attitudes in the Organizational Context. In N. Bajgoric (Ed.), *Always-On Enterprise Information Systems for Modern Organizations* (pp. 159–183). Hershey, PA: IGI Global. doi:10.4018/978-1-5225-3704-5.ch008

Steenkamp, A. L. (2018). Some Insights in Computer Science and Information Technology. In *Examining the Changing Role of Supervision in Doctoral Research Projects: Emerging Research and Opportunities* (pp. 113–133). Hershey, PA: IGI Global. doi:10.4018/978-1-5225-2610-0.ch005

Stipanović, C., Rudan, E., & Zubović, V. (2022). Reaching the New Tourist Through Creativity: Sustainable Development Challenges in Croatian Coastal Towns. In M. Valeri (Ed.), *New Governance and Management in Touristic Destinations* (pp. 231–245). IGI Global. https://doi.org/10.4018/978-1-6684-3889-3.ch014

Tabach, A., & Croteau, A. (2017). Configurations of Information Technology Governance Practices and Business Unit Performance. *International Journal of IT/Business Alignment and Governance*, *8*(2), 1–27. doi:10.4018/IJITBAG.2017070101

Talaue, G. M., & Iqbal, T. (2017). Assessment of e-Business Mode of Selected Private Universities in the Philippines and Pakistan. *International Journal of Online Marketing*, *7*(4), 63–77. doi:10.4018/IJOM.2017100105

Tam, G. C. (2017). Project Manager Sustainability Competence. In *Managerial Strategies and Green Solutions for Project Sustainability* (pp. 178–207). Hershey, PA: IGI Global. doi:10.4018/978-1-5225-2371-0.ch008

Tambo, T. (2018). Fashion Retail Innovation: About Context, Antecedents, and Outcome in Technological Change Projects. In I. Management Association (Ed.), Fashion and Textiles: Breakthroughs in Research and Practice (pp. 233-260). Hershey, PA: IGI Global. https://doi.org/ doi:10.4018/978-1-5225-3432-7.ch010

Tantau, A. D., & Frăţilă, L. C. (2018). Information and Management System for Renewable Energy Business. In *Entrepreneurship and Business Development in the Renewable Energy Sector* (pp. 200–244). Hershey, PA: IGI Global. doi:10.4018/978-1-5225-3625-3.ch006

Teixeira, N., Pardal, P. N., & Rafael, B. G. (2018). Internationalization, Financial Performance, and Organizational Challenges: A Success Case in Portugal. In L. Carvalho (Ed.), *Handbook of Research on Entrepreneurial Ecosystems and Social Dynamics in a Globalized World* (pp. 379–423). Hershey, PA: IGI Global. doi:10.4018/978-1-5225-3525-6.ch017

Teixeira, P., Teixeira, L., Eusébio, C., Silva, S., & Teixeira, A. (2021). The Impact of ICTs on Accessible Tourism: Evidence Based on a Systematic Literature Review. In C. Eusébio, L. Teixeira, & M. Carneiro (Eds.), *ICT Tools and Applications for Accessible Tourism* (pp. 1–25). IGI Global. doi:10.4018/978-1-7998-6428-8.ch001

Trad, A., & Kalpić, D. (2018). The Business Transformation Framework, Agile Project and Change Management. In M. Khosrow-Pour, D.B.A. (Ed.), Encyclopedia of Information Science and Technology, Fourth Edition (pp. 620-635). Hershey, PA: IGI Global. https://doi.org/ doi:10.4018/978-1-5225-2255-3.ch054

Trad, A., & Kalpić, D. (2018). The Business Transformation and Enterprise Architecture Framework: The Financial Engineering E-Risk Management and E-Law Integration. In B. Sergi, F. Fidanoski, M. Ziolo, & V. Naumovski (Eds.), *Regaining Global Stability After the Financial Crisis* (pp. 46–65). Hershey, PA: IGI Global. doi:10.4018/978-1-5225-4026-7.ch003

Trengereid, V. (2022). Conditions of Network Engagement: The Quest for a Common Good. In R. Augusto Costa, F. Brandão, Z. Breda, & C. Costa (Eds.), *Planning and Managing the Experience Economy in Tourism* (pp. 69-84). IGI Global. https://doi.org/10.4018/978-1-7998-8775-1.ch004

Turulja, L., & Bajgoric, N. (2018). Business Continuity and Information Systems: A Systematic Literature Review. In N. Bajgoric (Ed.), *Always-On Enterprise Information Systems for Modern Organizations* (pp. 60–87). Hershey, PA: IGI Global. doi:10.4018/978-1-5225-3704-5.ch004

Vargas-Hernández, J. G. (2017). Professional Integrity in Business Management Education. In N. Baporikar (Ed.), *Management Education for Global Leadership* (pp. 70–89). Hershey, PA: IGI Global. doi:10.4018/978-1-5225-1013-0.ch004

Varnacı Uzun, F. (2021). The Destination Preferences of Foreign Tourists During the COVID-19 Pandemic and Attitudes Towards: Marmaris, Turkey. In M. Demir, A. Dalgıç, & F. Ergen (Eds.), *Handbook of Research on the Impacts and Implications of COVID-19 on the Tourism Industry* (pp. 285–306). IGI Global. https://doi.org/10.4018/978-1-7998-8231-2.ch014

Vasista, T. G., & AlAbdullatif, A. M. (2017). Role of Electronic Customer Relationship Management in Demand Chain Management: A Predictive Analytic Approach. *International Journal of Information Systems and Supply Chain Management, 10*(1), 53–67. doi:10.4018/IJISSCM.2017010104

Vieru, D., & Bourdeau, S. (2017). Survival in the Digital Era: A Digital Competence-Based Multi-Case Study in the Canadian SME Clothing Industry. *International Journal of Social and Organizational Dynamics in IT, 6*(1), 17–34. doi:10.4018/IJSODIT.2017010102

Vijayan, G., & Kamarulzaman, N. H. (2017). An Introduction to Sustainable Supply Chain Management and Business Implications. In M. Khan, M. Hussain, & M. Ajmal (Eds.), *Green Supply Chain Management for Sustainable Business Practice* (pp. 27–50). Hershey, PA: IGI Global. doi:10.4018/978-1-5225-0635-5.ch002

Vlachvei, A., & Notta, O. (2017). Firm Competitiveness: Theories, Evidence, and Measurement. In A. Vlachvei, O. Notta, K. Karantininis, & N. Tsounis (Eds.), *Factors Affecting Firm Competitiveness and Performance in the Modern Business World* (pp. 1–42). Hershey, PA: IGI Global. doi:10.4018/978-1-5225-0843-4.ch001

Wang, C., Schofield, M., Li, X., & Ou, X. (2017). Do Chinese Students in Public and Private Higher Education Institutes Perform at Different Level in One of the Leadership Skills: Critical Thinking?: An Exploratory Comparison. In V. Wang (Ed.), *Encyclopedia of Strategic Leadership and Management* (pp. 160–181). Hershey, PA: IGI Global. doi:10.4018/978-1-5225-1049-9.ch013

Wang, J. (2017). Multi-Agent based Production Management Decision System Modelling for the Textile Enterprise. *Journal of Global Information Management, 25*(4), 1–15. doi:10.4018/JGIM.2017100101

Wiedemann, A., & Gewald, H. (2017). Examining Cross-Domain Alignment: The Correlation of Business Strategy, IT Management, and IT Business Value. *International Journal of IT/Business Alignment and Governance, 8*(1), 17–31. doi:10.4018/IJITBAG.2017010102

Wolf, R., & Thiel, M. (2018). Advancing Global Business Ethics in China: Reducing Poverty Through Human and Social Welfare. In S. Hipsher (Ed.), *Examining the Private Sector's Role in Wealth Creation and Poverty Reduction* (pp. 67–84). Hershey, PA: IGI Global. doi:10.4018/978-1-5225-3117-3.ch004

Yablonsky, S. (2018). Innovation Platforms: Data and Analytics Platforms. In *Multi-Sided Platforms (MSPs) and Sharing Strategies in the Digital Economy: Emerging Research and Opportunities* (pp. 72–95). Hershey, PA: IGI Global. doi:10.4018/978-1-5225-5457-8.ch003

Yaşar, B. (2021). The Impact of COVID-19 on Volatility of Tourism Stocks: Evidence From BIST Tourism Index. In M. Demir, A. Dalgıç, & F. Ergen (Eds.), *Handbook of Research on the Impacts and Implications of COVID-19 on the Tourism Industry* (pp. 23–44). IGI Global. https://doi.org/10.4018/978-1-7998-8231-2.ch002

Yusoff, A., Ahmad, N. H., & Halim, H. A. (2017). Agropreneurship among Gen Y in Malaysia: The Role of Academic Institutions. In N. Ahmad, T. Ramayah, H. Halim, & S. Rahman (Eds.), *Handbook of Research on Small and Medium Enterprises in Developing Countries* (pp. 23–47). Hershey, PA: IGI Global. doi:10.4018/978-1-5225-2165-5.ch002

Zacher, D., & Pechlaner, H. (2021). Resilience as an Opportunity Approach: Challenges and Perspectives for Private Sector Participation on a Community Level. In A. Zehrer, G. Glowka, K. Schwaiger, & V. Ranacher-Lackner (Eds.), *Resiliency Models and Addressing Future Risks for Family Firms in the Tourism Industry* (pp. 75–102). IGI Global. https://doi.org/10.4018/978-1-7998-7352-5.ch004

Zanin, F., Comuzzi, E., & Costantini, A. (2018). The Effect of Business Strategy and Stock Market Listing on the Use of Risk Assessment Tools. In *Management Control Systems in Complex Settings: Emerging Research and Opportunities* (pp. 145–168). Hershey, PA: IGI Global. doi:10.4018/978-1-5225-3987-2.ch007

Zgheib, P. W. (2017). Corporate Innovation and Intrapreneurship in the Middle East. In P. Zgheib (Ed.), *Entrepreneurship and Business Innovation in the Middle East* (pp. 37–56). Hershey, PA: IGI Global. doi:10.4018/978-1-5225-2066-5.ch003

About the Contributors

Shilpa Deo has been awarded NET with JRF in Economics by UGC. She has been awarded PhD in Economics by Gokhale Institute of Politics & Economics. She has been working as an Assistant Professor at School of Management (UG), MIT World Peace University. She has been extensively doing research in her interest areas and has also won "Best Research Paper Award" for paper presentation at an International Conference. She has several publications to her credit in national and international journals. She is also serving as a Research Fellow at Centre for International Trade and Business in Asia, James Cook University, Australia.

A. V. Senthil Kumar is working as a Director & Professor in the Department of Research and PG in Computer Applications, Hindusthan College of Arts and Science, Coimbatore since 05/03/2010. He has to his credit 11 Book Chapters, 250 papers in International Journals, 15 papers in National Journals, 25 papers in International Conferences, 5 papers in National Conferences, and edited 8 books (IGI Global, USA). He is an Editor-in-Chief for International Journal titled "International Journal of Data Mining and Emerging Technologies", "International Journal of Image Processing and Applications", "International Journal of Advances in Knowledge Engineering & Computer Science", " International Journal of Advances in Computers and Information Engineering" and "International Journal of Research and Reviews in Computer Science".. Key Member for India, Machine Intelligence Research Lab (MIR Labs). He is an Editorial Board Member and Reviewer for various International Journals.

* * *

Abdurazzag Ali Aburas is working at University of KwaZulu Natal, School of Engineering, Howard college campus, Durban, South Africa. Recently, he gives consultation for IT Company. He received research fund from school of engineering in 2018. At present time, he is coordinator of big data research group (UKZNBD). He has supervised a number of PhD and MSc research project (2006-2011) and currently establish new PhD and MSc research project at UKZN (2018). He has new book published based Engineering Education (2013) and completed 2nd book titled Human Mobile Interaction (2018) and his third book on Bigdata in progress.

Güneş Akgül is master student at Adana Alparslan Türkeş Science and Technology University and she works as a tourist guide in Cappadocia, Turkey.

Arda Can Aktürk received his bachelor's degree in Economics from Istanbul Technical University and a master's degree in International Trade from Boğaziçi University. He is interested in macroeconomics, international competition, and public policies. Nowadays he is a textiles and raw materials trader in Turkey.

Fatma Feyza Gündüz is currently an Assistant Professor at the Department of International Trade and Finance, Adana Alparslan Türkeş Science and Technology University in Turkey. Her fields of study are statistical and econometric models and their applications. In 2018, she was a visiting professor at University Niccolò Cusano in Rome, Italy. She has many studies in international and national indexed journals and books. She has presented papers at various international and national conferences and meetings.

Mehtap Isik has BSc degree in Mathematics, MA and PhD degrees in Economics from Bogazici University. She worked as a Risk analyst at Citibank, Istanbul. Later, she joined the Department of International Trade as a full-time faculty member. Her research interests include microeconomic theory, game theory, social network theory, international economics and development, political economy, environmental economics, urban economics and transportation economics. She also lectures in some of these subjects at Department of International Trade and Institute of Social Sciences, Bogazici University.

Neelima K. received her M.Tech degree in Embedded Systems from JNTUA Ananthapuramu in 2015, and is now currently working as Assistant Professor in Sree Vidyanikethan Engineering College, Tirupati. Her current research interests include Information Theory, VLSI, and Image Processing.

Gayathri R. is currently an Assistant Professor at School of Management, SASTRA Deemed University in India. An excellent orator with a Doctorate in Economics (2013) from Bharathidasan University, India. Her areas of interest include International Business, Marketing and Business Ethics. She handles courses such as Economics and Marketing. She has a rich academic experience of 20 years in teaching and 7 years in Research. Her focus is on contemporary social research, and she is a co-investigator in the funded project funded by the Ministry of Rural Development, Government of India. She has presented papers at international and national level conferences and seminars. She has published a number of research articles and case studies in referred Scopus indexed journals.

Karthikeyan S., BSc, MBA, is currently pursuing PhD (Full Time) at School of Management, SASTRA Deemed University, India in the area of Investors Psychology .He received his master's degree in Business Administration at SASTRA Deemed University, Tamilnadu in India. He has 5 years of Industry & 8 years of academic experience. He has rich experience in handling specialized business courses in Finance and HR to both Under-Graduate and Post-Graduate students. He has presented and published a number of research articles in national and international conferences.

Sushil Sharma is currently an Associate Provost at University of Texas. He was earlier working as an Associate Dean and a Professor of Computer Information Systems (CIS) in the Miller College of Business at Ball State University. Dr. Sharma has the unique distinction of earning two doctoral degrees. He has over 20 years of administrative leadership experience and more than 25 years of experience in higher education. Dr. Sharma served as the Chair for the Department of Information Systems and Operations Management (2008–2012) and Executive Director of the MBA and other Certificate Programs (2011-2013). A Leadership Fellow in Higher Education through the Management Development Program at Harvard University, he has co-authored/edited/co-edited twelve (12) books and published over ninety (90) refereed research papers in the most reputed national and international MIS journals. In addition, he has published forty-five (45) refereed chapters in various books and has presented and published over 135 papers in various national and international conferences. Dr. Sharma's research has appeared in several highly ranked journals in the MIS field, including Decision Support Systems, Communications of the Association for Information Systems, European Journal of Information Systems, Information Systems Frontiers, Journal of Information Privacy & Security (JIPS), Electronic Commerce Research Journal, and Information Management and Computer Security.

Chennapalli Subhas received M.Tech Degree in Electronics Instrumentation and Communication Systems from Sri Venkateswara University and Ph. D degree in wireless communications from JNTUA Ananthapuramu. He is a member of IEEE, ISTE, IETE and IEICE. He is currently working as Professor of ECE and Vice-Principal in JNTUA College of Engineering, Kalikiri. He has published over 35 journal papers, 12 papers in conference proceedings and has guided 4 Ph.D

Scholars. His research interests are in Error Detection and Correction Codes, and Communication Systems.

C. Vijayabanu is currently Professor at School of Management, SASTRA Deemed University in India. She obtained her Ph.D. in Commerce-Human Resource Management in 2000 at Bharathidasan University, India. Her current research interests focus on the areas behavioral studies –Personality, Perception: attitudes & values. She handles courses such as Human Resource Management, organizational behavior and specialization courses such as Change Management, Training & Development, etc. She brings to her classes enriched knowledge of 5 years of Research & 23 years of academic experience. She has produced five doctoral scholars successfully and currently Guiding 2 Ph.D. scholar. She has presented papers at international and national level conferences and seminars.She has published number of research articles and case studies in referred Scopus indexed journals. She has served on the Editorial Review Boards of several academic journals, including Business theory and practice, Journal of Management Social Science and Humanities and Journal of Business Economics and Management.

Index

H

I

M

O

P

R

S

T

www.ingramcontent.com/pod-product-compliance
Lightning Source LLC
LaVergne TN
LVHW061536290926
849162LV00004B/809

* 9 7 8 1 6 6 8 4 5 2 8 9 9 *